WAR CRIME OR JUST WAR ?

THE IRAQ WAR
2003 -2005

A CASE FOR INDICTMENT

NICHOLAS WOOD

EDITED BY ANABELLA PELLENS

South Hill Press

Dedicated to the Iraqi People

Published by SOUTH HILL PRESS
20 South Hill Park Gardens
London NW3 2TG

Typeset by Ben Bayliss

Printed and Bound by

Mackays of Chatham plc
Chatham

ISBN 0-9528443-1-1

CONTENTS

PREFACE.

This book grew out of conversations with Rob Murthwaite while we were composing a letter for Stop the War Coalition to be sent to the International Criminal Court at The Hague. He argued from the humanist point of view that humans were not aggressive primates: they did not need curbing by laws to prevent them acting like beasts: only some men behaved like beasts. After all, he said, two million marched against the war with Iraq, and he didn't consider himself the same as Blair and Bush. I argued from the opposite point of view: that we were genetically aggressive primates, who were all capable of violence, and that we needed laws to curb this aggression.

Unfortunately Rob's work on human rights law prevented him from helping to write this book, but many of the ideas are his. We both felt very angry about the war, as we felt it was obscene, and had been foisted onto us by deceit. Robert feels that the denial of the Magna Charta was one of the most terrible things that have happened under Blair's leadership, as this document is the foundation of all modern democracies. I felt especially upset about the war as I had worked in Iraq, and found Iraqis a dignified people, who deserved better than Saddam and who do not deserve to be bombed or maimed, least of all the many children.

So this book developed out of two years of becoming involved in politics, working in the House of Commons in a humble capacity, and observing events. I have been privileged with the kindness and encouragement of several MPs who have to remain anonymous. At first I wasn't aware that the Commons Committees were open to the public and you could actually see and hear Jack Straw or Clare Short speaking. I have bombarded MPs with a series of postcards and written countless letters to the press. Some letters did get printed by *The Independent* and my friends suggested that I turn them into a book. In a small way letters are sometimes effective. The aim is to make a modest contribution towards stopping the knee jerk rush to war, and protesting at its conduct. Geoffrey Robertson, QC, has pointed out the importance of the Pinochet case in causing unease among our leaders. In the two years of this war, I have come to think this is the most optimistic development in the prevention of war.

Since I am an archaeologist, I became fascinated by the importance of British archaeologists in the creation of the concept of Iraq as a nation and their involvement in spying and actual warfare. It also astonished me that the RAF had been bombing Iraq off and on for nearly ninety years. There is more to this Iraq War than meets the eye.

Having worked in Saudi Arabia, I have also been appalled at the imposition of American culture on that country. The crude, spiritually bankrupt, McDonalds and Dunkin Donuts; the American style villas being a complete antithesis to the traditional courtyard houses that have developed over thousands of years to cope with the very high temperatures; the twelve-lane highways without proper pavements compared with the winding shaded streets of traditional Arabic housing, all filled me with dread. The young intellectual Wahabi sees this aspect of America, and doesn't like what he sees. I fear that many Americans fail to understand this, and too many Americans are ignorant of the world outside their country. This cultural assault by America is something that needs to be addressed as well as its bellicosity.

Of course there are moments in writing a book when you wonder why you bother. At this point Anabella Pellens entered the scene. Being Argentine she knows what imprisonment and disappearances mean, and has been invaluable as an editor. She also pointed out that, because much of the book is based on the spoken word reported week by week in newspapers, it could in future be used as a historic reference.

I have also been fortunate to count on the help of Hani Lazim who checked the brief history of Iraq. Philippa Youngman kindly gave initial advice on the structure of the book.

Chris Coverdale first introduced me to the complexities of the International Criminal Court in the Stop the War campaign. We discussed long and hard how we could persuade MPs to make claims to the ICC, to the point of purchasing our Eurostar tickets to The Hague. But this was in vain as it turned out. But Chris has not given up jumping over the many hurdles to this Criminal Court with great persistence. He very kindly agreed to vet my chapter on the Laws and Customs of War, and wrote the introduction to the incorporation of the Rome Statute of the ICC into British Domestic Law. The rest of the book will contain errors which are all mine. It is to be hoped that some readers will feel inclined to make their own claims, first to the British Courts, then to the Prosecutor at the address on the back of the book.

My friends have been very supportive with showers of e-mails and references which have helped make the text more factual. I have had weekly discussions with my lifelong friend Peter Day, geographer and student of all things classical Greek, on such topics as the impossibility of a young soldier under fire being able to discriminate. Peter has dissected Blair's use of language. He argues that to declare that a Security Council veto is "unreasonable" and therefore invalid, is a step on the way to dictatorship, and to qualify every recent remark with "genuinely" means that Blair subconsciously realises no one believes a word he says any more. Peter was responsible for spotting Chirac's speech of 10 March 2003 in a French Government website; a printout of which I sent to Clare Short. Claire Short was astonished by its content as it was very different from the version offered by the Prime Minister in that crucial debate on 18 March 2003. So much so that it led to the French Ambassador going to Number 10 to protest.

I am indebted to the late Sir Harry Hinsley, who, as my tutor, gave me a love of books and history, and with whom I continue having daily dialogues in my head. I think he would have approved of this book.

This book, on purpose, is based on extracts from press reports quoting what was actually said. I have thus relied on some very brave journalists who have risked and even lost their lives in Iraq.

Without my wife Sara's financial support I would not have been able to produce this book. We have also discussed the war every day for two years. The fact that she is a classicist and a political prize-winner in America in her youth, has meant her advice and arguments are sometimes formidable.

I take full sole legal responsibility for the contents of this book.

Nicholas Wood
London, February 2005.

INTRODUCTION.

This is an angry book. How dare a Prime Minister abuse his office and drag Britain into a war with cunning and deceit? How dare he withhold Foreign Office papers – critical of the decision to go to war – from the Cabinet discussion? How dare he privately enter into deals with President Bush, without involving Cabinet and Parliament? How dare he lie about France?

Tony Blair has dragged us into a war that has killed tens of thousands of Iraqis and maimed four times as many; very many of them children with arms and legs torn off, breasts forever burnt, stomachs full of scars, eyes blinded. Depleted uranium dust now blows about Iraq with a radioactive life measured in millions of years.

Every time I read about a Muslim tortured with a broom handle, or savaged by dogs so that he wets himself as part of a US soldiers' "game", I feel personally violated. When Tony Blair says useful information is being obtained at Guantanamo Bay, I think what a vile man he is. When I see photographs of Iraqi children with their limbs torn off in their fathers' arms I weep. The outrageous destruction of Fallujah is of biblical proportions. Why has my country been dragged into this? We were told it was to eliminate weapons of mass destruction which could be targeted against this country within 45 minutes. That was a lie.

It is questionable whether Mr Blair and Mr Bush actually had any first-hand experience of Iraq before 2002. (Their presidential-style visits to countries involve being whisked from airports to expensive palaces or castles in bullet-proof limousines.) Did they know anything about Iraq's history, its geography, its tribal and religious divisions or its prosperity in the seventies? That it had been a model for UNESCO literacy programmes, that it was a secular state with religious tolerance, that Jews lived in harmony with Muslims and Christians, and that it had the best record for women's emancipation in any Middle Eastern country? Or did they only know what they wanted to know: the world of realpolitik and of Saddam's profligacy

1

and brutality, his danger to Israel, and his nationalisation of oil? It is my belief that if they had known anything beyond the bigoted poison poured in their fundamentalist Christian ears by the neo-cons (and realised what a charming, intelligent, dignified people the Iraqis can be, and how beautiful their children are) they would have done anything to avoid a war. They might even have come to love Iraq, the Iraqis and the fast-flowing Euphrates by Babylon. They might have respected other peoples' culture and values, and followed Chirac's wisdom, "war is always a final resort, always acknowledgement of failure, always the worst solution, because it brings death and misery." The West could have disposed of Saddam through legal means; or accommodated him, as they did Gaddafi; or waited for an implosion, as happened in the USSR.

This book is an attempt to illustrate how the perpetrators of this war could be brought to justice. As British we cannot distance ourselves from what has happened because we have paid our taxes, and we enjoy the benefits of wealth created by being the second biggest arms manufacturer in the World. We are all guilty, but it is still possible to say that we don't like what we see.

As I was writing this introduction, the Iraq war was not going to plan. A British hostage was awaiting beheading. On September 21, 2004 – eighteen months after the war began – guerrilla and political resistance to the US and UK occupation was growing and Tony Blair, the British Prime Minister, declared that there was a second war going on in Iraq. The first war had succeeded in its aim of toppling Saddam Hussein; the second was a war against the forces of terrorism that were gathering in the *crucible* of Iraq.

But what exactly was the war plan? As Clausewitz said, with his personal experience of fighting in the Napoleonic wars, "War is always the servant of policy... without a sound policy, success in war is improbable." In fact there were many plans and motives for going to war with Iraq. First there was the fine motive of ridding a country of a brutal dictatorship, and the installation of a democracy. Quite what form this democracy was supposed to take is, two years after occupation, a matter of speculation. As we have seen, the questions of a democratic government in Iraq (in a religious and racially divided Iraq) were spelled out by Gertrude Bell in 1920. Her observations remain true today with 20% Sunnis, 20% Kurds, and 60% Shia, and a minority of 700,000 Christians. The Coalition had clearly not studied this problem; or rather Mr Blair had arrogantly binned Foreign Office memos on the subject. The Foreign Office warned Blair in secret letters – which have only now come to light – that there were grave dangers in attacking Iraq[1]. A new regime installed in place of that of Saddam could quickly revert to old ways and to the acquisition of weapons. Terrorism would increase rather than decrease. Mr Bush could have been advised that 60% Shia majority would probably turn Iraq into a fundamentalist Islamic state with close ties to Iran. Hardly the US desired outcome. *Freedom and Democracy* also means – in American eyes – a free market for American commercial interests.

Then there is the second motive: Oil. In 1973 another British Prime Minister, Edward Heath, was warned by a secret intelligence document[2] that the United States had very similar plans for a pre-emptive invasion of a Middle Eastern country, in order to have a secure base to control the price and supply of oil, as a reaction to the setting up of the OPEC cartel. This war had nothing to do with ridding countries of dictators, especially of dictators installed by the US. In 2002, in one of his speeches prior to the war, President George W. Bush declared that one of the aims of war was to break OPEC. At the successful outcome of the initial invasion, a Provisional Administration was set up in Iraq by the Pentagon. One of its first initiatives was to privatise the nationalised oil assets and switch these to the advantage of American companies. This act of theft is contrary to The Hague and Geneva Conventions and the Nuremberg Charter of 1945.

Third is the question of Israel. Over the years there have been various feasibility studies by the United States and Israel for establishing water pipe lines from the River Euphrates to Israel. There have been communications between Israel and the Kurds over the creation of an independent Kurdish state, sympathetic to Israel, in Northern Iraq. There were very real concerns since Saddam was supplying money to Palestine and had launched Scud missiles against Israel during the 1992 Gulf War. And then there is the desire by the extreme Zionist lobbies to expand Israel eastwards, *even unto the Euphrates*.

Fourth is US military dominance. American bases had to be withdrawn from Saudi Arabia because the regime there was looking

3

increasingly shaky – and had spawned Osama Bin Laden, leader of al-Qa'ida and his collection of terrorists who could fly but not land planes. After the 11 September 2001 (9/11) bombing of the World Trade Centre twin towers, there was a need to combat al-Qa'ida, and to appear victorious. In the words of one American officer "as you know we were subject to a very big attack and thousands of our people were murdered." The novelty of this form of terrorism put the US in a quandary which is virtually insoluble, especially as various pigeons were coming home to roost. In the 1980s the US had supplied money and arms to the Taliban and Osama, in order to win the Cold War against Russia by proxy in Afghanistan. It had created a Frankenstein monster in addition to 10,000 well-armed fighters who were at a loose end once the Russians pulled out of that quagmire. The US therefore attacked Afghanistan to flush out the Taliban and al-Qa'ida from the mountains. But this was not enough. An example had to be made of another Muslim country to demonstrate the overweening power of American arms. Iraq was the obvious choice – and had been targeted by the neo-cons of the US prior to 9/11 in their imperialist manifesto published by *Project for the New American Century* in September 2000. In Iraq was a further Frankenstein monster of America's own making.

The Western leaders' knowledge of Iraq was very limited. Advice from Middle Eastern experts went unheeded. The consequences of what was beginning to be an anti-Muslim war at home and abroad were discounted. The wisdom of Clausewitz lay forgotten. Plans for after the war were either shambolic or non-existent. The Coalition ended wandering around in a quagmire of violence unleashed by their own recklessness.

Amnesty International and the Red Cross have pointed out that fifty per cent of Iraqis were children under the age of 13. UNICEF warned in 2002 that 33% of Iraqi children were malnourished. After 12 years of UN sanctions they were near to starvation. Diseases had killed an estimated half million children in the chaotic Iraqi hospitals. Some 60% of the population relied on food handouts. Water, sewerage and electricity systems were fragile; any military action was only going to make these matters worse. You don't start bombing a country in this condition.

Using the terms of Nazi Germany, *Shock and Awe* was launched on a poorly equipped country. On 14 March 2003, cruise missiles were fired from UK and US warships against Baghdad. The invasion was all but over by 1st May 2003 and Saddam's statue in Baghdad was toppled. But then the Coalition's troubles began. There was no agreed plan of what to do next. To the astonishment of Blair and Bush, the Iraqi people did not greet the invaders with rejoicing and flowers, but with booby traps and looting. Another Clausewitz dictum came into play: *If you don't occupy all the territory, you haven't conquered it.*

What is now unbelievable, but sickeningly true, is that the Western allies did not fight on moral high ground and demonstrate that they were following The Hague and Geneva Conventions. Nor did they follow the Principles of Nuremberg[3]. Nor did the leaders follow the Articles of the newly set up International Criminal Court at The Hague. Instead of a display of justice and freedom based on the 1215 Magna Charta, the basis of all modern democracies, the same prisons and methods of Saddam Hussein were adopted. The leaders of the Coalition Forces declared that many of the international conventions for the conduct of war were inapplicable. With crass folly, Donald Rumsfeld, the US Secretary of Defense, even suggested that prisoners, held by the US Army for interrogation, should stand for eight to ten hours instead of four as laid down in a memo for his signature[4].

Bush unwisely called this war a *crusade*. With poor leadership from fundamentalist Christian backgrounds, it was almost inevitable that a Christian God would be evoked to protect the young soldiers going into battle. This has meant that in two years – Iraqis, who were supposed to be freed by this war – have become the *enemy* allied to Satan. The Commandments *Thou shalt not kill*, and *Love thy neighbour as thyself* are forgotten in the adrenalin of battle.

Methods were adopted of brutality, sexual crudity, sadism, injustice, racial humiliation and wanton destruction of Iraqi homes, of the heritage of Islam and ancient civilisations, as well as a callous disregard for children's life and health; all of which overshadowed any of the fine motives for going to war. The Muslim world daily views these atrocities on television and newspapers, and can come to only one conclusion: *These war crimes beggar belief.* If we are to allow them to take place without any protest, we are as guilty as any

5

of those who took part in barbaric acts during war. We will find that these experiments in cruelty will become the norm. Is this what we want?

This book is divided into two parts. First, the background to the war. Second, case studies that set out how, in the author's view, the many breaches of the Laws and Customs of War have come about. In this context, the first chapter deals briefly with the history of Iraq and its oil. What emerges from this review of Iraq is the depth of the UK's involvement in its history and the number of times the RAF has bombed Iraq since 1920. Then follows an examination of the most important Hague and Geneva Conventions dealing with the conduct of war and of the Principles of Nuremberg, where it was held that the leaders were responsible for the conduct of wars, however far they were removed from the battle front. The Nuremberg Tribunal established that *crimes against peace*, and *crimes against humanity* were punishable, as well as *war crimes*. The 1998 house arrest of General Pinochet in the UK is discussed in some detail, as it illustrates how there is no Statute of Limitations on a torturer, and how State Immunity can be overruled. That allies in war are legally in partnership is also discussed, as are Clare Short's revelations about the workings of 10 Downing Street. They show how in seven years the Prime Minister has moved away from Cabinet Government to personal Government.

In the second part of the book, the case studies speak for themselves. It is almost as if Mr Blair, Mr Hoon, Mr Bush, and Mr Rumsfeld had gone through The Hague and Geneva Conventions ticking them off to make sure no breach is missing.

Finally, the book concludes with the various steps that can be taken to bring the instigators of this war to justice, and to provide some monetary compensation to Iraqis.

---

[1] Jack Straw, Foreign Secretary, *Independent*, March 2003.
[2] State Papers, 1973.
[3] Nuremberg Charter, 1945
[4] Pentagon action memo, *Counter-Resistance Techniques*, approved by SECDEF on 2 December 2002.

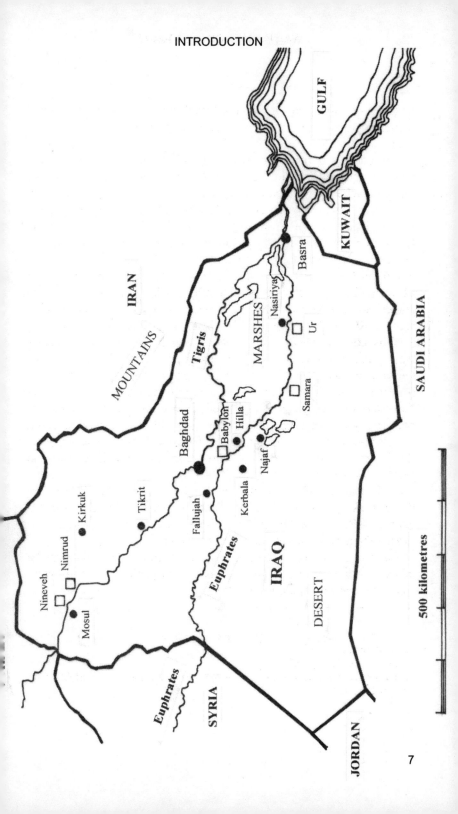

WAR CRIMES OR JUST WAR?

CHAPTER 1
BRIEF HISTORY OF IRAQ & ITS OIL.

PREHISTORY At Hit, on the Euphrates, and south of Musil, bitumen outcrops are worked from antiquity. Oil and bitumen are used for waterproofing boats, as a building material (see Uruk temples), in *Greek fire*, for sticking bricks, as background for ivory and gold decoration, and as oil for lamps.

1810 Claudius James Rich British representative of the East India Company makes archaeological surveys of Iraq.

1845 The British archaeologist, Austen Henry Laylard, excavates in Nimrud and Nineveh and (having paid Turkish officials) crates up whole sections of palaces for transport to the British Museum. (Imagine Napoleon boxing up half of Stonehenge and using it as a triumphal arch to the Louvre) .

1871 German oil exploration experts visit Iraq, including Kirkuk, Qaiyara and Tuz Khurmatu. Oil rights are transferred to the Turkish Sultan's Privy Purse.

1897 The Mesopotamian petroleum fields are described in the "Geographical Journal" of the Royal Geographical Society.

1900 German archaeologists excavate Babylon. German commercial and diplomatic interests are established in Baghdad and Basra.

1902 HMS Lapwing comes to the protection of Kuwait against Turkish forces. (Kuwait was part of Basrah Wilayat in the Ottoman Empire. The British, in agreement with the Sultan, went in there to counter German gains of railway and oil rights.)

1903 Imperial Ottoman Baghdad Railway Company is formed (backed by Germany and Britain) to connect Turkey with Baghdad and Basra. A twenty-metre strip allotment is allocated for oil exploration along the railway.

1907 German explorers confirm oil deposits at Mosul.

1912 Churchill and First Sea Lord Admiral Fisher order British Navy to convert warships from coal to oil power. Shell, Deutches

9

Bank, British National Bank of Turkey and Gulbenkian, form a consortium – African and Eastern Concessions – to exploit oil.

1913 HMS Alert is anchored off the coast at Ashar, southern Iraq, as Arab nationalism escalates against Turkey. Kuwait's independence from Turkey is recognised in Anglo-Turkish agreement of 1913 (a secret agreement with the Sheikh of Kuwait meant Kuwait did not become independent until 1963). This gives Britain a foothold in the Basra region.

1915 British commence military operations against Turkey from Basra area. Turks counterattack and damage oil pipelines.

1916 Sykes Picot Agreement allocated British sphere of influence in Mesopotamia, and France in Syria and Lebanon.

1917 Turks are defeated. British occupy Baghdad, with Black Watch in the Vanguard. Royal Navy fuels from Basra.

1920 Churchill, Bell, Lawrence and other British diplomats install Faisal as King of Iraq. The RAF bombs rebels. On 19 February, Churchill advocates the use of gas bombs, *calculated to cause disablement of some kind but not death*. "I do not understand this squeamishness about the use of gas against uncivilized tribes." British advisors are embedded in the Iraqi government.

1921 British Iraqi Petroleum Company, a consortium of the Shell Group, Anglo Persian, the French Government's Compagnie Francaise des Petroles, the American Near East Development Corporation and Mr Gulbenkian, have total oil monopoly in Iraq.

1924 British Trusteeship Treaty with Iraq is lodged with the League of Nations. Kurdish rebellion in Sulaymania and Halabja region under Shaykh Mahmud is put down by RAF bombing raids and the Iraqi army and police. Problems of tribal raids on the Syrian border are resolved by the RAF.

1925 Turkey's dispute over Mosul area boundary with Iraq is determined by the League of Nations. Christians are expelled from Turkey into the Mosul area. Problems of tribal raids on the disputed Syrian border are resolved by the RAF and Iraqi chief Ajiil-al Yawar.

1927 Drilling begins at Kirkuk oil fields in Northern Iraq. British company builds 900-foot steel bridge over the Euphrates at Fallujah.

1929 British School of Archaeology is founded in Iraq as a memorial to Gertrude Bell. Digs at Ur, Kish, Nineveh, Tirkalan, Ctesiphon, Warqa, Tall Lu, Tall Billi, Samarra and Khorsabad.

1930-32 Further Kurdish claims for a separatist state put down by the RAF, Iraqi army and Assyrian levies. (*Bomber Harris* of Dresden fame was one of the pilots dropping mustard gas bombs on Kurdish villagers). Assyrians demand for *Millet* autonomy rejected by the League of Nations.

1932 British Mandate ends. British Administrators leave Iraqi government.

1933 King Faisal I died. Ghazi, his playboy son, popular – and friend of military officers – is crowned.

1934 Iraq begins exporting oil in major quantities. Shia tribes in southern Euphrates region, from Hilla to Nasiriya, are in constant revolt against predominantly Sunni government. Revolt is put down by Iraqi army.

1936 Iraqi army, under Bakr Sidqi, stage successful coup against civil government and bomb Baghdad.

1938 The area south of Basra, including oil terminals, is granted as an oil concession to the British-owned Basra Petroleum Company.

1939 King Ghazi (anti British and pro German and against Palestine British rule favouring Zionism) crashes his car into an electricity pole and dies. British Consul at Mosul stoned to death by rioters (it is believed that Ghazi's killing was organized by British intelligence).

1940 During Second World War, division in government between pro Axis and Pro British allies comes to a head.

1941 British Army secures Basra region after heavy bombardment. The British Arab Legion under Glubb Pasha moves in from Jordan to the Euphrates and secures Iraq Petroleum Companies oil pumping station at Rutba. The RAF and Fleet Air Arm bomb the Iraqi Army in Habbaniya, Fallujah area, and nightly bomb Nasiriya, Amara, Samawa, Dwaine, Armadi, Qarnah, and Mosul. The Iraqi Army is defeated by predominantly British Indian troops. Iraqi administration is allowed to carry on.

1945 Growth of Anti-British communism produces secretly printed al-Qa'ida newspaper.

1946 Pro-Palestinian anti-British riots. West held to be unjust in supporting Zionism. Sixteen-inch oil pipe link from Kirkuk to Haifa and Tripoli is constructed.

1947 The *Portsmouth Treaty* for two RAF bases in Iraq is cause of riots. Treaty is abandoned. Royal Navy continues to fuel from Basra.

1948 Iraq joins Arab war against newly formed Israeli state. Later retreats.

1950 Oilfield southwest of Basra is exploited by British Petroleum Company.

1951 British build subsidiary port at Umm Qasr for oil terminal pipelines. Waterway to Basra is also dredged. Between 1/2 and 2/3s of the shipping tonnage is British.

1958 *The Free Officers*, led by Brigadier Abdel Karim Kassem with support from the newly formed Patriotic United Front, which includes the Communist, Democratic Patriotic, Ba'ath and Istiqlal (Independence) parties, stage a military coup and overthrow King Faisal (the British-supported monarch). Britain proposes to Foster Dulles, US Foreign Secretary, making Kuwait a Crown Colony. Foster Dulles replies "what a very good idea".

1959 Iraq leaves Baghdad Pact (a US, Turkish, Iranian, Pakistani and British cold war alliance).

1960 Kassem initiates first OPEC Conference in Baghdad (to protect oil producers' interests against Western exploitation) by fixing the price of oil among member states.

1961 Kassem sets up Iraq National Oil and kicks out the British Iraq Petroleum Company (IPC). Iraq makes overtures to USSR. Kuwait becomes independent from Britain. Iraq claims Kuwait is part of Iraq. Britain sends in troops to defend Kuwait.

1963 Kassem murdered in Ba'ath Party coup helped by CIA.

1968 A group of army officers (including Saddam Hussein) takes over.

1972 The Ba'ath government nationalises Iraqi Oil and prohibits foreign ownership of companies. OPEC quadruples the price of oil and stops shipping oil to America as a reprisal for its support of Israel.

1973 The US Pentagon has secret plans to invade Kuwait or another Arab state to seize oil fields in order to break the OPEC cartel. The Plan is abandoned when oil pricing crisis ends.

1975 Treaty between Iran and Iraq divides the Shatt-al-Arab waterway. Important to both countries for access to the Persian Gulf.

1979 In February the Shah of Iran flees to Egypt. Ayatollah Khomeini becomes leader of Iran. In July Saddam Hussein becomes president of Iraq and Commander in Chief after killing most of the Ba'athist leadership.

1980 Iraq invades Iran.

1987 US Navy protects Kuwait oil tankers through Persian Gulf. Kuwait is an ally of Iraq in the Iraq-Iran war (Kuwait was selling oil on behalf of Iraq and lots of armaments came to Iraq through Kuwait. It provided over US$10 billion for Saddam's war). The Iran Contra gate becomes apparent.

1988 Kurds shoot dead 150 unarmed Iraqi prisoners of war. Iraq uses gas during attack on Hallabja killing 5,000 Kurds, USA refused to discuss the issue at the UN or the Security Council.

1989 British and Americans stop all forms of credit for Iraq and USA demands that Iraq reduce its army to a third and get rid of all weapons sold – by them – to Iraq during the war with Iran.

1990 Saddam invades Kuwait (on the nod from US ambassador in Baghdad) because Kuwait is beginning to extract Iraq's oil from under a disputed border. (Kuwait sold Iraq's debt to American companies, who started demanding money at a time when oil-pumping from all US oil-producing client states was at a maximum and the price per barrel was at its lowest).

1991 The Gulf War. Iraq defeated by US and coalition including UK. Kurds and Shias encouraged to revolt by US and UK. No fly zones created by US and UK. Sanctions imposed on Iraq by UN. Humanitarian crisis over the next 12 years, during which an estimated 500,000 children and a million adults die.

2003 The Iraq War. Oilfields seized by US and UK. Oil Ministry in Baghdad protected by US.[1]

A PIECE OF CAKE: THE TRAGEDY OF IRAQ.
COMMENTARY ON THE HISTORY OF IRAQ.

The serious British pillage of Iraq began in 1845, when the British archaeologist, Austen Henry Laylard, excavated Nimrud and Nineveh and – having paid off Turkish officials – crated up whole sections of these Assyrian palaces for transport to the British Museum. From then on there was a scramble between British, French, German and American archaeologists to excavate, record and cart away the artefacts of the cradle of civilization. European museums became stuffed full of sections of palaces, statues, Babylonian cuneiform tablets, cylinder seals and gold jewellery from Uruk. Detailed maps were produced that turned out to be of immense value when the British military campaigns commenced in 1914.

What emerges, from a study of Iraq's brief and tragic history, is the almost continuous British resort to the use of RAF bombers. The justification of going to war because Saddam Hussein had bombed 5,000 of his own people in Hallabja with gas must be mirrored by the RAF bombing of Iraqis and Kurds in 1917, 1920, 1924, 1925, 1930, 1931, 1932, 1941, 1991, 1998 and 2003. Not all of these bombings could have been *to free the Iraqi people*.

For nearly one hundred years Mesopotamia (as it was then called) has been regarded by the British Government as a cake from which slices can be cut, or a trough of food. In 2003 the Foreign Secretary, Jack Straw, when commenting in Cabinet about British contracts in Iraq said, "We took the risks and bore the costs, we cannot let the French and Germans get their noses in the trough."[2] In 2003 Sir Jeremy Greenstock, the Prime Minister's Special Envoy for Iraq, in Baghdad said that British contractors should have *a slice of the action*. (The Foreign Office spokesperson said this was in the context that British contractors were experts at reconstruction.)

During the First World War, at a War Council on 1915, Prime Minister Asquith, said of the collapse of the Turkish Empire that if "... we were to leave the other nations to scramble for Turkey without taking anything for ourselves, we should not be doing our duty." In 1914 Lord Curzon had said "The effect of taking it [Baghdad] would be prodigious throughout Asia, and it would be a valuable piece when the game of chess begins." On 22 March 1915, Lord Crew said that he could foresee trouble with France "when the cutting of the cake begins."[3]

What was this cake? Iraq was strategically placed between Egypt and India. Various other nations had their eye on this easy access to India (the jewel in the crown of the British Empire). Germany was especially interested in building a railroad from Turkey to Baghdad and eventually Basra to have access to the Persian Gulf. Britain countered these moves by sending various gunboats to lie off Kuwait and Basra and finally, with the outbreak of the First World War, to occupy the Basra area with troops. After a series of advances and retreats, the Turks were finally driven out of Mesopotamia. The first troops to occupy the Baghdad railway station were the Black Watch, the same regiment which was to play a propaganda role in the American assault on Fallujah some eighty years later.

In 1918 the victors of the First World War – surveying the defeated lands of the Ottoman Empire in the Middle East – had the satisfactory task of slicing up the cake and establishing their spheres of interest. (In an extraordinary fashion, these events eighty-six years ago seem a dress rehearsal for the Iraq War of 2003. It appears almost as if the UK and US cannot keep their hands off Iraq.) At the time, a key role was played by archaeologists who in effect acted as spies in the region. Gertrude Bell was an English aristocrat who – through her archaeology – established herself as an indispensable advisor to the British Government; together with T.E. Shaw (Lawrence of Arabia), another archaeologist who, during his first archaeological excavation at Carchemish, spent his spare time looking at German engineers on the Baghdad Istanbul Railway through a pair of large binoculars. Gertrude Bell learnt fluent Arabic and was a highly intelligent observant person who, because of her sex, was able to enter the inner sanctum of Iraqi homes, as well as carry out measured surveys of antiquities.

Back in Europe, the Anglo French Armistice of 1919, naïvely and altruistically, declared of the newly occupied territories: "The indigenous population should exercise the right of self determination regarding the form of national government under which they should live." Gertrude Bell was aghast and wrote in a paper for the Foreign Office entitled *Self Determination in Mesopotamia*: "The publication of the Anglo French declaration was regrettable. Previous to its appearance, the people of Mesopotamia, having witnessed the successful termination of the war, had taken it for granted that the country would remain under British control. The declaration opened up other possibilities which were regarded almost universally with anxiety, but provided opportunities for political intrigue to the less stable and fanatical elements."

In March 1919 Gertrude Bell returned to Britain and met with Mr Balfour, the British Foreign Secretary, to discuss the Middle East. She also attended the Paris Peace Conference, where lobbying took place for the creation of a Zionist state. French demands for Syria, American interests in Saudi Arabia and British interests in Iraq, Jordan and Kuwait were also addressed.

Gertrude Bell was lobbying for the creation of an Iraqi state. A commentator at the time said to her: "But Gertrude! You are flying in the face of four millennia of history if you try to draw a line around Iraq and call it a political entity!" She then returned to Iraq and wrote a memorandum to influence Colonel Wilson, the Deputy Chief Political Officer in Mesopotamia, who in turn said that it was "impossible to create a new sovereign Mohammedan State... The warlike Kurds numbering half a million will never accept an Arab ruler. The Shia, numbering 1 3/4 million would not accept Sunni domination - and no form of Government has yet been envisaged which does not involve Sunni domination."

By March 1920 Iraq was in revolt against the Frangi (the European usurper). It began with tribal conflicts in the middle Euphrates and spread as religious leaders stirred up hatred. The holy cities of Najaf and Karbala suffered most. A British (occupiers) peacekeeping force put down the rebellion with many casualties on both sides. Gas bombs were used by the British air force against military and civilian targets. An early attempt at autonomy by the Kurds was abandoned by the British. The allies – Britain, France and Russia – agreed in advance on the division of the Ottoman Empire. The October 1917 revolution exposed the plan; British and French victors had to redraw the map to divide the area excluding the Russians. The USA was given a share in the Persian Oil Company, and later in Iraqi Oil, as payback for their late involvement in the war.

On 15 December 1920 Gertrude Bell wrote: "Council decided that Congress should consist of 100 members, of whom 20 should be elected by sheiks of the tribes. There would also be four Jewish and five Christian representatives. Sayid Talib Pasha [the provisional government Interior Minister]... has been trying to ingratiate himself with Shias and nationalists... but... none trust his intentions." Talib, who was seeking the throne, was later arrested for incitement to rebellion by the British Governor –who got rid of him sending him into exile. "The situation that confronted H.M. Government in Iraq at the beginning of 1921 was a most unsatisfactory one." wrote Winston Churchill, the new UK Colonial Secretary.

Gertrude Bell then wrote her *Review of the Civil Administration of Mesopotamia*. This was published as a government paper, with weekly intelligence summaries from Iraq and Syria. On 14 January 1921 she wrote "Under Electoral Law... the suggestion [for tribal representation] met with considerable opposition, at the bottom of which lay the rooted objection of the propertied and conservative classes to admit the tribesmen, who are regarded as little removed from savages, to share in the councils of the state." Eighty years later, in January 2004, this fundamental division of society is still a stumbling block.

In February 1921 Bell attended the Cairo Conference on the Middle East with Lawrence, Churchill and others. The managing director of the Anglo-Persian Oil Company was also present in Cairo at the time, lobbying the conference. Emir Faisal, who had fought alongside Lawrence in the Hejaz and whose brother was to be installed as King of Transjordan, was asked to be a candidate for the throne of Iraq. Faisal was crowned on 23 August 1921 after a 96% popular vote for the single candidate. Sayid Talib had been moved out of the way. Bell said, "We've got our King crowned[4]".

The new king had to rely on the Sunni aristocracy as his power base, though he did try to enfranchise the population by encouraging the people of Tikrit (Saddam's hometown) to enter the army. Faisal was in effect the puppet king of British interest, which had a large Embassy in Baghdad situated on the banks of the Tigris in the old Ottoman Palace. Through the Sunni establishment the British had a monopoly on Iraq's oil in the Iraqi Petroleum Company (IPC). The British had promised the Iraqis a 20% participation in oil concessions, but did not keep this promise. The British also monopolised Iraqi trade. Faisal's son, Ghazi, with the help of General Bakr Sidiqi, staged a coup in 1936 to govern the country militarily. About the same time, Saddam Hussein was born in a humble mud brick dwelling.

The Iraqi military were beginning to think about putting an end to Britain's dominance. They looked towards Germany and the rise of the Third Reich as a possible solution to this dominance. This was of course bad news to the British, who solved the problem in the usual way: by resorting to RAF air strikes.

After the Second World War, the German interest pressure was replaced by the USSR's strategic and economic interest during the

Cold War. Under Kassem, the Iraqi Government had become a left-leaning government and this posed a dangerous situation for America and Britain. There was also the threat to all Western interests in the Middle East posed by Muslim fundamentalism in Iran and Wahabism in Saudi Arabia. (The Wahabis were used by the USA to combat the USSR by proxy in Afghanistan.) In some regions even Islam and Nationalism was backed by the US as a force against Communism and progressive movements. In 1963 Saddam Hussein was inserted into this power game. A shrewd gun-toting thug groomed (by the CIA in Egypt around 1961) to promote a secular anti-Iranian State. His Ba'ath party membership was recruited heavily from the old reactionary classes to counter the Communist and Shia revolutionary movements during and after the Cold War.

Initially, during the 1980s, Iraq seemed to be turning into a model of enlightenment for Western purposes. UNICEF went there to study how the Ba'ath Party was achieving such high levels of literacy among children. Schools and hospitals were built. Women were placed in positions of power. Christian churches were built. Jews, Christians, Sunnis and Shias were able to coexist. The fact that Saddam Hussein, relied on torture, imprisonment and death was overlooked and even encouraged by the West, who made immense profits selling arms and equipment to the regime (with preferential tariffs and financial guarantees paid by UK taxpayers). Then things started to go wrong. Saddam was becoming too powerful and was supporting the Palestinians. He was a pan Arab. His weapons were a threat to Israel. He was an important member of OPEC. He posed the question: *Why should the West have its oil cheaply?* He nationalised the oil fields. He prevented foreigners from owning Iraqi companies. Here was an anti-American and anti-British philosophy that was becoming dangerously successful. Ba'athism might spread to the whole Persian Gulf Region. Israelis might be pushed into the sea. His occupation of Kuwait became the *causa belli* for the West.

But when surveying the brief history of Kuwait, we see that this *causa belli* was a rotten apple. Kuwait was no democracy. It had been considered for annexation by the British in 1958. It had been on the USA's 1973 list of countries to invade. It was probably about to extract oil from under the Iraqi border. When Saddam approached the American Ambassador in Baghdad and asked what the American reaction would be if he invaded Kuwait in 1990, she replied that America would regard it as the internal affairs of Arab States and that it would therefore not concern America. She had, "no opinion on Arab-Arab conflicts like your border disagreement with Kuwait." She added that she was going on two weeks holiday and could not be contacted. This piece of unimaginable diplomatic folly probably resulted in a million deaths and years of misery for Iraq which has not ended yet.

In the 1920s the borders had been drawn up, figuratively speaking, with a wooden ruler over glasses of port in the British Foreign Office. When we also consider that the Royal Air Force had bombed Iraq for various reasons throughout the twentieth century, we must conclude that the 1991 and 2003 wars were not about moral rectitude but about the conflict of two great power blocks – the West and the Arab – over the same piece of cake. Nothing more, nothing less. However, the war of 2003 had even less moral justification as it was probably primarily a demonstration of US firepower against Osama Bin Laden – who actually hated all that Saddam Hussein stood for.

Having now started the War with Iraq (described by the elder statesman and Tory ex-Foreign Minister, Douglas Hurd, at Chatham House in 2004 as *an act of great folly*), the UK and US have arrogantly fallen into a quagmire from which they will find it hard to extract themselves. The moral high ground – on which they declared battle – was to free the Iraqi people and bring democracy. This high ideal, however, has brought massive misery. In its own backyard of Northern Ireland, the British Government has been unable to broker a final agreement after a century of strife. The resolution of problems has only begun to occur because the Catholic birth rate has been higher than that of Protestants and a demographic balance has been achieved. In Iraq such a situation is not possible. Kurds represent approximately 20% of the population, Sunnis 20% and Shias 60%.

The historical perspective reveals the immense complexity of Iraq and the lack of success of the British-imposed rule based on the 1921 Westminster model of democracy. In 1953 Stephen Longrigg, produced a study, *Iraq 1900 to 1950*, for the Royal Institute for International Affairs. In it he said, "It was difficult in 1950 not to anticipate that Cabinet Government would long continue, and with it the rootless precariousness of a regime which seemingly at any time a successful intrigue, or a military coup d'etat of too familiar pattern, could subvert[5]." Nor did Longrigg think that the conditions for an imposed parliamentary democracy existed in Iraq. This was percipient as in 1958 Kassem and his *Free Officers* were to stage a military coup that foreshadowed Saddam Hussein's rise to power.

This very scholarly work by Stephen Longrigg should have been read by Mr Blair before he began his adventures. The Foreign Office experts (and those who had experience of Iraq) did warn the Prime Minister, prior to the war, of the complexities of Iraq's political, religious, and racial scene. This advice clearly was not heeded. Even Mr Straw, the Foreign Secretary, was deeply concerned about the hornets' nest that is Iraq. But his role had really been usurped by Mr Blair in his very personal desire to go to war, as the following secret papers leaked to the press show.[6]

An *Eyes Only* options paper on Iraq, prepared by the Cabinet Office Overseas and Defence Secretariat, was given to Mr Blair on Friday 8 March 2002. "The greater the investment of Western forces, the greater our control over Iraq's future, but the greater the cost and the longer we would need to stay... The only certain means to remove Saddam and his elite is to invade and impose a new government, but this would involve nation building over many years."

Replacing Saddam with another *Sunni strongman* would allow the allies to withdraw their troops quickly. This leader could be persuaded not to seek WMD in exchange for large scale assistance in reconstruction. "However there would then be a strong risk of the Iraqi system reverting to type. Military coup could succeed coup until an autocratic Sunni dictator emerged who protected Sunni interests. With time he could acquire WMD". A representative Iraqi government if it were to survive "...would require the US and others to commit to nation building for many years. This would entail a substantial international security force." Since Israel and Iran had WMD, even a representative Iraqi government "would probably try to acquire its own."

Fifty-two retired British Diplomats wrote to the Prime Minister in 2004 saying his post invasion policy in Iraq was a recipe for anarchy. "To describe the resistance as led by terrorists, fanatics and foreigners is neither convincing nor helpful. Policy must take account of the nature and history of Iraq, the most complex country in the region.

However much Iraqis may yearn for a democratic society, the belief that one could now be created by the Coalition is naive[7]." The conflict between the Sunnis, Shias and Kurds continues to this day.

KUWAIT.

While delving in the libraries of The Royal Geographical Society and Chatham House, I was also surprised by the continuous British interest in Kuwait. This adds to the hypocrisy of the outrage of the British government that Saddam Hussein should make demands on Kuwait and invade it in 1991. Interest in Kuwait began with the Anglo-Kuwait agreement of 1899. This small harbour state had been established in the early nineteenth century. Shayk Mubarak gained the throne by killing his brother in 1896. He acknowledged Turkish authority, but asked for British protection. The 1899 Protectorate gave the British a foothold in Mesopotamia. In 1902, at the request of Shayk Mubarak, HMS Lapwing came to guard Kuwait against Turkish forces. Kuwait's independence from Turkey was recognised in the Anglo-Turkish agreement of 1913 but since Mubarak also had date palm groves and a large house in Basra, the British were able to claim a foothold there as well, which was convenient for the construction of the new oil pipeline from Persia (Iran). British forces occupied the Basra area in 1914 at the start of the First World War. By 1920 there were continuous Bedouin tribal raids across the ill-defined dessert borders between Kuwait, Saudi Arabia and Iraq. Saudi Arabia made raids on Kuwait which were defeated by the RAF. In 1937 there were border disputes between Iraq and Kuwait, which were not resolved until 1991. In 1938 Iraq had claimed annexation of Kuwait because of border smuggling. The British Ambassador intervened. In 1958 Selwyn Lloyd, British Foreign Minister, said to Foster Dulles, American Foreign Secretary, that Britain was thinking of making Kuwait a colony. Foster Dulles replied with "that would be a good idea". Britain ended the protectorate status in 1961. In 1963 the borders of Kuwait were defined after claims by Iraq. In 1973 there were secret US plans to invade Kuwait and seize its oilfields as a counter blow to OPEC. Less than twenty years later Saddam Hussein claimed that Kuwait was drilling under the Iraqi border, and therefore drawing oil from Iraq's oil deposits. Events leading to the *Mother of all battles* and the 2003 Iraq War began.

It can be argued that, in the time scale of the last one hundred years, Kuwait has been primarily dominated by the West and only for a very brief period by Iraq. In 1920, British strategic map makers had planned Kuwait as a permanent stranglehold on Iraq's access to the sea.

The preliminary British boundary of Kuwait was drawn on the map as a circle 130 miles diameter. The surveyors realised this was a tall order in the desert sand, and drew it as a series of straight lines between points. Such boundaries were initially meaningless to Bedouin tribesmen driving their goats and sheep, but became more meanigful when the boundary lines were found to run through the middle of an oil field.

---

[1] A brief summary of complex issues related by Said K Aburish in *Saddam Hussein the Politics of Revenge*, London: Bloomsbury Publishing, 2000.

[2] Clare Short, *An Honourable Deception*, London: Free Press, 2004, p205 et seq.

[3] John Fisher, *Curzon and British Imperialism in the Middle East*, London: Frank Cass, 1999, p6 et seq.

[4] H.V.E Winstone, *Gertrude Bell*, London: Quartet Books, 1980, p190 et seq.

[5] Stephen H Longrigg, *Iraq 1900 to 1950*, London: Oxford University Press, 1953, p397.

[6] Michael Smith, *Daily Telegraph*, 18 September 2004.

[7] BBC News. 29 April, 2004. http://news.bbc.co.uk/1/hi/uk_politics/3660837.stm

CHAPTER 2
LAWS & CUSTOMS OF WAR: A SUMMARY

We shall briefly examine the main laws relating to the crimes against peace and the conduct of war.

Mindful of American atrocities against Red Indians, Abraham Lincoln asked Dr Leiber to draw up a code to limit bloodshed in the Civil war of 1863. The *Leiber Code* was one of the first written codes of war. Others followed and became complex as the means of waging war became more ingenious and violent. The most important were the Hague Conventions of 1907. Until the Nuremberg trials of 1946 the laws and customs were self-policing and were more often observed in breach than in compliance. The Charter of the Nuremberg Tribunal 1945 established the culpability of leaders, and crimes against humanity. The Geneva Conventions followed in 1949 and in 1977 their Protocols. These were designed to curb the excesses of war and especially to protect the Red Cross. They are largely self-policing, save for Protocol I Additional to the Geneva Conventions, Article 88(2), where extradition was made possible; but never (as far as we know) practiced. This deficiency – for what's the point of having laws of behaviour if there is no calling to account? – caused the UN to establish the International Criminal Court at The Hague in 2003. It remains to be seen if this is a paper tiger. Meanwhile, there was an extraordinary development when, in 1998, General Pinochet was arrested in the UK for crimes he had committed in Chile 20 years previously. He was kept under house arrest in a suburb of London for a year. As we shall see, this may be the method by which justice may be visited on war criminals, and compensation obtained for their victims, in the future.

THE MAGNA CARTA, 1215. HABEAS CORPUS

Magna Carta or The Charter of Liberties was granted by King John to his subjects, in the year 1215.

(39) *No free man shall be seized or imprisoned, or stripped of his rights or possessions, or outlawed or exiled, or deprived of his standing in any other way, nor will we proceed with force against him, or send others to do so, except by the lawful judgement of his equals or by the law of the land.*

(40) *To no one will we sell, to no one deny or delay right or justice.*

Violation of the principle of no imprisonment without the due process of law, as first laid down in 1215, was established at Guantanamo Bay by the Americans in 2002, and adopted in Iraq during the invasion and subsequent occupation. Not only have PoWs been imprisoned but also civilians, often on the slenderest of pretexts. The detainees have been neither granted access to lawyers nor charged with any offence. Their whereabouts after several months' captivity is often unknown. Their names are misspelled and not properly recorded. They have often been subject to physical (as well as psychological) torture.

ESTABLISHMENT OF THE GENEVA CONVENTIONS AND THE RED CROSS.

In 1846 A Geneva Convention was established for the Amelioration of the Condition of the Wounded in Armies in the Field. This in turn led to the establishment of the International Committee of the Red Cross based in Geneva. During the 1870-71 Franco Prussian War and the 1898 Spanish American War, by and large the conditions of the convention were followed because it was in the interest of the combatants, on both sides, not to leave the injured to die in agony but to carry them to field hospitals.

The Red Cross became an important organisation in times of war and in human disasters. The use of the Red Cross emblem ensured some sort of protection from attack. After the First World War (1914 -1918), because of various deficiencies in The Hague Convention of 1907, a revised convention was drawn up in Geneva in 1925 adding to its terms. Thus when the German high command breached the Geneva Convention they were also breaching the Hague Convention of 1907. By 1949, after the experiences of the Second World War, these Conventions were considered inadequate. The 1949 Conventions became much larger in scope than The Hague Convention of 1907 and in many ways they are over elaborate. The Signatories have to police themselves which, of course, is a grave weakness.

Nevertheless, 132 countries signed up to the Conventions and, diplomatically at least, have recognised its provisions as a humane way of conducting wars. They have also recognised that grave breaches are considered internationally as war crimes. Thus, the destruction of a city the size of Fallujah for the sake of eliminating 1,000 to 3,000 rebels, driving out a population of a quarter of a million, destroying the water supply, preventing Red Crescent ambulances from collecting the wounded from the city and targeting a clinic killing twenty doctors, are all considered internationally as breaches of the Geneva Conventions and as such *war crimes*. Now, whatever the Blair and Bush governments say about Fallujah, the fact of these breaches hangs like an albatross around their necks.

THE HAGUE CONVENTION 1907.

RESPECTING THE LAWS AND CUSTOMS OF WAR ON LAND.

This Convention was a means of codifying laws and customs which had been discussed at various peace conferences towards the end of the nineteenth century. In one respect its aims were altruistic – to diminish the evil effects of war on the innocent, the prisoners and the wounded. In another, its aims were self serving – if the war does not go well, and you take me as a prisoner, I want to be treated humanely; so I, in return, will promise to treat you humanely and respect your families and property. The cynic will say it was a development of mediaeval chivalry: laying down rules for the game of war. Certainly it was followed by the most horrendous two world wars, when millions were killed and cities flattened, but it did have a moderating influence in some areas. The conventions became incorporated in

Rules of Engagement carried in soldiers' pockets. (If you are caught, give name, rank and number only) When someone put up his hands with a white flag, it was most often accepted that he had surrendered, and would not be subject to shooting or torture. Likewise, medical units were respected and rape and pillage discouraged.

Some generals, notably the very pious Montgomery, were sticklers for the rules to the great advantage of the inhabitants of places they conquered. His respect for The Hague Convention IV of 1907 meant that, behind the scenes of the theatre of war, there was not administrative chaos and rebellion as is seen in Iraq today. This was actually to his military advantage. Had the Ba'athist police and administration not been disbanded in direct breach of the Hague Convention IV, the US and UK forces would probably not have had to fight on all fronts as they are today. In addition, there are other Hague laws and customs which immediately stand out as having been broken by the US /UK Coalition; such as the seizure of the state's assets, torture of prisoners, wanton destruction of property and the use of weapons likely to cause great suffering. All of which qualify the Coalition leadership to stand trial for war crimes and the belligerent states to pay compensation to Iraq. Since might is right, the likelihood of this happening at the moment is slim; however, events could change with time and the basis for trial and compensation and retribution may come about within this established legal basis.

Another effect of the Hague Convention IV is that it was used as a framework for what was internationally accepted as customary conduct in war. This basis was expanded in the Nuremberg Charter of 1945 for the prosecution of the Nazi leadership. It also formed the basis of the Geneva Conventions of 1949, under the guardianship of the International Red Cross. Some would say the Geneva Conventions have become too complex in comparison with The Hague Conventions.

SUMMARY OF MAIN CLAUSES RELEVANT TO THE IRAQ WAR.

Seeing that while seeking means to preserve peace and prevent armed conflicts between nations, it is likewise necessary to bear in mind the case where the appeal to arms has been brought about... thinking it important... to revise the laws and customs of war... inspired by the desire to diminish the evils of war, as far as military requirements permit, [they] are intended to serve as a general rule of conduct for the belligerents in their mutual relations and in their relations with the inhabitants.

Article 1: *The Contracting Powers shall issue instructions to their armed forces... in conformity with the Regulations... annexed to the present Convention.*

Article 3: *A belligerent party which violates the provisions ... shall ... be liable to pay compensation.*

REGULATIONS

Section I: On Belligerents.

Article 1: *1. To be commanded by a person responsible for his subordinates. 2. To have a fixed distinctive emblem. 3. To carry arms openly.*

Article 3: *The armed forces of belligerent parties may consist of combatants and non-combatants. In the case of capture by the enemy, both have a right to be treated as prisoners of war.*

Article 4: *Prisoners of war... must be humanely treated, All their personal belongings, except arms, horses, and military papers, remain their property.*

Article 6: *The State may utilize the labour of prisoners of war... The tasks shall not be excessive, and shall have no connection with the operations of the war.*

Article 7: *... prisoners of war shall be treated as regards board, lodging, and clothing on the same footing as the troops of the Government who captured them.*

Article 9: *Every prisoner is bound to give... his true name and rank.*

Article 14: *An inquiry office for prisoners of war is instituted on the commencement of the hostilities in each of the belligerent States... It is the function of this office to reply to all inquiries about prisoners.*

Article 15: *Relief societies for prisoners of war... shall receive from the belligerents... every facility... within the bounds imposed by military necessity.*

Article 18: *Prisoners of war shall enjoy complete liberty in exercise of their religion...*

SECTION II: Hostilities

Article 22: *The right of belligerents to adopt means of injuring the enemy is not unlimited.*

Article 23: *... it is especially forbidden...*

(a) *To employ poison or poisoned weapons;*

(b) *To kill or wound treacherously.*

(c) *To kill or wound an enemy who, having laid down his arms, or having no longer means of defence, has surrendered at discretion;*

(d) *To declare that no quarter will be given;*

(e) *To employ arms, projectiles, or materials calculated to cause unnecessary suffering;*

(g) *To destroy or seize the enemy's property, unless such destruction or seizure be imperatively demanded by the necessities of war;*

(h) *To declare abolished, suspended or inadmissible in a court of law the rights and actions of the nationals of a hostile party...*

Article 25: *The attack or bombardment, by whatever means, of towns, dwellings, or buildings which are undefended is prohibited.*

Article 27: *In sieges... all necessary steps must be taken to spare, as far as possible, buildings dedicated to religion, art, science or charitable purposes, historic monuments, hospitals, and places where the sick and wounded are collected, provided they are not being used at the time for military purposes.*

Article 28: *The pillage of a town or place... is prohibited.*

Article 42: *Territory is considered occupied when it is actually placed under the authority of the hostile army.*

Article 43: *The authority of the legitimate power having in fact passed into the hands of the occupant, the latter shall take all the measures in his power to restore, and ensure, as far as possible, public order and safety, while respecting, unless absolutely prevented, the laws in force in that country.*

Article 44: *A belligerent is forbidden to force the inhabitants of territory occupied by it to furnish information about the army of the other belligerent or its means of defence.*

Article 46: *Family honour and rights, the lives of persons, and private property, as well as religious convictions and practice, must be respected. Private property cannot be confiscated.*

Article 47: *Pillage is formally forbidden.*

Article 55: *The occupying State shall be regarded only as administrator and usufructuary of public buildings, real estate,*

forests, and agricultural estates belonging to the hostile State, and situated in the occupied country. It must safeguard the capital of these properties, and administer them in accordance with the rules of usufruct.
Article 56: *The property of municipalities, that of institutions dedicated to religion, charity and education, the arts and sciences, even when State property, shall be treated as private property. All seizure of, destruction or wilful damage done to institutions of this character, historic monuments, works of art and science, is forbidden, and should be made the subject of legal proceedings.*

THE UNITED NATIONS CHARTER, 1945.

Article 2(3) requires that international disputes be settled *by peaceful means in such a manner that international peace and security, and justice, are not endangered.* Article 2(4) requires that countries refrain from *the threat or use of force against the territorial integrity or political independence of any state, or in any other manner inconsistent with the Purposes of the United Nations.* Article 33 requires that parties to a dispute *shall seek a solution by negotiation, inquiry, mediation, conciliation, arbitration, judicial settlement, resort to regional agencies, or other peaceful means.*

CHARTER OF THE NUREMBERG TRIBUNAL, 1945.

In 1945 the USA, the USSR, and the UK agreed to set up a tribunal to try those responsible for war crimes during the Second World War. The trials were held in Courtroom 600 at Nuremberg. Justice Jackson, the Chief US Prosecutor said "The privilege of opening the first trial in the history for crimes against peace of the world imposes a grave responsibility." It was with high ideals that over a thousand personnel were involved for more than three years in preparing and carrying out trials supposed to help prevent aggressive wars from happening again. It was not only an expression of existing international law but in itself a contribution to international law. The trials of the leaders of the National Socialist Party, the SS, SD, the Gestapo and the Army opened on 18 October 1945. Twenty-one individuals were indicted. Many witnesses were called for prosecution and defence. Considerable documentary evidence, including 1,809 affidavits, was submitted. Records of the Judgements were compiled in twenty two volumes. Tape recordings were made of all the proceedings.

Acts which were described as crimes included planning and executing a war of aggression in violation of international treaties. The Hague Convention (I), 1899, was sited: *before an appeal to arms... to have recourse, as far as circumstances allow, to the good offices of mediation of one or more friendly Powers*. Also sited was the Hague Convention for the Pacific Settlement of International Disputes, 1907, and the Kellog Brand Pact of 1928. These Conventions all aimed at preventing aggressive war. It is noticeable that in many ways the setting up of the International Criminal Court at The Hague in 2003 was a regressive step, in that it will not consider the illegality of going to war – as the Rome Statutes have not defined aggressive war.

The Charter of the International Military Tribunal set up in 1946 defined crimes which came in the jurisdiction of the Tribunal as: (a) *Crimes against Peace: namely, planning, preparation, initiation or waging of a war of aggression or a war in violation of international treaties, agreements or assurances, or in participation in a common plan or conspiracy for the accomplishment of any of the foregoing.* (b) *War Crimes namely, violation of the laws or customs of war. Such violations shall include, but be limited to murder, ill treatment or deportations to slave labour or for any other purpose of civilian population of or in occupied territory, murder or ill treatment of prisoners of war or persons on the seas, killing of hostages, plunder of public or private property, wanton destruction of cities, towns or villages, or devastation not justified by military necessity.* (c) *Crimes against Humanity: namely, murder, extermination, enslavements... or persecution on political, racial or religious grounds... Leaders, organisers, instigators and accomplices participating in the formulation or execution of a common plan or conspiracy to commit any of the foregoing crimes are responsible for all the acts performed by any persons in the execution of such a plan.*

The Judgements of Nuremberg made it clear that they were aimed primarily at the leadership. This leadership was often far from the battlefield; was often personally squeamish about acts of violence; was sentimental towards animals and children; lived in luxurious surroundings; had religious convictions – but gave commands and issued ideas of behaviour that resulted in very grave crimes indeed. While a few individual minor players (such as Werhmacht soldiers, camp commandants, and bureaucrats who organised transports) were subsequently tried, it was the leaders who were considered ultimately responsible for the conduct of all operations.

If we apply the same logic to the Iraq war, Mr Hoon, the Secretary of Defence, cannot shelter behind the fact that a few UK soldiers are being court-martialled for offences against Iraqis. These acts should never have taken place in the first place. Looting, which should not have been allowed in Basra, was actually encouraged by Mr Hoon in the first twenty four hours. Mr Hoon has been directly responsible also for the use of cluster bombs and depleted uranium, defending their use on the grounds of military expediency. The Nuremberg judges made it quite clear that they did not accept Goering's defence of military expediency coming before humanitarian considerations.

Another important emphasis of the Nuremberg Judgements was the prosecution of those responsible for planning an aggressive war using lies and conspiracy. It is clear that the UK Parliament was mislead by deception into taking Britain to war. While there is no desire to repeat the death penalty for such conspiracy, there is absolutely no reason why Mr Blair should not be tried for recklessly planning an illegal war, which has resulted in thousands of Iraqi deaths, and countless wounded and traumatised civilians, many of whom are children.

It was also emphasised at Nuremberg, that the economic exploitation of a country was a grave crime punishable with death. In Chapter 7 we discuss the stripping of Iraqi assets by the Coalition. The desire of the US to exploit Iraqi oil, following a programme set out back in 1973 to break the power of the OPEC cartel and ensure abundant oil, was one of the motivations of this war.

Some will say 'Why bother with the Nuremberg trials that took place sixty years ago?' There are those still alive today who were old enough to remember when the Nuremberg trials took place. To those grey beards, the Nuremberg trials were very important. Monsters were brought to justice after years of near starvation. I remember what it is to be hungry, and to crouch with my mother and aunts under the stairs during a bombing raid.

In 1946 Nuremberg Courtroom number 600 contained high ideals that this would be the end of wars. In the last two years we have seen the same examples all over again: Lies; denial that the Geneva Conventions apply to them; exploitation of the assets of another country; and torture. A press officer using vile language and who is ruthless. ALL THIS WAS SUPPOSED TO HAVE STOPPED IN 1945.

One thousand people were employed to compile the Nuremberg Protocols in twenty Blue books. No one opens them any more. They should do so. People will argue that the Nazi crimes were in a scale out of all comparison to Iraq. In one way they are right. But to little Ali Ismail Abbas, who lost his parents and all his limbs in the first weeks of the war, they are wrong. They are also wrong if depleted uranium dust proves in the long run to make large areas of Iraq uninhabitable. We don't know. To my mind Fallujah is in the same category as Lidice. A genuine film document, made by a German soldier, survived: it shows laughing Germans taking great pleasure in burning down Lidice. The great joy many German war criminals felt during their actions is something they would not remember after the war. [1]

There is no reason why the judgements of Nuremberg should not be considered relevant to the war in Iraq. Our concern is to avoid civilian deaths, disease and starvation, the torture of prisoners, the destruction of property and infrastructure, imprisonment without trial, economic theft, religious intolerance, racial hatred and humiliation. This desire should be no different now from what it was in 1946. People should to be allowed to live in peace and to choose their own destiny. Those who destroy that peace should be brought to justice.

SUMMARY OF NUREMBERG JUDGEMENTS.

THE INDICTMENT:
Crimes against Peace, War Crimes, and Crimes against Humanity, and of a Common Plan or Conspiracy to commit those Crime.

THE JUDGEMENTS:

GOERING. *Crimes against peace:* Commander-in-Chief of the Luftwaffe. He testified: "My point of view was decided by political and military reasons only." After his own admissions to this Tribunal, from the positions which he held, the conferences he attended, and the public words he uttered, there can remain no doubt that Goering was the moving force for aggressive war second only to Hitler. He was the planner and prime mover in the military and diplomatic preparation for war which Germany pursued. *War crimes and crimes against humanity:* The record is filled with Goering's admissions of his complicity in the use of slave labour. As Plenipotentiary. Goering was the active authority in the spoliation of conquered territory, plundering, shooting and desettling populations in occupied territories: persecution of Jews: the direction of the final solution.
Found guilty on all four counts. To be hanged. (He committed suicide hours before he was to be hanged.)

HESS. Hitler's successor designate after Goering. *Crimes against peace:* The Fuhrer's deputy, was active in planning aggressive war. Guilty: life imprisonment. *War crimes*: Not guilty.

RIBBENTROP. Reichsminister for Foreign Affairs. *Crimes against peace:* Planned aggressive war. The way in which he carried out discussions with Poland makes it clear that he did not enter them in good faith. Guilty. *War crimes and crimes against humanity:* Planned economic and political policies in occupied territories; planned final solution. Guilty: To be hanged.

KEITEL. Chief of Staff of Armed Forces. *Crimes against peace:* planned aggressive war, including making use of a possible "incident", such as the assassination of a German minister in Prague, to preface an attack. Guilty. *War crimes and crimes against humanity:* Ruthless treatment of prisoners; looting of cultural property in occupied territories; liquidation of Poles and Jews; ordered attacks on a single German soldier to be met with putting to death 50 to 100 communists; saboteurs' families to be executed; civilians guilty of resistance to be shot; authorised the use of PoWs as slave labour. Defence: Obeying superior orders. Guilty: To be hanged.

KALTENBRUNNER: Leader of SS in Austria. *Crimes against peace:* active in intrigue against illegitimate government of Austria; took no part in planning aggressive war. Not guilty. *War crimes and crimes against humanity:* In charge of Gestapo, SD and criminal police; ordered executions in concentration camps; shooting of prisoners; organised slave labour; leading part in the final solution Guilty: To be hanged.

FRICK: General Plenipotentiary for the administration of the Reich. *Crimes against peace:* Not guilty. *War crimes and crimes against humanity:* knowledge of atrocities committed in concentration camps. Knowledge of insane, sick and elderly put to death. Guilty: To be hanged.

STREICHER: publisher of an anti-Semitic weekly. *Crimes against peace:* Not guilty. *Crimes against humanity:* Known as Jew baiter number one; wrote anti-Semitic articles in *Der Sturmer*; supported Jewish pogrom; as early as 1938 called for the annihilation of Jewish race. Guilty: To be hanged.

ROSENBERG: Head of Foreign Affairs. *Crimes against peace:* Played an important part in planning aggressive war; planned occupation of Eastern territories. Guilty. *War crimes and crimes against humanity:* Responsible for plunder of public and private property in occupied territories; plundered railways and art collections; carried out forced labour and extermination of Jews; declared that The Hague Laws of Land Warfare were not applicable in the Occupied Eastern territories. Guilty: To be hanged.

FRANK: In charge of Legal Affairs. *Crimes against peace:* Not guilty. *War crimes and crimes against humanity:* Willing and knowing participant in the use of terrorism in Poland; in the economic exploitation of Poland in a way which led to the death by starvation of a large number of people; in the deportation to Germany as slave labourers of over a million Poles; and in a programme involving the murder of at least three million Jews. Guilty: To be hanged.

FUNK: Minister of Economics, later President of the Reichsbank and President of the Continental Oil Company. *Crimes against peace:* Participated in the economic preparation for certain of the aggressive wars but not a leading figure. Not guilty. *War crimes and crimes against humanity:* Planned exclusion of Jews from economic life of

Germany; agreed with Himmler that the Reichsbank should benefit from gold and jewels taken from Jewish victims; he participated in the economic exploitation of occupied territories; was responsible for the exploitation of the oil resources of occupied territories in the East; responsible for the seizure of the gold reserves of Czechoslovakian National Bank; responsible for the liquidation of the Yugoslavian National Bank; helped plan slave labour. Guilty: life imprisonment.

SCHACHT: Commissioner of Currency, later President of the Reichsbank. *Crimes against peace:* Central figure in Germany's rearmament programme – not considered by the tribunal as in itself a crime. Not guilty.

DOENITZ: Commander in Chief of the German Navy. *Crimes against peace:* Built and trained U- boat arm, but not aware of aggressive war policy. Not guilty *War crimes:* Unrestricted submarine warfare contrary to Naval Protocol of 1936; ordered killing of survivors of shipwrecked vessels; employed slave labour for the production of ships; advised Hitler not to denounce Geneva Conventions but to break them at will. Guilty: Ten years imprisonment.

RAEDER: Chief of Naval Command. *Crimes against peace:* Built and directed German Navy; planned invasion of Norway. Guilty. *War crimes:* Responsible for sinking the *Athenia*, an unarmed British passenger liner; carried out unrestricted submarine warfare; machine gunned survivors and executed commandos even though they were in uniform. Guilty: Life imprisonment.

VON SCHIRACH: Reich Youth Leader. *Crimes against peace:* Not guilty. *Crimes against humanity:* Control of civilian war economy in Austria, carried out murder, enslavement and deportation of Jews. Guilty: Twenty years imprisonment.

SAUCKEL: *Crimes against peace:* Not guilty. *War crimes and crimes against humanity:* Overall responsibility for slave labour programme, and transport of slave labour. Guilty: To be hanged.

JODL: Chief of Operations staff of Armed Forces. *Crimes against peace:* In a strict military sense, he was the actual planner of the war. Claimed he had to obey Hitler. Guilty. *War crimes and crimes against humanity:* Planned to eliminate Soviet commissars without trial; argued against Hitler denouncing Geneva Convention; ordered the evacuation of all persons in Northern Norway and the burning of their houses; signed an order that Hitler would not accept an offer of surrender of Leningrad or Moscow, insisting that they be completely destroyed. Defence: Following superior orders. Guilty: To be hanged.

VON PAPEN: Vice Chancellor. *Crimes against peace:* Not guilty.

SEYSS-INQUART: Austrian Minister of Security. *War crimes and crimes against humanity:* In Austria organised confiscation of Jewish property and deportation. In Norway, Poland and Netherlands, as Administrator, organised shooting of hostages; persecution of Jews and reprisals against resistance; pillage of private property in Netherlands and use of forced labour. Guilty: To be hanged.

SPEER: Hitler's architect and confidant, Reich Minister for armaments. *Crimes against peace:* Not guilty. *War crimes and crimes against humanity:* Used slave labour. Guilty: Twenty years imprisonment.

VON NEURATH: Minister of Foreign Affairs. *Crimes against peace:* Aware of preparations for aggressive war. Guilty. *Criminal activities in Czechoslovakia:* Organised production for German war effort, sent students to concentration camps. Guilty: Fifteen years imprisonment.

FRITZCHE: Radio commentator later Head of Propaganda Ministry. *Crimes against peace:* Present at Goebbel's daily staff conferences. Not guilty. *War crimes and crimes against humanity:* Prosecution maintained he incited and encouraged the commission of war crimes by deliberately falsifying news, to arouse in the German people those passions which lead to the commission of atrocities. It was decided that he was not aware that the news was false. Not guilty

BORMAN: Secretary to Hitler. *Crimes against peace:* Not guilty. *War crimes and crimes against humanity:* Administered entire civilian war effort; ruthless exploitation of occupied territories; planned slave labour, annihilation of populace and economic exploitation; prohibited decent burials for Russian prisoners of war; organised lynching of prisoners. Guilty: To be hanged.

A striking thing about these cases is that those found guilty came from a wide variety of professions, not all military. There were journalists, financiers, an architect and politicians, as well as the military. They all were involved in one way or another in the planning and execution of an illegal war.

From these judgements we can draw parallels with the Iraq war. The use of false press releases – especially to deny wrongdoing – comes to mind; as does the denial that the Geneva Conventions apply; the admittance of a "mistake"; economic exploitation, especially of oil; conspiracy to wage war using false claims (and not making use of diplomacy in good faith); reprisals against civilian population and property; torture of prisoners.

Bearing in mind that Fallujah was a city of a quarter of a million inhabitants, that the Iraq Body Count runs at approximately 30,000 civilian deaths as a direct result of the war, and that there has been widespread torture and ill treatment of Iraqi prisoners; the atrocities are on the same scale as some of those committed in the Second World War. For instance, the Nazi reprisal for Himmler's death was killing 360 civilians at Lidice and then burning down the village. In Fallujah, in reprisal for the killing of four American contractors, 600 died in the first raid; eventually 70% of the buildings were damaged or destroyed in a city nearly the size of Cardiff [population: 315,000].

THE GENEVA CONVENTIONS OF 1949 AND THEIR PROTOCOLS.
BRIEF SUMMARY OF ARTICLES RELEVANT TO THE IRAQ WAR:

Extracts from **THE GENEVA CONVENTION I FOR THE AMELIORATION OF THE CONDITION OF THE WOUNDED AND SICK IN ARMED FORCES IN THE FIELD, 12 AUGUST 1949.**
Article 3: (1) *Persons taking no active part in the hostilities, including members of armed forces who have laid down their arms ...* or are wounded [shall not be subject to] (a) *violence to life and person in particular... cruel treatment and torture;* (c) *outrages upon personal dignity;* (2) *The wounded and sick shall be collected and cared for.*

Article 12: *Women shall be treated with all consideration due to their sex.*
Article 15: *At all times... Parties to the conflict shall, without delay... search for the dead and prevent their being despoiled.*
Article 16: *Parties... shall record as soon as possible, in respect of each wounded sick or dead person of the adverse Party falling into their hands, any particulars which may assist in his identification... the information shall be forwarded to the Information Bureau described in Article 122... They shall likewise collect and forward through the same bureau one half of a double identity disc, last wills or other documents of importance to the next of kin.*
Article 19: *Fixed establishments and mobile medical units... may in no circumstances be attacked... their personnel shall be free to pursue their duties.*
Article 22: *The following conditions shall not be considered as depriving a medical unit... of protection. (1) That the personnel of the unit... are armed, and that they use their arms in their own defence.*
Article 24: *Medical personnel... shall be respected and protected in all circumstances.*
Article 26: *The staff of the National Red Cross Societies and that of other Voluntary Aid Societies... employed on the same duties as the personnel named in Article 24, are placed on the same footing.*
Article 28: *Personnel designated in Articles 24 and 26... shall be authorized to visit periodically the prisoners of war in labour units or hospitals outside the camp.* Article 35: *Transports of wounded and sick or of medical equipment shall be respected and protected...*
Article 36: *Medical aircraft... shall not be attacked.*
Article 38: *... the red cross* [or the red crescent] *on a white background... is retained as the distinctive sign of the Medical Service of armed forces.*
Article 46: *Reprisals against the wounded, sick personnel, buildings or equipment protected by the Convention are prohibited.*

The following Articles are crucial to an understanding of the legal responsibilities of the Parties in a conflict and especially the legal partnership of allies in a war. Article 49: *The High Contracting Parties undertake to enact any legislation necessary to provide effective penal sanctions for persons committing or ordering... any of the grave breaches of the present Convention... It may also, if it prefers, and in accordance with the provisions of its own legislation, hand such persons over for trial to another High Contracting Party concerned, provided such high contracting party has made out a prime facie case... Each High Contracting Party shall take measures necessary for the suppression of all acts contrary to the... Convention.*

Article 50: *Grave breaches to which the preceding Article relates shall be those involving any of the following acts, if committed against persons or property protected by the Convention: wilful killing, torture or inhuman treatment, including biological experiments, wilfully causing great suffering or serious injury to body or health, and extensive destruction and appropriation of property, not justified by military necessity and carried out unlawfully and wantonly.*

Article 51: *No High Contracting Party shall be allowed to absolve itself or any other High Contracting Party of any liability incurred by itself or by another high Contracting Party in respect of breaches referred to in the preceding article.*

Article 52: *At the request of a Party to the conflict, an inquiry shall be instituted...*

Extracts from **THE GENEVA CONVENTION III RELATIVE TO THE TREATMENT OF PRISONERS OF WAR, 12 AUGUST 1949.** The conditions of this Convention are very similar to Article 49, 51, and 52 of the Geneva Convention I. This convention is especially relevant to conditions in Abu Ghraib.

Article 13: *Prisoners of war must at all times be humanely treated.* Article 14: *Prisoners of war are entitled in all circumstances to respect for their persons and their honour.* Article 22: *Prisoners of war may be interned only in premises located on land and affording every guarantee of hygiene and healthfulness. Except in particular cases... they shall not be interned in penitentiaries.*

Article 25: *Prisoners of War shall be quartered under conditions as favourable as those for the forces of the Detaining Power who are billeted in the same area... The foregoing provisions shall apply in particular to the dormitories of prisoners of war as regards both total* surface and minimum cubic space, and the general installations bedding and blankets.

Article 26: *The basic daily food rations shall be sufficient in quantity, quality and variety... Sufficient drinking water shall be supplied to prisoners of war.*

Article 29: *The Detaining Power shall be bound to take all sanitary measures necessary to ensure the cleanliness and healthfulness of camps... Prisoners of war shall have for their use day and night, conveniences which conform to the rules of hygiene...*

Article 34: *Prisoners of war shall enjoy complete latitude in exercise of their religious duties...*

Article 122: *Upon the outbreak of a conflict and in all cases of occupation, each of the Parties to the conflict shall institute an official Information Bureau... The information shall make it possible quickly to advise the next of kin concerned.*

Extracts from **THE GENEVA CONVENTION IV RELATIVE TO THE PROTECTION OF CIVILIAN PERSONS IN TIME OF WAR, 12 AUGUST 1949.** This is particularly relevant to the attacks on Fallujah in April and November 2004.

Article 33: *No protected person may be punished for an offence he or she has not personally committed. Collective penalties and likewise all measures of intimidation or of terrorism are prohibited. Pillage is prohibited; Reprisals against protected persons and their property are prohibited.*

Article 53: *Any destruction by the Occupying Power of... property belonging individually or collectively to private persons or to the State... is prohibited, except where such destruction is rendered absolutely necessary by military operations.*

Article 55: *... the Occupying Power has a duty of ensuring the food and medical supplies of the population.*

Article 56: *To the fullest extent of the means available to it, the occupying Power has the duty of ensuring and maintaining... the medical and hospital establishments and services.*

Extracts from **THE HAGUE CONVENTION FOR THE PROTECTION OF CULTURAL PROPERTY IN THE EVENT OF ARMED CONFLICT, 14 MAY 1954.** This Convention is especially relevant to the destruction of museums, libraries and archaeological sites in Iraq; and to the attitude of Mr Donald Rumsfeld to such destruction.

The High Contracting Parties: ... Being convinced that damage to cultural property... means damage to the cultural heritage of the whole of mankind... have agreed the following provisions:

Definition of cultural Property

Article 1: (a) *... property of great importance to the cultural heritage of every people, such as monuments of architecture... archaeological sites... works of art; manuscripts, books...* (b)(a) *museums, large libraries...*

Article 4: (1) *The High Contracting Parties undertake to respect cultural property... by refraining from any use of the property... and... from any act of hostility directed against such property.* (3) *The... Parties further undertake to prohibit, prevent and, if necessary, put a stop to any form of theft, pillage ... and any acts of vandalism directed against cultural property.*

Article 28: *The High Contracting Parties undertake to prosecute and impose penal or disciplinary sanctions upon those... who commit or order to be committed a breach of the present Convention.*

Extracts from **PROTOCOL I ADDITIONAL TO THE GENEVA CONVENTIONS OF 1949 AND RELATING TO THE PROTECTION OF VICTIMS OF INTERNATIONAL ARMED CONFLICTS, 8 JUNE 1977**. This Protocol is particularly relevant to the use of depleted uranium weapons and cluster bombs, and the attacks on Fallujah.

Article 35: (1) *In any armed conflict, the right of the Parties to the conflict to choose methods or means of warfare is not unlimited,* (2) *It is prohibited to employ weapons... of a nature to cause superfluous injury, or unnecessary suffering,* (3)*... to employ methods or means of warfare which are intended, or may be expected, to cause widespread long-term and severe damage to the natural environment.*

Article 40: *It is prohibited to order that there shall be no survivors.*

Article 44: (2)*... violations of (rules of international law applicable in armed conflict) shall not deprive a combatant of his right to be a combatant, or, if he falls into the power of an adverse Party, of his right to be a prisoner of war* (3) *provided he carries his arms openly:*

(a) *during each military engagement*, [N.B. These Articles intended to cover guerrilla fighters.]

Article 51: (5) *...the following types of attack are to be considered indiscriminate:* (a) *an attack by bombardment... which treats as a single military objective a number of clearly separated... objectives located in a city, town, village... containing... concentrations of civilians or civilian objects; and* (b) *an attack which may be expected to cause incidental loss of civilian life, injury to civilians, damage to civilian objects... which would be excessive in relation to the concrete and direct military advantage anticipated.* (6) *Attacks against the civilian population... by way of reprisals are prohibited.*

Article 54: (1) *Starvation of civilians as a method of war is prohibited.* (2) *It is prohibited to attack, destroy, remove... drinking water installations.*

Article 55: (1) *Care shall be taken... to protect the natural environment against widespread, long-term and severe damage.*

Article 86: *Failure to act* (1) *The High Contracting Parties and the Parties to the conflict shall repress grave breaches... of the Conventions... which result from a failure to act when under a duty to do so.* (2) *The fact that a breach of the Conventions or of this Protocol was committed by a subordinate does not absolve his superiors from penal disciplinary responsibility.*

Article 88: (1) *The High Contracting Parties shall afford one another the greatest measure of assistance in connexion with criminal proceedings brought in respect of grave breaches of the Conventions or this Protocol.* (2)... *The High Contracting Parties shall cooperate in the matter of extradition. They shall give due consideration to the request of the State in whose territory the alleged offence has occurred.*

Article 91: *Responsibility. A Party to the conflict which violates the provisions of the Conventions or of this Protocol shall, if the case demands, be liable to pay compensation. It shall be responsible for all acts committed by persons forming part of its armed forces.*

This Protocol toughened up the Geneva Conventions of 1949 in relation to advanced weapons (including those that destroy the environment), prohibition of indiscriminate attacks and recognition that guerrillas share the right to PoW status. Ratification of Article 91 is important because it lays members of the UK Government and

Military open to extradition, trial, and penalties for grave breaches of the Geneva Conventions and Protocols. (While the UK became a Contracting Party in 1998, the US did not ratify). Article 86 is also important because it places responsibility for individual soldiers' actions on the leaders and commanders as was laid down at Nuremberg in 1945.

PROTOCOLS TO THE CONVENTION ON PROHIBITIONS OR RESTRICTIONS ON THE USE OF CERTAIN CONVENTIONAL WEAPONS WHICH MAY BE DEEMED TO BE EXCESSIVELY INJURIOUS OR TO HAVE INDISCRIMINATE EFFECTS, GENEVA 1980.
1997 OTTAWA CONVENTION – MINE BAN TREATY.

In the 1980s there were attempts to ban land mines. These mines are very cheap to produce and, having plastic casings, very difficult to detect. They are made in vast numbers by China, Israel, the US and the UK, among others. They have been especially used in Africa, and Afghanistan, blowing off the limbs of children and farmers long after they have been laid. The United Nations land mine treaties are so bound up with caveats that they are virtually impossible to enforce; especially as there is no outright ban on their use. The Protocols are also self-policing and end with Article 14: Compliance, which is a feeble consultation process. Large 2,000 lb cluster bombs used by the UK and the US are really simultaneous distributors of unmarked land mines, incendiary devices and flechette fragmentation bomblets. Because of their nature they are indiscriminate, yet their use is justified by Mr Hoon, our Defence Secretary on grounds of military expediency. Lady Diana Spencer must be turning in her grave. We notice that the United States once again backs out of ratifying protocols that outlaw some of the most horrendous weapons. Obviously Protocol III was aimed at outlawing napalm.

Protocol II, Article 3 says of land mines: (8) *The indiscriminate use... is prohibited. Indiscriminate use is any placement of such weapons; (b) which employs a method or means of delivery which cannot be directed at a specific military objective; or (c) which may be expected to cause incidental loss of civilian life... which would be excessive in relation to... direct military advantage anticipated.*

Protocol III on the Use of Incendiary Weapons, Article 1: (1) *"Incendiary weapon" means any weapon or munition which is primarily designed to set fire to objects...*Article 2: (1) *It is prohibited in all circumstances to make the civilian population... the object of attack...* (2) *any military objective located within a concentration of civilians the object of attack.* (Not ratified by US.)

Protocol IV Article 1 says: *It is prohibited to employ laser weapons... to cause permanent blindness...* (Not ratified by US)

Amended Protocol II (1996) Article 10: (1) *Without delay after the cessation of active hostilities, all mine fields, mined areas, mines, booby-traps and other devices shall be cleared, removed or destroyed or maintained in accordance with Article 3 and... Article 5 of this Protocol.* Article 14: *Compliance* (4) *The High Contracting Parties undertake to consult each other and to cooperate with each other bilaterally, through the Secretary-General of the United Nations or through other appropriate international procedures, to resolve any problems that may arise with regard to the interpretation and application of the provisions of this Protocol.*
In its Technical Annex, Articles 2 (c) and 3 (c) give parties the option of declaring, at the time of notifying consent to be bound, that they will defer, for up to nine years, compliance with its provisions regarding detectability, self destruction, and self deactivation of land mines.

In 1984, the United Nations drew up a Convention against Torture and Other Cruel, Inhuman and Degrading Treatment or Punishment which requires state parties to arrest, prosecute and punish those who have committed torture, where the alleged offender is present in any territory under its jurisdiction, or to extradite to a state which will prosecute such offenders. This Convention was generally ratified by UN members including Chile.

SUMMARY OF THE 1991 GULF WAR RULES OF ENGAGEMENT POCKET CARD CARRIED BY US SOLDIERS.

A. *Do not engage anyone who has surrendered*

B. *Avoid harming civilians,*

C. *Hospitals churches shrines... will not be engaged except in self defense.*

D. *Hospitals will be given special protection.*

E. *Booby traps may be used... to impede the progress of enemy forces. They may not be used on civilian... property.*

F. *Looting and taking of war trophies are prohibited.*

G. *Avoid harming civilian property unless necessary to save US lives.*

H. *Treat all civilians and their property with respect and dignity.*

I. *Treat all prisoners humanely and with respect and dignity.*

THE HAGUE TRIBUNAL, 1993.

The Geneva and Hague Conventions did not actually have functioning mechanisms for bringing war criminals to justice. Thus, in 1993, by Resolutions 808 and 827, the United Nations set up The Hague Tribunal, to try alleged war criminals linked to the break up of Yugoslavia in the 1990s. Cynics have suggested that as there had been widespread media publication of atrocities committed by the Parties, this Tribunal was set up to make it appear that something was being done. In 2001, Slobodan Milosevic, former president of Yugoslavia and Serbian leader was extradited to The Hague Tribunal in return for reconstruction finance to Serbia. Even though this was an ad hoc court, it took on a momentum of its own. The Prosecution indictments were based on breaches of the Geneva and Hague Conventions, and the Nuremberg Charter relating to war crimes, genocide, and crimes against humanity (especially rape, which had been widely practiced in the Former Yugoslavia). In 1994 The Hague Tribunal was extended in scope to include the trial of those guilty of war crimes in Rwanda. In 2005 The Hague Tribunal is still sitting.

The Rome Statute of the International Criminal Court, 2002.

In the United Nations it was, however, felt that the time had come to set up a permanent International Criminal Court outside state sovereignty. In 1998 120 States ratified the Statute of Rome to set up the ICC at The Hague. The Statute entered into force on 1 July 2002. The United States refused to sign it since there was a possibility that American soldiers might be brought to trial. Indeed, the establishment of this court poses a threat to state sovereignty. While the Security Council can request the prosecutor to instigate a case; it can also (under Article 16) veto an investigation for a period of one year. The Security Council can extend this period every year. It can only investigate a wrongdoing if the State, in which the alleged guilty party is, does not bring the alleged guilty party to justice – either through refusal or inability. It is therefore *complementary* to State Parties, as affirmed in Article 20, *Ne bis in idem* (double jeopardy). While the Prosecutor can begin an investigation, there has first to be a pre trial hearing where it is decided whether or not to commence an investigation. The ICC Prosecutor can issue a warrant for arrest. He also has power to punish a guilty party with life imprisonment and have property assets confiscated. Victims can claim compensation. (Think of the Hammoudi family in Basra, who wish to claim compensation personally from Mr Blair. In theory, this would be possible).

The US position is even clearer. The American Servicemen's Protection Act of 2001, was drawn up to prohibit military aid to supporters of the Rome Statute, and to give the US President power to bomb any country which detains US soldiers on ICC arrest warrants. European reaction to this bill was so bad that President Bush withdrew it. What he appears not fully to realise is that the Nuremberg Charter laid stress on the indictment of leaders, such as Rumsfeld, not on the likes of Lindie England, a scapegoat if ever there was one.

However, there are optimists who see this as a very important step towards establishing a world human rights court, and it may – like The Hague Tribunal – gather an unstoppable momentum of its own. Time will tell. At the moment, it is considering around 500 to 1000 claims in respect of Iraq alone. The building and staff have had to expand to cope. Initially, all these claims have only received an acknowledgement, while the Prosecutor decides what to do with them.

What this book attempts to do is to demonstrate that, within the terms of the Rome Statute of the International Criminal Court, there are grounds to investigate whether war crimes have been committed by Mr Blair and his close associates; and that there was knowledge and intent in their actions. Whether or not such a prosecution happens is a matter of public and international pressure.

The ICC in The Hague has jurisdiction over four distinctive crimes: the crime of genocide, crimes against humanity, war crimes and the crime of aggression.

Article 6 defines the crime of genocide as: ...*any of the following acts committed with intent to destroy, in whole or in part, a national, ethnical, racial or religious group, as such:* (a) *Killing members of the group;* (b) *Causing serious bodily or mental harm to members of the group;* (c) *Deliberately inflicting on the group conditions of life calculated to bring about its physical destruction in whole or in part;* (d) *Imposing measures intended to prevent births within the group;* (e) *Forcibly transferring children of the group to another group.*

Article 7.1 defines crimes against humanity as: ...*any of the following acts when committed as part of a widespread or systematic attack directed against any civilian population, with knowledge of the attack:* (a) *Murder;* (b) *Extermination;* (c) *Enslavement;* (d) *Deportation or forcible transfer of population* (e) *Imprisonment or other severe deprivation of physical liberty in violation of fundamental rules of international law;* (f) *Torture;* (g) *Rape, sexual slavery, enforced prostitution, forced pregnancy, enforced sterilisation, or any other form of sexual violence of comparable gravity;...*(k) *Other inhumane acts of a similar character intentionally causing great suffering, or serious injury to body or to mental or physical health.*

47

Article 7.2 continues with further important definitions of the elements of a crime against humanity: (a) *"Attack directed against any civilian population" means a course of conduct involving the multiple commission of acts referred to in paragraph 1 against any civilian population, pursuant to or in furtherance of a State or organisational policy to commit such attack;...* (e) *"Torture" means the intentional infliction of severe pain or suffering, whether physical or mental, upon a person in the custody or under the control of the accused; except that torture shall not include pain or suffering arising only from, inherent in or incidental to, lawful sanctions:*

Article 8, defines war crimes to mean *grave breaches of the Geneva Conventions* and violations of customary international war law. It defines these in a further 50 sub clauses.

Jurisdiction over the crime of aggression will only come into force when it has been clearly defined. The earliest this can occur is 2009.

Article 27, entitled *Irrelevance of official capacity*, lays the blame fairly and squarely on the shoulders of the political leaders responsible for such crimes. It states: *This Statute shall apply equally to all persons without any distinction based on official capacity. In particular official capacity as a Head of State or Government, a member of a Government or parliament, an elected representative or a government official shall in no case exempt a person from criminal responsibility under this Statute, nor shall it, in and of itself, constitute a ground for reduction of sentence.*

Article 29 states that there is no statute of limitations.

Article 30 relates to the mental element of a crime and helps the court to determine the offender's intent. (2) *...a person has intent where:* (a) *In relation to conduct, that person means to engage in the conduct;* (b) *In relation to a consequence, that person means to cause that consequence or is aware that it will occur in the ordinary course of events.*

Article 32 states: (1) *A mistake of fact shall be a ground for excluding criminal responsibility only if it negates the mental element required by the crime.* (2) *A mistake of law as to whether a particular type of conduct is a crime within the jurisdiction of the Court shall not be a ground for excluding criminal responsibility. A mistake of law may, however, be a ground for excluding criminal responsibility if it negates the mental element required by such a crime, or as provided for in article 33.*

How far under Article 32 mistake of fact or mistake of law come into operation because of falsehoods is something that requires considerable investigation. If Ministers of the Crown and Members of Parliament, who voted for the Iraq war, and armed service personnel were lied to, then one can conclude that Article 32 (1) comes into force, and that this is a ground for excluding criminal responsibility for some members of the UK administration and military. Since the UK involvement in the war was very personal to Mr Blair it might be discovered that everyone was duped in some way or another into supporting the Prime Minister. However, that would not exonerate those who realised they had been duped but still continued to support Mr Blair, refusing to act against the Prime Minister from fear of jeopardizing their personal position or a desire not to "rock the boat". But one can, for instance, sympathise with General Sir Mike Jackson, head of the British army when he said, "I spent a good deal of time recently in The Balkans making sure Milosevic was put behind bars. I have no intention of ending up in the next cell to him in The Hague."[2]

THE INTERNATIONAL CRIMINAL COURT ACT 2001. INCORPORATION OF THE ROME STATUTE INTO BRITISH DOMESTIC LAW.

In July 1998 Britain became a founding signatory to the inter-governmental treaty known as the Rome Statute of the International Criminal Court. Britain's Foreign Secretary, Robin Cook, announced in the House of Commons that the government intended to introduce legislation to enable the UK to ratify the Statute and comply with its obligations. The UK subsequently enacted The International Criminal

Court Act in 2001 which as well as recognising the authority of the International Criminal Court in the Hague, incorporated the three crimes of 'genocide, crimes against humanity, and war crimes' into British domestic law for the first time.

The ICC has been set up to investigate and prosecute genocide, crimes against humanity and war crimes committed anywhere in the world by nationals of signatory states. It also has jurisdiction over crimes, wherever committed, which are referred to it by the UN Security Council. It is however complementary to national courts. Signatory states, such as Britain, retain jurisdiction unless they are unable or unwilling to investigate and prosecute a crime themselves. The ICC prosecutor must defer to a state's courts unless the ICC determines that the state is unwilling or unable to carry out an investigation or prosecution.

THE AIMS OF THE ICC ACT

The Foreign and Commonwealth Office's notes explain that its principal aims are:

To incorporate ICC Statute offences into domestic law so that UK authorities will always be able to investigate and prosecute ICC crimes committed by UK nationals, residents or persons subject to UK service jurisdiction.
To make provision to enable the UK to meet its obligations under the ICC statute enabling it to ratify the statute. These obligations include provisions concerning the arrest and surrender of persons wanted by the ICC, assistance with investigations and provisions to serve prison sentences in this country.

THE ICC ACT

The complete Act is in six parts with ten Schedules.
Part I defines certain terms in the Act.
Part II provides for the arrest and surrender of suspects.
Part III provides for co-operation with ICC investigations.

Part IV provides for ICC prison sentences, fines, forfeitures and reparations.

Part V incorporates the ICC offences of genocide, crimes against humanity and war crimes into domestic law.

Part VI provides for the territorial extent and application of the Act.

The Pinochet Case, 1998. Extradition as a Method of Bringing Justice.

In 1998 General Pinochet, the former dictator and mass murderer of Chile, made the mistake of wandering into what he thought was a friendly state; he came to Harley Street in London to have treatment for a bad back. He was not aware that the Association of Progressive Prosecutors had brought a civil action in Spain against him and known Argentinian torturers. (The Argentine junta had used CIA methods of torture in Pinochet's brainchild, *Operation Condor*). Nor was he aware of, or bothered himself with, the fact Spain had signed an extradition treaty with the UK. The Spanish police issued an arrest warrant, which was passed to the extradition squad of Scotland Yard, who in turn applied for a domestic UK warrant for arrest under the Extradition Act 1989. On 16 October 1998 Pinochet was arrested at the clinic by the Scotland Yard anti-terrorist squad before he had time to flee back to Chile the following morning.

On 11 December 1998, a humiliated Pinochet, had to appear in a London Court, where he gave his name – and where the extradition warrant was read out. His case was reviewed by two panels of Law Lords. On 24 March 1999, the House of Lords judged that torturers... *may be punished by any state because the offenders are "common enemies of all mankind and all nations have an equal interest in their apprehension and prosecution."... The Torture Convention was agreed ... to provide an international system under which... the torturer could find no safe haven.* The torturer thus became *hostis humanis generis* (an enemy of all mankind) and the victim then had the right to sue the torturer if he came by accident within the jurisdiction of the state in which he resided, or into a state that had an extradition treaty with his own state.

On 8 October 1999 The Bow Street Magistrate ordered his extradition to Spain. Pinochet suddenly became ill and, with compassion, was allowed home. As he stepped down from the plane in Santiago he staged a remarkable recovery from a stroke and senile dementia. However, in 2005 it looks as if he is finally being tried in Chile, and facing those of his victims who are still alive.

While in London, General Pinochet seemed to have got away with his crimes. But he was effectively imprisoned for one year, between October 1998 and October 1999. Admittedly the standards of accommodation were more pleasant than Guantanamo Bay, and he was able to take frequent tea breaks with Mrs Thatcher in his suburban residence in Surrey. However, the fact remains he was under house arrest, and harboured the constant and ever-growing fear that he would be flown to Spain to explain himself to his victims. This fear may well have grown into a real illness, (which naturally disappeared as soon as his destination became Santiago).

The importance of this case, which is, in the opinion of Queen's Counsel Geoffrey Robertson, one of the most significant Human Rights cases in the 20th Century, is that it puts an end to state sovereign immunity from future prosecution for crimes of torture, for leaders such as Rumsfeld and Blair. Nor is there a statute of time limitation.

Six British nationals were detained without trial, in Guantanamo Bay, between 2001 and 2005. They were all subject to the most foul torture with methods approved by Secretary of Defense Rumsfeld.

On 4 June 2003, at Prime Minister's Question Time, in reply to a question on Guantanamo Bay by Mr. Charles Kennedy (Leader of the Liberal Democrats), the Prime Minister replied: ... "Obviously, that situation [detention without trial] cannot continue indefinitely, although it is complicated by the fact that the information is still coming from the people detained there. I cannot say more than that. The information is important."

Mr Rumsfeld and Mr Blair can no longer shelter behind the fact that it was not they but their subordinates who carried out the torture at Guantanamo Bay, Abu Ghraib or anywhere else. Mr Rumsfeld already has had to cancel a trip to Germany because of fear of arrest. In their retirement they should take great care where they spend their holidays.

Did the Prime Minister have an opportunity at the summit to raise again the position of the nine British citizens held at Camp Delta? They are in a legal no man's

land. In response to the Father of the House in a different context, he referred to the need for trials. No charges have even been brought against those British citizens. That is contrary to all the principles of international justice to which our country subscribes. If the boot were on the other foot, and we were holding American citizens in a similar fashion, all hell would have broken lose on Capitol hill and we would not have heard the end of it. Did the Prime Minister have any opportunity to raise that fundamental concern about our own passport holders with the President and representatives of the United States?

The Prime Minister: That last issue did not come up at the summit, but we have raised it with the US Government I have said what I have said about it already. Obviously, that situation cannot continue indefinitely, although it is complicated by the fact that information is still coming from the people detained there. I cannot say any more than that. That information is important.

The information coming from Guantanamo Bay is important. Hansard 4 June 2003

BIBLIOGRAPHY:
The conventions and protocols outlined in this chapter can be found in: Adam Roberts and Richard Guelff, *Documents on the Laws of War*, OUP, 2000.
A more detailed exposition of the Pinochet arrest can be found in: Geoffrey Robertson QC, *Crimes Against Humanity, The Struggle for Global Justice* London: Penguin, 1999.

---

[1] http://en.wikipedia.org/wiki/Lidice
[2] Richard Norton-Taylor, *Guardian*, 23 February 2005.

CHAPTER 3
ALLIES IN WAR AS PARTNERS.

Legally, the ongoing Iraq War is a joint enterprise between the US and the UK. American actions are a joint responsibility of the USA and the UK. If war crimes are committed by one party, they are also the responsibility of the other party, if the other party knowingly aids and abets the joint criminal enterprise.

RELEVANT LAW AND CONVENTIONS: The International Law Commission, Articles on Responsibility of States (2001), Article 16 provides that: *A State which aids or assists another State in the commission of an internationally wrongful act by the latter is internationally responsible for doing so if: (a) That State does so with knowledge of the circumstances of the internationally wrongful act; and (b) The act would be internationally wrongful if committed by that State.*

.

EVIDENCE OF PARTNERSHIP: In May 2004, Jack Straw, the UK Foreign Secretary, tried to distance Britain from the actions of its ally, the USA. When a fellow Labour MP said that Britain must share the shame of the US over brutality against prisoners, Mr Straw replied, "I do not accept your suggestion that the responsibility for dealing with matters that lie within the US sector is also shared by the UK[1]." As a lawyer, Mr Straw should be aware that this is not the case.

There is a common misconception that the British participation in the Iraq War is somehow nobler than the American role and that, therefore, the UK's role can be divorced from the American. Having operated for thirty years in Northern Ireland, UK forces are probably much better trained in sensitive urban guerrilla warfare than their US counterparts. However, the divorce is not legal.

There are five main factors which nullify this divorce. The joint planning of the war, political collaboration, joint military action in the theatre of war, joint administration in the occupation, joint exploitation of economic resources and assets, and joint financial benefit from such activities, such as the provision of mercenaries or seizing assets. As we will see in Chapters 4 and 5 (*Deceit & a Conspiracy for War* and *The Rht Hon Clare Short & Clausewitz*), there was considerable joint military planning and shared knowledge of preparations for the common purpose of attacking Iraq.

Politically, before and since the war, the British Prime Minister has gone out of his way to *stand shoulder to shoulder* with Bush, even in his darkest hours – immediately after the revenge killings of 600 Iraqis in Fallujah and the revelations of torture at Abu Ghraib. Nor did the British Government disassociate itself from the US Administration when it was discovered that its Defence Secretary, Donald Rumsfeld, had personally authorised different types of torture, and had even asked in writing for the torture to be more extreme[2]. This was a moment when the UK could have declared that enough was enough and pulled its troops out of Iraq (as Spain did), for that is the only true way of disassociating Britain from the USA.

The UK Government had been warned early on by Amnesty International and the Red Cross that torture and other abuses were being carried out in the 17 US-run prisons in Iraq. British-held captives had been handed over to these prisons. Only when photographs were leaked to the press were the public made aware of these scandals. It was then discovered that UK soldiers had also been involved in wanton killing and torture. Considering that the war was ostensibly to liberate Iraq, the Coalition leaders should have been scrupulous in their application of the laws and customs of war. In fact, the US Administration made it clear that they thought that the Geneva Convention did not apply to a whole range of prisoners. The atmosphere of torture and abuse came straight from the US President and Defence Secretary, Donald Rumsfeld, yet the UK Government did nothing about it.

Militarily, the two main participants in the war are in close partnership. UK soldiers protect the MSL (Main Supply Line from Kuwait to the American Forces) along which all ammunition, food, water, and other logistic supplies must travel. British troops man the border control with Kuwait. British troops hold the Southern Sector of Iraq, thus allowing American forces to operate in the Central Theatre[3]. Because there is less hostility in the South, the numbers of British troops are much smaller than the 140,000 Americans, yet they are still sustaining casualties in rough proportion. In a crude legal comparison, the US is the armed bank robber, and the UK provides the getaway car.

There have also been combined military operations. The SAS operate alongside the US army in special operations inside the American sector. The *aggressive patrolling* of the Tikrit area – which proved such a disaster and which was also contrary to the Geneva Convention – was a combined operation. The preliminary attacks eliminating Iraqi air defences were carried out by UK planes together with American planes. The first week of invasion was initiated by the *Shock and Awe* bombardment of Baghdad using cruise missiles fired from UK as well as American warships[4].

The Economic exploitation of Iraq has been a joint enterprise, though largely to the advantage of American companies. It was considered it would be a *sine qua non* of a democratic Iraq that nationalised assets should be privatised, with American companies given priority in running these assets. The UK has been eager to join in this pillage, but has only been fed a few crumbs from these contracts. One of the most important tasks of the British Army was to seize the southern oil fields of Iraq quickly and guard them from sabotage. One area where British companies have financially benefited is in the provision of mercenaries to carry out security duties. Many of these mercenaries are former UK soldiers, especially SAS. At least one UK ex MP has personally benefited financially from these contracts. There are estimated to be at least 10,000 mercenaries in Iraq, none of them bound by the Geneva Conventions.

In October 2004 there was a request for a reserve battalion of 650 British troops to move into an area south of Baghdad previously occupied by US troops. This would free the US army to carry out its mission to defeat insurgents in Fallujah in a November 2004 assault. In Parliament on 18 October 2004 the Liberal Democrat MP, Jenny Tonge asked, "If we refuse the American request, what penalties are we likely to incur?" Mr Hoon, the Defence Secretary replied, "There will be no penalty but we will have failed in our duty as an ally...

Were we to refuse the request it would go to the heart of our relationship not only with the US, but with other members of the alliance."[5]

Our Defence Secretary, who is a barrister as well as an MP, thus confirms the legal position – in contradiction to Mr Straw, our Foreign Secretary – that allies in war are in partnership. If war crimes are committed, the war crimes of one partner are the war crimes of the other partner, if the partner has a knowing common purpose in a joint criminal enterprise. The joint actions which can lead to liability for a crime in international law are: One; participation in a common purpose. Two; participation in a common purpose, where the other partner, or both commit a crime that was not necessarily first agreed on, but which has a risk of occurring. (eg. in an armed bank robbery that gets out of hand, and a policeman is shot dead by mistake). Three; by aiding and abetting an illegal act, by practical assistance, encouragement, or moral support. Thus, violations by the USA become the responsibility also of UK nationals, "notwithstanding that such violations may have been committed by US forces[6]."

By the end of October 2004, 650 British troops had moved into the area immediately south of Baghdad in support of the major American assault on Fallujah in November. While their contribution militarily was negligible, their presence politically was of considerable importance. On CNN websites (used as propaganda prior to the Bush Republican re-election), some 25% of the pictures shown, of the battle for Fallujah in November 2004, were of the British Black Watch soldiers.

These British soldiers were some hundred miles away at Camp Dogwood *supporting* the Americans. The Black Watch suffered five deaths. They wore caps with distinctive red cockades. They appealed to the Scottish nationalism of many Americans who have a sentimental attachment to kilts and bag pipes. They are an impressive elite force – very well equipped – that carried out a night raid on a small town a few miles from their base. This action some would be proud to call a *surgical strike* without deaths on either side. For the Iraqis, marched off with blankets over their heads leaving their howling wives and children behind, their view of the experience was somewhat different. Interestingly, it was the Black Watch Regiment which first entered Baghdad Main Railway Station in 1917, pushing the Turkish army northwards.

CONCLUSION: The Iraq War is a joint illegal enterprise between two major players: the US and the UK. American and UK actions are a joint responsibility of the US and the UK. If this partnership becomes sundered by troop withdrawal, or the end of hostilities, the war crimes already committed will still have to be accounted for by either party, or both.

---

[1] Colin Brown, *Independent*, 13 May 2004.
[2] Pentagon action memo (unclassified), *Counter-Resistance Techniques*, approved by SECDEF on 2 December 2002.
[3] Rageh Ommar, *Revolution Day,* London: Viking, 2004, p205.
[4] BBC film archive, March 2003.
[5] Hansard, 18 October 2004.
[6] Peacerights, *Report of the Inquiry into the alleged commission of War crimes by Coalition Forces in the Iraq War during 2003*, London, 8-9 November 2003.

WAR CRIMES OR JUST WAR?

CHAPTER 4
DECEIPT & A CONSPIRACY FOR WAR.

The real *causae belli* for the Iraq War were not given. The Charter of the United Nations allows self-defence under Article 51, but it does not allow pre-emptive self-defence unless supported by a Security Council resolution. Mr Blair claimed that intelligence showed Iraq had weapons of mass destruction posing an *imminent* 45-minute threat to UK nationals. Paul Wolfowitz, the US Deputy Secretary of Defense, said that the WMD threat was used as a cause for going to war for *bureaucratic reasons*. He was right. There were no weapons.

Hans Blix, the UN weapons inspector, was asked to find these weapons. He found none, but was recalled before he had completed his task so that *Operation Shock and Awe* could begin before it turned too hot in Iraq. At the time, Dr Blix did not realise he was being used by the US and the UK as part of a prearranged plan to trap Saddam Hussein. The real reasons for going to war were complex and required deceit; hence they were *crimes against peace* – punished with death at Nuremberg in 1946.

RELEVANT LAWS AND CONVENTIONS: The Charter of the United Nations, Article 2(3) requires that international disputes be settled by peaceful means so *that international peace and security, and justice, are not endangered.* Article 2(4) requires that Members refrain *from the threat or use of force against the territorial integrity or political independence of any state, or in any other manner inconsistent with the Purposes of the United Nations.* Article 33(1) requires that parties to a dispute first *seek a solution by negotiation, enquiry, mediation, conciliation, arbitration, judicial settlement, resort to regional, agencies... or other peaceful means.* Not until all such means are exhausted should force be used.

Charter of the Nuremberg Tribunal, Principle VI (a) *Crimes against peace: (i) Planning, preparation, initiation or waging of a war of aggression or a war in violation of international treaties, agreements or assurances; (ii) Participation in a common plan or conspiracy for the accomplishment of any of the acts mentioned under (i).*

In 1973, the then British Prime Minister, Edward Heath, was warned by secret MI6 Intelligence that the Americans had a plan to invade a Middle Eastern country in order to break the OPEC cartel and reduce the price of oil per barrel. The US also wished to establish a firm military presence in the area in order to secure future oil supplies, and ensure that Israel was not attacked.[1] The oil fields of Kuwait, Saudi Arabia, and Abu Dhabi were possible targets. Mr Heath was also warned that the Pentagon might ask Britain to join in this attack, but that Iraq might react unfavourably to such a move. In the event there was no such attack. The world oil crisis ended with a reduction in OPEC price levels and new supplies being found in the North Sea and elsewhere.

Saddam Hussein had initially been nursed by the CIA. He had certainly been supported with military equipment – including biological and chemical agents – by America in the 1980s, even after his chemical attack on the Kurdish town of Halabja. The US supported Saddam in his war against Iran as a matter of realpolitik. Large amounts of money were made from this relationship based on oil and munitions. However, things started to go sour when Saddam backed Palestine financially. The last straw came when he invaded Kuwait.

The Gulf War served to kerb his power and to impose stringent sanctions, which reduced much of Iraq's population to hunger and poverty (with a very high level of child mortality, probably in the region of half a million). Actually, it was also in the US's interest to keep a weakend dictator in Iraq as a buffer against Iranian activities. As we now know, Saddam Hussein largely complied with the United Nations resolutions banning him from having weapons of mass destruction and long range rockets. By 2002 Saddam Hussein had no weapons of mass destruction and efforts were being made to lift the UN sanctions – not least because they were having a dire effect on

Iraqi children. As these events were starting to take shape, Al Qa'ida attacked the twin towers on American soil.

An intellectually weak President of the USA had been listening to fundamental Christians and a very powerful Zionist Imperialist neo-conservative lobby: The Project for the New American Century. The neocons had advocated a pre-emptive war against Iraq in their September 2000 report *REBUILDING AMERICA'S DEFENSES: Strategy, Forces and Resources for a New Century.* 9/11 provided their opportunity. (In 1998, Madeleine Albright, US Secretary of State, had already said of Iraq, "If we have to use force, it is because we are America; we are the indispensable nation. We stand tall, and we see farther into the future."[2]) President Bush had to show the US public that America was able to combat a new and frightening form of terrorism. Again the Pentagon appealed to Britain to support its actions. A deal was struck between the American President and the British Prime Minister, who had been a Fulbright Scholar in his youth and who – like Bush – was a fundamental Christian. To show the folly of attacking American territories and the virtues of democracy, private enterprise, and global markets, a massive demonstration of American power would be made against a Middle Eastern country. Afghanistan first, then Iraq was the deal. Iraq was a soft target. Its skies were already dominated by US and UK fighter planes, its airfields and military installations regularly bombed. In the circumstances, quite how Saddam was supposed to wield his weapons of mass destruction was never explained.

But what was to be the excuse for such a drastic illegal step? On 17 March 2002, Wolfowitz was invited to lunch at the British ambassador's residence. Their discussions are described in a letter to Blair's foreign policy advisor. "I opened by sticking very closely to the script that you used with Condi Rice. We backed regime change, but the plan had to be clever and failure was not an option. I then went through the need to wrongfoot Saddam on the inspectors and the Security Council Resolutions and the critical importance of the Middle East peace plan. If all this could be accomplished skilfully, we were fairly confident that a number of countries could come on board."[3] Pressure would then be put on Saddam to allow UN

Weapons Inspector, Hans Blix, into the country. Saddam would probably obstruct the UN team, and this failure to comply would be the *causa belli*.

The cynical conspiracy was thus set in motion. British and American intelligence were hard put to find any evidence of weapons of mass destruction. Intelligence caveats were ignored. Possibilities became certainties. Smudgy satellite photographs were produced. A ten year-old PhD thesis was used. Dossiers were printed. Saddam, Mr Blair said, had the capability of striking UK territory within 45 minutes. Tanks were out on British streets around Heathrow Airport.

Things in early 2003 were not going to plan however. The Prime Minister was forced into a position, by his public pronouncements and Parliament, where he had to seek a second resolution from the UN Security Council to go to war. Resolution 1441 was not considered by many (including the Secretary General, Koffi Annan, and the British Ambassador, Sir Jeremy Greenstock) as a trigger for war. France's position, supported by Germany and Russia (both Security Council members), was that Hans Blix should be given more time to complete his inspections. This was perfectly reasonable as Hans Blix was making progress and Saddam Hussein was even dismantling some medium range missiles. The French President said on 10 March 2003 that France would veto such a new resolution at that particular moment in time, and that war should be avoided if at all possible. However, if Hans Blix failed, war would be inevitable – but it wasn't at that moment.[4] Now, this proved a massive problem for Blair as the armies were geared up for war and dates had already been pencilled in for mid March at the latest (later it would be too hot in Iraq to fight). What then to do?

Blair lied. The gamble was that British MPs had not read the text of the French President' s interview on French TV of 10 March (and probably would not have had an English translation). Thus, on 12 March, Blair said in Parliament that such a veto would be *unreasonable* and that there was a country that was going to veto the resolution under *any circumstance*, which was simply not true. Bush joined in this chorus, and the Americans declared that the French were *cowards* and *cheese-eating surrender monkeys*. By 18 March 2003 Blair's lie was perpetuated many times over in the debate for going to war. The French President was named and mocked in the debate by both main parties. The debate succeeded in its aim and Hans Blix's team were ordered to leave Iraq.

In all probability a crucial factor in obtaining a Labour majority was the fact that Blair had persuaded Clare Short not to resign from the Cabinet prior to 18 March 2003, using the supposed fact that war was inevitable because of the French position. When, in May that year, I sent Clare Short a copy of the full text French Diplomatique translation of the President's interview, she replied she was amazed.

In the summer of 2003, the chairman of the Foreign Affairs Committee, the Speaker of the House of Commons and the chairman of the Parliamentary Standards Committee were all shown the disparity between the Prime Minister's account and what the French President actually said. In her deposition to the Foreign Affairs Committee, Clare Short included the full text translation of the French President's interview. None of these officials of the House of Commons – public servants of the taxpayer – chose to call the Prime Minister to the House to explain this disparity, as is in their power.

It should be understood that the decline of parliamentary standards carries very grave consequences. It may be considered extreme to say that in 1932 there were only 13 debates in the Reichstag. But it is true to say that an institution is quickly trampled underfoot if it is not sustained. It is also true to say that complicity in an illegal act of war is also considered a *war crime*.

In this rush to war, it was necessary to lie about the plans and also to lie about the reactions of other European states. Parliament was misled into war. In a performance before the United Nations, Colin Powell and Mr Straw used an imaginary bottle of anthrax to demonstrate that Saddam was a major threat to world peace. At the time both statesmen already had grave doubts about the nonsense they were propounding. However, this was the usual refrain of leaders about to embark on an aggressive war in the cause of peace.

But it was all lies. There were no weapons. Intelligence experts who broke ranks and said it was nonsense were vilified. Dr Kelly so much so that he killed himself. Journalists were sacked from the BBC for telling the truth. Foreign Office and Government Communications Headquarters staff who dared voice what was going on were sacked. The House of Commons was dragged into accepting these lies. War was declared on a false pretext just in time before the weather changed in Iraq. Troops that had been assembled for months were unleashed and the *Shock and Awe* bombardment of Baghdad commenced with ear-shattering explosions and lurid scenes reminiscent of Martin's paintings of *The Last Days of Babylon*. For ten days and nights the ground shook, glass windows were torn out of their frames and the latest technology of death was hurled at the long-suffering human guinea pigs below. Children with limbs ripped off, were laid to rest in blood soaked blankets. Meanwhile Saddam Hussein left the city by motor car.

But the Coalition leaders – Blair and Bush – were able to walk towards their lecterns (with arms spread slightly from their bodies, as if ready to draw imaginary guns from their holsters) and pronounce victory. It was all over in a few weeks. Except for the guerrilla war. Two years later the road from Baghdad airport to the city is still unsafe but at the time, the US public were impressed; the war against Al Qa'ida was being won. The trouble of course was that Saddam's secular State had had no truck with Osama Bin Laden.

At Nuremberg in 1946, a radio commentator by the name of Fritzche was accused of *crimes against peace* and of *war crimes* (by inciting and encouraging the former) by deliberately falsifying news to arouse in the German people those passions which lead to atrocities. It was decided that Fritzche was not aware that the news was false, and he was therefore acquitted. No such defence could be put forward by Blair since he was the author of the news. Mr Blair claimed he was privy to secret intelligence (which of course "he could not divulge") that Saddam Hussein had weapons of mass destruction that could be unleashed on Cyprus within 45 minutes. When the tabloid papers splashed this news on their front pages, Blair and Hoon knew the news to be false but made no attempt to correct it. Blair's second dossier on Saddam's weapons capability (known as the *Dodgy Dossier*) was cobbled together from a students PhD thesis (which referred to events in Iraq twelve years earlier) under the pretence that the matters described were the very latest intelligence. This dossier – which was an official Government document – was never withdrawn, even though it was a pack of lies.

This propagation of false news happened early on in the conflict. Straw and Blair declared that two major bombings (part of the *Shock and Awe* air strikes) that hit two market places in Baghdad, and in which many civilians were killed, were self-inflicted by the Iraqis. (Even though Robert Fisk, a distinguished British journalist, found American markings on the shrapnel of the missiles.) This knee-jerk transfer of blame to the enemy was very similar to that described in the trial of Saukel and Raeder at Nuremberg in 1946. When, during the invasion period, two British soldiers were shot in a fire fight in Basra, Blair misleadingly claimed (contrary to the eye-witness account of the British officer in charge) that they had been dragged out of a vehicle and executed by the mob. This false statement – accompanied by dramatic vocal effects – formed an important part of Blair's speech at Camp David in early 2003. The *Sun* newspaper and *Kilroy*, the popular TV programme, picked it up and whipped up public sentiment for aggressive prosecution of the war. The accusation was subsequently retracted.

When later that year Mr Blair, en route to China, heard that Dr Kelly (who had made known to the BBC his misgivings about Saddam's weapons programme) had killed himself; Mr Blair's reaction was to say he had no part in the naming of Dr Kelly. In fact, it later transpired Mr Blair had chaired three separate meetings to discuss exactly how to name Dr Kelly. The builder who has bunged up our drain, the gardener who has trod on our favourite plant, the playground bully, they will all deny their misdeeds. Their denials are unimportant. Mr Blair's deceits are very important.

Mr Blair has become enmeshed in his own deceits. In 2002 he said in various speeches that most people agreed the world would be a better place without Saddam Hussein, but that regime change per se was not an option, it would in fact be illegal. The Prime Minister and the Secretary of Defence, Mr Hoon, got in a tremendous muddle about this legality:

25 FEBRUARY 2003. Mr Blair: "Even now, today, we are offering Saddam the prospect of voluntary disarmament through the UN. I detest his regime—I hope most people do—but even now, he could save it by complying with the UN's demand."[5]

18 MARCH 2003. Mr Blair: "I have never put the justification for action as regime change. We have to act within the terms set out in 1441 – that is our legal base."[6]

MAY 2003. Mr Hoon said of the Government's argument that the threat from Iraqi weapons of mass destruction was the main reason for going to war, "That was the reason we gave, which I stand by, for taking military action against Saddam Hussein's regime. We are confident WMDs are there. We now have to find them... Bear in mind that we also committed ourselves to stay within international law, as we interpreted it in the UK, and the threat posed by WMD was the reason for taking action."[7]

But a year later Mr Blair was saying: "It was a difficult choice. I took the choice. I stand by it. But let us be clear about this also: if the right hon. Gentleman [Mr Kennedy] had had his way, Saddam Hussein and his sons would still be running Iraq. That is the case and that is why I took the stand that I did. I take it now, and I, at least, will stick by it."[8]

At Nuremberg, those accused of lying in *crimes against peace* were hung.

FRIDAY, 8 MARCH 2002. Mr Blair is given a *Secret UK Eyes Only* options paper, prepared by the Cabinet Office Overseas and Defence Secretariat.

"The greater the investment of Western Forces, the greater our control over Iraq's future, but the greater the cost and the longer we would need to stay. The only certain means to remove Saddam and his elite is to invade and impose a new government, but this would involve nation-building over many years."

Replacing Saddam with another *Sunni strongman* would allow the allies to withdraw their troops quickly. This leader could be persuaded not to seek WMD in exchange for large scale assistance in reconstruction.

"However there would then be a strong risk of the Iraqi system reverting to type. Military coup could succeed coup until an autocratic Sunni dictator emerged who protected Sunni interests. With time he could acquire WMD". A representative Iraqi government if it were to survive "would require the US and others to commit to nation building for many years. This would entail a substantial international security force." Since Israel and Iran had WMD, even a representative Iraqi government would probably try to acquire its own. The U.S. had lost confidence in containment, said the paper.

"The success of Operation Enduring Freedom, distrust of UN sanctions and inspection regimes, and unfinished business from 1991 are all factors" but there would be major problems finding a legal justification to use military force, as "subject to law officers' advice, none currently exists." Since the threat of Saddam using chemical or biological weapons was no greater than in the recent past, regime change had no basis in international law, and there was no evidence of Iraq backing international terrorism, "this makes moving quickly to invade legally very difficult," the paper concluded.

The problem was "Washington believes the legal basis for an attack on Iraq already exists. Nor will it necessarily be governed by wider political factors. The US may be willing to work with a much smaller coalition than we think desirable." Mr Blair should "consider a staged approach, establishing international support, building up pressure on Saddam and developing military plans." The policy should be to push hard for the return of the weapons inspectors, "winding up the pressure on Iraq." If Saddam refused to admit the inspectors, or if they were admitted and subsequently expelled, that could provide legal justification for large scale military action. "Saddam would try to prevent this, although he has miscalculated before." The options paper also said that "If an invasion is contemplated this autumn, then a decision will need to be taken in principle six months in advance."

MONDAY, 11 MARCH 2003. Three days after receiving the options paper, at a Downing Street press conference with the visiting Vice President Cheney, Mr Blair said, "No decisions have been taken...but that there is a threat from Saddam Hussein and the weapons of mass destruction that he has acquired is not in doubt at all." Mr Cheney only insisted that UN weapons inspectors be allowed back in with "a go anywhere, any time kind of regime."

In Washington Mr Bush had reportedly told one aid: "F*** Saddam. We're taking him out".

Sir Christopher Meyer, British Ambassador to the US, warned from Washington that the President's desire to get rid of Saddam should not be underestimated. Mr Blair now sent Sir David Manning, his foreign policy adviser, to Washington to explain the UK's problems. Sir David Manning briefed the British Ambassador, and outlined the strategy to Condoleezza Rice, Mr Bush's national security adviser. (Sir David, who had been stranded in Washington on September 11 2001, had forged a good working relationship with Miss Rice, dealing together with the immediate aftermath of the al-Qa'ida attacks.)

THURSDAY, 14 MARCH 2002. Sir David sends a memo to Downing Street late in the evening, which is forwarded by fax to Barcelona (EU summit 14 -17 March). It read:

"Prime Minister, I had dinner with Condi on Tuesday, and talks and lunch with her and an NSC [National Security Council] team on Wednesday (to which Christopher Meyer also came). These were good exchanges and particularly frank when we were one-on-one at dinner. We spent a long time at dinner on Iraq. It is clear that Bush is grateful for your support and has registered that you are getting flak.

"I said that you would not budge in your support for regime change but you had to manage a press, a Parliament and a public opinion that was very different than anything in the States, and you would not budge on your insistence that, if we pursued regime change it must be very carefully done and produce the right result. Failure was not an option. Condi's enthusiasm for regime change is undimmed. But there were some signs, since we last spoke, of greater awareness of the practical difficulties and political risks.

"From what she said, Bush has yet to find the answers to the big questions: how to persuade international opinion that military action against Iraq is necessary and justified; what value to put on the exiled Iraqi opposition; how to co-ordinate a US/allied military campaign with international opposition (assuming there is any); what happens on the morning after?

"Bush will want to pick your brains. He will also want to hear whether he can expect coalition support. I told Condi that we realised that the Administration could go it alone if it chose. But if it wanted company, it would have to take account of the concerns of its potential coalition partners."

He also said he had warned Miss Rice that the weapons inspectors issue was key and had to be handled in a way that would persuade Europe in particular that America realised the war had to be legal.

"Renewed refusal by Saddam to accept unfettered inspection would be a powerful argument." It was of "paramount importance" that the allies also dealt with the Middle East issue.

Unless they did they could find themselves "bombing Iraq and losing the Gulf." There were signs that the Prime Minister's visit to the ranch would be useful. "No doubt we need to keep this in perspective. But my talks with Condi convinced me that Bush wants to hear your views on Iraq before taking decisions.

"He also wants your support. He is still smarting from the comments by other European leaders on his Iraq policy. This gives you real influence: on the public relations strategy; on the UN and weapons inspections; and on US planning for a military campaign. This could be critically important. I think there is a real risk that the Administration underestimates the difficulties. They may agree that failure isn't an option, but this does not mean that they will avoid it."[9]

FRIDAY, 15 MARCH 2002. Latest Joint Intelligence Committee assessment said that "Intelligence on Iraq's weapons of mass destruction (WMD) and ballistic
missile programmes is sporadic and patchy... From the evidence available
to us, we believe Iraq retains some production equipment, and some small
stocks of CW agent precursors, and may have hidden small quantities of
agents and weapons... There is no intelligence on any BW agent production
facilities."[10] (At this time Blair was in Barcelona for the EU summit, talking to the French President, Jacques Chirac, and the German Chancellor, Gerhard Schroeder.)

SUNDAY, 17 MARCH 2002. On British TV, Clare Short denounced (with a hint of resignation) that "blind military action against Iraq doesn't deal with the problem." One hundred Labour MPs had signed a House of Commons motion opposing the war.[11] In Washington, the

US Deputy Secretary of Defense, Paul Wolfowitz, was invited to lunch at the British Ambassador's residence. The ambassador wrote to Sir David Manning about the meeting: "I opened by sticking very closely to the script that you used with Condi Rice. We backed regime change, but the plan had to be clever and failure was not an option.

"I then went through the need to wrongfoot Saddam on the inspectors and the UN Security Council Resolutions and the critical importance of the Middle East peace plan. If all this could be accomplished skilfully, we were fairly confident that a number of countries could come on board."[12]

MONDAY, 18 MARCH 2002. Ian Duncan Smith declared "Saddam must go". An ICM poll found more than half the country were against Britain supporting a US-led invasion. Mr Straw told the PM there was no way that any meaningful declassified report on Iraq could be published.[13]

FRIDAY 22 MARCH 2002. (That weekend, 23-24 March, Mr Straw had to compose note for PM ahead of his visit to Crawford, Texas.) Peter Ricketts, Straw's policy director, sent Straw a confidential memo "By sharing Bush's broad objective The Prime Minister can help shape how it is defined, and the approach to achieving it. In the process he can bring home to Bush some of the realities which will be less evident from Washington. He can help Bush make good decisions by telling him things his own machine probably isn't.

"The truth is that what has changed is not the pace of Saddam Hussein's WMD programmes, but our tolerance of them post-11 September. I am relieved that you have decided to postpone publication of the unclassified document.

"My meeting yesterday showed that there is more work to do to ensure the figures are accurate, and consistent with those of the US.

But even the best survey of Iraq's WMD programmes will not show much advance in recent years on the nuclear, missile or chemical weapons/ biological weapons fronts: the programmes are extremely worrying but have not, as far as we know, been stepped up.

"US scrambling to establish a link between Iraq and al Qa'ida is so far frankly unconvincing.

"To get public and Parliamentary support for military options we have to be convincing that the threat is so serious/imminent that it is worth sending our troops to die for."

The second problem was "the end state". What sort of Iraq would we be left with? "Regime change does not stack up. It sounds like a grudge between Bush and Saddam."

What was to stop any new leader acquiring weapons of mass destruction? "It would be almost impossible to maintain UN sanctions on a new leader who came in promising a fresh start."[14]

130 Labour MPs have now signed the early day motion against war and, according to a MORI poll, 52% of the population opposed joining the US in a war against Iraq.

MONDAY, 25 MARCH 2002. Mr Straw forwards a note to the Prime Minister marked *Secret and Personal*. "The rewards from your visit to Crawford will be few. The risks are high, both for you and the Government.

"I judge that there is at present no majority inside the Parliamentary Labour Party for any military action against Iraq, (alongside a greater readiness to surface their concerns).

"Colleagues know that Saddam and the Iraqi regime are bad. But we have a long way to go to convince them as to: the scale of the threat from Iraq and why this has got worse recently: what distinguishes the Iraqi threat from that of eg. Iran and North Korea so as to justify military action; the justification for any military action in terms of international law; and whether the consequence of military action really would be a compliant law-abiding replacement government."

Mr Straw said neither the extent of threat nor reasons for tackling it now were clear. It was doubtful that America would be considering action if it were not for 9/11.

But at the same time there "was no credible evidence" to link Iraq to Osama Bin Laden and al-Qa'ida. British strategy had to be based on international law, using Iraq's "flagrant breach" of the UN imposed obligation to allow the weapons inspectors unfettered access. It should concentrate initially on strengthening the sanctions regime and insisting that weapons inspectors be allowed the "go anywhere, anytime" regime Mr Cheney had demanded.

"I know that there are those who say that an attack on Iraq would be justified whether or not weapons inspectors were readmitted," the Foreign Secretary said. "But I believe that a demand for the unfettered readmission of weapons inspectors is essential, in terms of public explanation, and in terms of legal sanction for any military action."

But there were two "potential elephant traps" he warned. The first was the point that regime change per se was no justification for military action.

The second, the question of whether or not it would require a new mandate. "The US are likely to oppose any idea of a fresh mandate," Mr Straw said, "on the other side, the weight of legal advice here is that a fresh mandate may well be required."

Mr Straw said post war Iraq would cause major problems, no one had a clear idea what would happen afterwards "There seems to be a larger hole in this than anything." Most American assessments argued for regime change as a means of destroying WMD.

"But none has satisfactorily answered how that regime change is to be secured, and how there can be any certainty that the replacement regime will be any better. Iraq has no history of democracy so no one has this habit."[15]

FRIDAY, 5 APRIL 2002. Crawford, Texas summit. In his pre-summit interview, Mr Blair told NBC that he and the President were "not proposing military action at this point in time." In his corresponding pre-summit interview with ITN Mr Bush said, "I made up my mind that Saddam needs to go."

There was, in fact, little doubt that the Crawford summit was a council of war. "I explained to the Prime Minister that the policy of my government is the removal of Saddam, and that all options are on the table, Mr Bush said later. "The world would be better off without him and so will the future."

SATURDAY, 6 APRIL 2002. In a speech in the George Bush Senior Presidential library, Mr Blair said that the Iraqi dictator had to allow the weapons inspectors in "any time, any place... But leaving Iraq to develop weapons of mass destruction in flagrant breach of no less than nine separate United Nations Security Council resolutions, refusing still to allow weapons inspectors back to do their work properly, is not an option."[16]

IRAQ INTERVIEW GIVEN BY M. JACQUES CHIRAC, PRESIDENT OF THE REPUBLIC, TO "TF1" AND "FRANCE 2"

THE PRESIDENT - Not sufficiently. But it isn't for you or for me to decide that, that's for the inspectors to whom the UN has entrusted the responsibility of disarming Iraq to say. The inspectors have to tell us: "we can continue and, at the end of a period which we think should be of a few months" - I'm saying a few months because that's what they have said - "we shall have completed our work and Iraq will be disarmed". Or they will come and tell the Security Council: "we are sorry but Iraq isn't cooperating, the progress isn't sufficient, we aren't in a position to achieve our goal, we won't be able to guarantee Iraq's disarmament". In that case it will be for the Security Council and it alone to decide the right thing to do. But in that case, of course, regrettably, the war would become inevitable. It isn't today.

http://www.elysee.fr/ang/actus/speeches_.htm

18 Mar 2003 : Column 767

The Prime Minister : First, the hon. Gentleman is absolutely wrong about the position on resolution 1441. It is correct that resolution 1441 did not say that there would be another resolution authorising the use of force, but the implication of resolution 1441—it was stated in terms—was that if Iraq continued in material breach, defined as not co-operating fully, immediately and unconditionally, serious consequences should follow. All we are asking for in the second resolution is the clear ultimatum that if Saddam continues to fail to co-operate, force should be used. The French position is that France will vote no, whatever the circumstances. Those are not my words, but those of the French President. I find it sad that at this point in time he cannot support us in the position we have set out, which is the only sure way to disarm Saddam. And what, indeed, would any tyrannical regime possessing weapons of mass destruction think when viewing the history of the world's diplomatic dance with Saddam over these 12 years? That our capacity to pass firm resolutions has only been matched by our feebleness in implementing them. That is why this indulgence has to stop—because it is dangerous: dangerous if such regimes disbelieve us; dangerous if they think they can use our weakness, our hesitation, and even the natural urges of our democracy towards peace against us; and dangerous because one day they will mistake our innate revulsion against war for permanent incapacity, when, in fact, if pushed to the limit, we will act. But when we act, after years of pretence, the action will have to be harder, bigger, more total in its impact. It is true that Iraq is not the only country with weapons of mass destruction, but I say this to the House: back away from this confrontation now, and future conflicts will be infinitely worse and more devastating in their effects.

http://www.publications.parliament.uk/pa/cm200203/cmhansrd/vo030318/debtext/30318-07.htm#30318-07_sp-min7

20 May 2003

from The Rt Hon Clare Short MP

Dear Nicholas Wood

Thank you very much for sending me a transcript of President Chirac's interview of 10 March. It is shocking that his commitment to war if inspection failed was not highlighted in our media and that Tony Blair's comments were misleading.

Thank you for bringing this to my attention.

Yours sincerely

[1] The Joint Intelligence Committee, State Papers, 1973.

[2] NBC *Today* show, 19 February 1998.

[3] Michael Smith, *Telegraph*, 18 September 2004.

[4] Iraq interview given by M. Jacques Chirac, President of the Republic, to "TF1" and "France 2", 10 March 2003; http://www.elysee.fr/ang/actus/speeches_.htm

[5] *Hansard*, 25 February 2003, Column 124;
http://www.publications.parliament.uk/pa/cm200203/cmhansrd/vo030225/debtext/30225-05.htm#30225-05_spmin1

[6] *Hansard*, 18 March 2003, Column 772;
http://www.publications.parliament.uk/pa/cm200203/cmhansrd/vo030318/debtext/30318-09.htm

[7] *Spectator*, 1st May 2003.

[8] *Hansard*, 13 October 2004, Column 280;
http://www.publications.parliament.uk/pa/cm200304/cmhansrd/cm041013/debtext/41013-03.htm#41013-03_spnew11

[9] Michael Smith, 'Secret papers show Blair was warned of Iraq chaos' and 'Failure is not an option, but it doesn't mean they will avoid it', *Telegraph*, 18 September 2004.

[10] Annex B of the Butler report, pp.167-168.

[11] 'Short warns over Iraq action', BBC News, 17 March 2002;
http://news.bbc.co.uk/2/hi/uk_news/politics/1877740.stm

[12] Michael Smith, 'Failure is not an option, but it doesn't mean they will avoid it', *Telegraph*, 18 September 2004.

[13] Ibid.

[14] Ibid.

[15] Ibid

[16] Ibid.

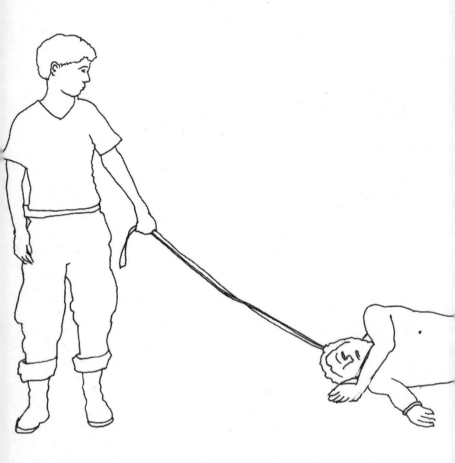

CHAPTER 5
THE RHT HON CLARE SHORT &
CLAUSEWITZ.

Clausewitz, the military strategist of the Napoleonic period, observed that "war is always the servant of policy... without a sound policy, success in war is improbable." This dictum can well be applied to the appalling lack of planning for the post invasion period in Iraq. For several months, in the corridors of the Pentagon and the cellars of the British High Command at Northwood military planning for the war had been intense. The question of what to do after a rapid invasion was considered only in a matter of weeks before the invasion began.

As Secretary of State for the Department of International Development (DfID), and charged with preparing for the aftermath of the war in Iraq, Clare Short had a unique insight into these events. What she saw – the Prime Minister's recklessness – eventually led to her resignation from the Government.

Her evidence shows the Cabinet meetings about Iraq were totally inadequate[1]; that this was very much Tony Blair's personal war; that he ignored expert advice, shunned discussion, listened only to his small cabal of unelected advisors, brushed aside problems and, worst of all, that he lied.

Because of the very large New Labour majority, Parliament became Blair's plaything. The fact that Parliament discussed fox hunting for a total of 700 hours and Iraq for only seven shows the depths to which it has plummeted. Many of his party's MPs became so concerned with maintaining their pleasant life style of oak-lined offices, superb cheap meals and six-digit expense bills, that many compromised their consciences. As a result, tens of thousands of Iraqis have died, thousands of children have been maimed and countless Iraqis have been vilely tortured. There are no accurate figures, since a complacent Mr Ingram did not think it necessary to count Iraqi deaths and casualties. Very few MPs voted against the Government.

In Chapter 4: *Deceit & a Conspiracy for War*, we have seen that there were many reasons, declared and undeclared, for this war. The preparations for a very rapid high-tech invasion were carefully worked out. Troops were trained and deployed in the Persian Gulf and Kuwait months in advance. In contrast, the aftermath was treated with scant regard. There was a major split between the US State Department and the Pentagon about the administration of Iraq. The State Department wanted to retain the Ba'ath Administration while removing its leaders, thereby conforming with the Hague Conventions of 1907 concerning the maintenance of civil administration. But the Pentagon wanted to dismiss the Ba'ath Administration and install a Provisional US Administration with sweeping powers to privatise the assets of Iraq to the advantage of American companies, and also to install permanent military bases in Iraq. A third political programme was proposed by Clare Short's Department: to run post-war Iraq under United Nations auspices. In order to keep Clare Short on his ship of war, the Prime Minister promised her this outcome. Unknown to her, Mr Blair had also promised Mr Bush to go along with the Pentagon plan. These conflicting political aims conform to Clausewitz' observation on lack of clear policy.

As we have seen, the Foreign Secretary, Jack Straw, was more percipient than Blair about the dangers of the Pentagon approach. Clare Short's department was also giving dire warnings which were ignored. The concept that Iraq, a country the size of France, could suddenly be run by 600 strangers, who couldn't even speak Arabic and who had only found Iraq on the map a few weeks earlier, is preposterous. Everyone was pulling in different directions. Planning was chaotic and divisive. Two years later the country is still in violent chaos.

At the Foreign Affairs Committee inquiry into events leading up to the Iraq War held on 17th June 2003 (to which I attended in the public seats), Clare Short described in her evidence that the Cabinet meetings about Iraq were totally inadequate. She said decisions were made in advance by Mr Blair in a small outside office with his cabal of unelected advisors (Sir David Manning, Jonathon Powell, Alistair

Campbell and Sally Morgan). Actual Cabinet meetings only lasted from forty five minutes to an hour. At these meetings each Minister in turn read out what was in effect a brief presentation report. There was very little time left for discussion or dissent. Iraq would be discussed only briefly. No proper minutes were kept. During the critical period of the summer of 2002, throughout the long parliamentary *recess* (holiday), from July to September, there were no Cabinet meetings at all. During this period, frantic secret preparations for the conflict were going on. There had been a special Cabinet set up to deal with major foreign policy issues called the Cabinet Defence and Overseas Policy Unit. The idea was for Ministers to meet the military and to discuss possible pitfalls, logistics, and humanitarian problems. It never met.

In July 2002 Clare Short asked for a Cabinet discussion on Iraq. None was granted until after the summer recess in September. By then Blair had committed the UK to ally itself with US policy. Gordon Brown, the Chancellor, told her that Blair had already asked Geoffrey Hoon in August to get ready 20,000 troops for Iraq. Clare Short also had access to secret MI6 intelligence, and was aware that Alistair Campbell was involved in producing a dossier, based on intelligence, with the claim that WMDS could be deployed within 45 minutes. She then asked for a further Secret Intelligence Service briefing on Iraq for her department. She was told 10 Downing Street would not allow it. She did however receive a briefing eventually and was told that Saddam did have hidden programmes for WMDS, but "there was nothing to suggest this threat was imminent or should be dealt with urgently."

She later discovered that Foreign Office and SIS papers on Iraq had been prepared for Cabinet discussion as early as March 2002, but had been withheld from view by Mr Blair.

Clare Short felt that war should be avoided; but if it was to happen, then the only way to prevent a humanitarian and political disaster in Iraq was to keep the backing of the United Nations. UN Resolution 1441 backing the weapons inspection by Hans Blix met her requirements. She was not aware that this was a ruse. (cf Chapter 4: *Deceit & a Conspiracy for War*). Contrary to the Attorney General's opinion of UN Resolution 1441, the UK Ambassador, Sir Jeremy Greenstock, said at the United Nations, in November 2002, on the adoption of 1441, "There is no automaticity in this Resolution. If there is a further Iraqi breach of its disarmament obligations, the matter will return to the Council for discussion as required in Operational Paragraph 12." This position was confirmed by Blair in Cabinet in November 2002. But as Clare Short says, he made one set of promises to his country, another to President Bush.[2]

In February 2003, a few weeks before the war began, her Department started preparations for the outcome of the war in earnest, liaising with the Red Cross, the UN, and other NGOs. In Parliament on 30 January 2003, Clare Short said that "order and stability were essential to avoid a humanitarian disaster. Bombing could damage water supplies and sanitation... There might be environmental damage from burning oil fields, and threats of chemical and biological weapons could be real."[3] She believed it was essential to have UN support in the reconstruction of Iraq, and that post conflict preparations were not ready. At the Cabinet meeting of 7 March she was again stressing this to the PM, who appeared to agree.

She felt the PM had a reckless disregard for detail. On 8 March Clare Short said she would resign, but the PM inveigled her back into the Government on the plea that she could not abandon ship at such a late stage. Her expertise was needed for the reconstruction of Iraq and it was all the fault of the French who were irresponsibly going to veto any UN proposal to go to war with Iraq. This, she subsequently discovered, was a lie.

In Clare Short's own words: "First instinct of No 10 is to lie. New Labour had moved, *to having no respect for the truth*."[4] These are strong words indeed coming from a Privy Councillor.

During the rapid invasion and its immediate aftermath, Clare Short attended War Cabinet meetings at 8.30 every morning and stressed the Red Cross reports, which said that electricity and water supplies were damaged and there were grave problems with keeping hospitals running. She raised the problems of disorder and looting. The MoD scorned these reports. Contrary to his promises to Clare Short, Blair went along with the Pentagon's idea of post-war Iraq: a Provisional US-run administration with an Office of Reconstruction and Humanitarian Assistance (ORHA), set up in late 2002 under General Jay Garner, arms salesman and retired General. The Americans wished to establish their own interim administration and bypass the

United Nations. The US had its eye on the oil. The predominantly-US team moved into the Green Zone compound in Baghdad and tried to govern Iraq from behind a high concrete wall illuminated by the flames consuming former Ba'ath Regime administrative buildings, amid the crackle of machine-gun fire and the thump of rocket propelled grenades. Amateur chaos commenced.

At a ministerial meeting chaired by Jack Straw on 10 April 2003, the Foreign Secretary said that it mustn't get out to the public that there were differences between the UK and the US regarding the interim administration under ORHA. He went on to argue, "We took the risks and bore the costs, we cannot let the French and Germans get their noses in the trough." The Foreign Office and No 10 wanted DfID to integrate with ORHA in Baghdad. Clare Short felt this was a recipe for disaster, as ORHA was so inefficient. It became clear to her that "the US was looking for a client state and long term military bases in Iraq" and that Jack Straw was beginning to regard Iraq as a commercial opportunity for Britain. On 12 May 2003 she resigned.

Hence the preparations for the humanitarian consequences of war were not uppermost in Blair's mind when he went to war. Fearing his project would come to naught, he withheld information from his Cabinet, thus missing the value of criticism. To ensure the well being of the people we were supposed to liberate, why were there no Hercules transport planes loaded to the brim with doctors, plumbers, electricians, firemen, policemen, oxygen cylinders and medical supplies to rush behind the soldiers into the children's hospitals? Why were only soldiers sent? Were they alone supposed to sort out the mess? Why was *Shock and Awe* allowed to target electrical supplies, when the consequences in a hot country that relied on pumped water and pumped sewage systems would be dire? The war might have been otherwise a lot quicker and cheaper, because Iraqis would have welcomed the Coalition as humanitarian liberators. Instead, in their minds and the mind of the Arab world, the Coalition became the invaders. Civilians were hooded, handcuffed, beaten and taught a lesson about al-Qa'ida. It is as if Mr Blair had no consideration for the Iraqi people, half of whom are children under 13 years old. He certainly didn't want those killed or maimed to be counted.

[1] Observations on the brevity of cabinet discussions from the Foreign Affairs Committee, Clare Short interview, 17 June 2003.
[2] Clare Short, *An Honourable Deception?*, London: Free press, 2003, p161.
[3] Hansard, 30 January 2003.
[4] Ibid, p181.

CHAPTER 6
A RUTHLESS GOVERNMENT.

One of the Law Lords, talking to an eminent QC, said that he had never in his thirty years experience of working for the British Government come across an administration that was as ruthless as the one under Tony Blair. Can this hearsay evidence be substantiated?

My tutor, Sir Harry Hinsley, who worked in Bletchley Park, said that he had met Hitler and found him to be most charming and gracious. Most dangerous people can put on the charm. Is Mr Blair the young, friendly, slightly naïve, athletic, inspired-by-Christ, caring, virtuous, moral person he would like us to believe (and probably sees in his mirror every morning)? Or has he a side to him which is cunning, hard as nails, and prepared to kill? From the events of the last three years, the two parts of Mr Blair seem probable.

In the run up to war, Mr Blair often repeated the mantra, "One of the unfortunate consequences of war are inevitable civilian casualties." He must therefore have been aware of the consequences of using cluster bombs and other modern lethal devices. Thus, in the terms of the Rome Statute of the International Criminal Court, Article 30: *Mental element*, he understood his actions and their probable results, therefore qualifying himself for trial for war crimes. The very term *civilian casualties* is a euphemism. Mr Blair could not bring himself to say *civilian death and maiming* (especially of children and babies). That would not have sounded quite the same to his audiences. But that was a certain consequence of using scattering projectiles on a population where 50% were under the age of thirteen.

In dealing with those who dissented from his policy of going to war, Mr Blair, advised by his kitchen cabinet of un-elected advisors (Jonathon Powell, Sir David Manning, Alistair Campbell and Sally Morgan), has been equally clear-headed. Let us take the case of the weapons scientist Dr David Kelly. He was a top advisor to the intelligence community on Saddam Hussein's weapons of mass destruction. He briefed a BBC journalist that the Government had

87

exaggerated the case for going to war in their published dossiers on the threat from weapons of mass destruction. This leak was reported by Andrew Gilligan one morning at 6:10 am on the BBC's *Today* programme. Andrew Gilligan did not cross-check this leak against any other source (as he should have done), but he knew he was talking to someone very high up in the Defence Establishment: an official MoD spokesman, who would never have lied on such an important matter. In addition, the field of experts on Saddam's WMD programme made up a very small group.

On the advice of Alistair Campbell, Mr Blair took this accusation extremely seriously. A scheme was organised to find Andrew Gilligan's source. Mr Hoon wrote to Gavyn Davies, the BBC chairman, naming Dr Kelly and challenging him to confirm he was Mr Gilligan's source. The BBC stood firm. It was at this point that Dr Kelly's name was leaked to the press.[1] Eventually Dr Kelly made a confidential confession to his line manager. How then to out Dr Kelly? His name would not be released to the press but, if any journalist asked the correct name, it would be confirmed. This childish method of course revealed his name within a few hours. Mr Blair was chairman of the panel that thought up this idea.

Dr Kelly was then subject to interviews and briefing by Mr John Scarlett, Chairman of the Joint Intelligence Committee, who had a reputation for fierce interrogation of KGB spies. Kelly also had meetings with Ministry of Defence officials. He said he had been "put through the wringer" and the "questioning was quite brutal". He felt he "was being treated like a fly."

Within the space of a few days, the Downing Street apparatus tried to discredit Dr Kelly. (They succeeded, beyond their purpose.) Dr Kelly was a minor bureaucrat... he was mentally unstable... he was a *Walter Mitty character*... unreliable... etc. Dr Kelly was summoned to the Foreign Affairs Committee to explain himself. Beforehand, MI6 had imposed very strict limits on what Dr Kelly could or could not say to the Committee. This compounded his ordeal. Tom Mangold, a television journalist and close friend, said

Mrs Kelly had told him her husband was deeply unhappy and furious at how events had unfurled. "She told me he had been under considerable stress, that he was very, very angry about what had happened at the committee, that he wasn't well, that he had been to a safe house, he hadn't liked that, he wanted to come home."[2] Two days later Dr. Kelly was dead, apparently by his own hand.

As a consequence of the *Today* programme, other players fell like ninepins. Greg Dyke, a popular Director General of the BBC was sacked. His superior, BBC Chairman Gavin Davies, also had to resign and Andrew Gilligan (the reporter of whom Alistair Campbell said, "We will fuck Gilligan.") was sacked. An insight into how Mr Campbell works occurred on 8 February 2005 when the PM's close advisor returned to office, after an absence of nine months. His first job was to promote an election advertisement of two (Jewish) Opposition leaders depicted as flying pigs. There were accusations of anti-Semitism. Mr Campbell typed out an e-mail to Labour's advertising agency. Unfortunately he pressed the wrong button and the message was delivered to the BBC's *Newsnight* team. It read: "... Now fuck off and cover something important you twats."[3]

The kitchen cabinet had had it in for the BBC from the start of the war; the Prime Minister sent a personal letter to Greg Dyke accusing the BBC of being biased against the war. "I believe, and I am not alone in believing, that you have not got the balance right between support and dissent..."[4] Mr Blair wanted his word spread, not the word of the millions all over the world who had marched in the previous months against the war. The integrity of the BBC as independent of Government control was at stake. Greg Dyke felt he was being bullied by Blair.

In his book, *Inside Story*, Mr Dyke writes. "The charge against Blair is damning. He was either incompetent and took Britain to war on a misunderstanding, or he lied when he told the House of Commons that he didn't know what the 45 minute claim meant. We were all duped. History will not be on Blair's side. It will show that the whole saga is a great political scandal."[5]

We now know (from leaked Foreign Office papers[6]) that the Prime Minister and his kitchen cabinet exaggerated the case for going to war, and that there were no weapons of mass destruction in Iraq.

Alistair Campbell's claim that the BBC had lied was incorrect. A large number of people believe that it was Mr Blair and Mr Campbell who were the liars.

Further whistleblowers were dealt with equally ruthlessly. Katherine Gun, a translator working at Government Communications Headquarters, came across an e-mail from the US National Security Agency "requesting help with a plan to bug the six *swing states*" on the UN Security Council – whose votes were vital to win the second UN resolution authorising the invasion of Iraq. "I was shocked", she said. "If the war went ahead as a result [of bugging] I knew hundreds of thousands of innocent people were going to die." Ms Gun released the e- mail to the public. She was arrested, imprisoned over night, and later charged under the Official Secrets Act. But her trial on 25 February 2004 never took place because the Government probably realised that Mr Blair, the Attorney General and Mr Straw might have to appear as witnesses for the Prosecution. She, of course, lost her job.[7]

The head of the nuclear, chemical, and biological branch of the Defence Intelligence Staff (DIS), Dr Brian Jones, confirmed Dr. Kelly's assessment that the Government's dossiers on Iraq were misleading and that Tony Blair's foreword "transformed probability into certainty". He said that "the Government's dossier [of September 2002] went much further than we wanted it to go." When the Foreign Affairs Committee reported that there had been no complaints from the intelligence community about the September dossier, he "knew it wasn't true" and had to act to defend the DIS. So he wrote a confidential memo to the deputy chief of Defence Intelligence, Martin Howard. He later said that "The next time I saw that letter was when it appeared on my television screen."[8] He was denied another expected contract in autumn 2004; in effect he was sacked.

Prior to the war, Elizabeth Wilmshurst, a Deputy Legal Advisor to the Foreign Office, went to the Attorney General, Lord Goldsmith, and advised him that there was no legal basis for going to war. She said: "I regret that I cannot agree that it is lawful to use force without a second Security Council resolution. I cannot in conscience go along with advice within the office or to the public or parliament – which asserts the legitimacy of military action without such a resolution, particularly since an unlawful use of force on such a scale amounts to the crime of aggression; nor can I agree with such action in circumstances which are so detrimental to the international order and the rule of law."[9] Her advice was rejected. She resigned from the Foreign Office.

George Galloway, the Labour MP who led the 18 March 2003 revolt of 150 backbench Labour MPs against the motion for going to war (and who described the actions of Mr Bush and Mr Blair waging war on Iraqis as that of *wolves*), was dismissed from the Labour party for which he had worked for thirty years. In his book *I'm not the only one* he says. "Tony Blair and his clique of highjackers who are flying Labour to destruction may wish the party had been aborted. They are certainly doing everything they can to coax it into euthanasia."[10]

Paul Bigley, brother of the kidnap victim Ken Bigley, who publicly protested in October 2004 that Mr Blair was responsible for his brother's kidnapping and beheading by an Iraqi military faction, had his apartment in Belgium ransacked by MI6 and FBI and his computers removed.

The Rht Hon Clare Short finally resigned from the cabinet when she decided that the war was *reckless*. It has subsequently been hinted by 10 Downing Street that she is suffering from mental problems, just as the Rht Hon Mo Mowlam was discredited over Northern Ireland. In her book *An Honourable Deception?* Clare Short, recording her diary, states that "First instinct of No 10 is to lie". And on 7 April 2003, "Feeling terribly pessimistic re TB... The period from late March until I resigned was a very miserable time for me. I had sacrificed a lot by responding to Tony Blair's pleadings to stay in government and had done so because I believed his promises... But it seemed to me that these promises were made to manipulate me."[11] Further on she quotes her reply to the Foreign Affairs Committee. "I believe that the Prime Minister must have concluded that it was honourable and desirable to back the US in going for military action in Iraq and that it was, therefore, honourable for him to persuade us through the various ruses and devices he used to get us there, so I presume he saw it as an honourable deception."[12]

There was a Downing Street briefing to the press that Clare Short would be deselected from her Birmingham constituency, which she has held for twenty one years. Of this she said "We now have a ruthless party machine run tightly from the centre."[13]

THE CASE OF CRAIG MURRAY. Extracts from a speech by Craig Murray, British Ambassador to Uzbekistan (2002-04)

"It was in my first few days in Uzbekistan that I was confronted with the pictures of Avazov, with Azimov boiled to death in Jaslyk prison. The University of Glasgow pathology department studied the detailed photos and concluded that this was immersion in, not spattering with, boiling liquid. There was a clear tidemark. The fingernails had also been pulled.

"So how should the West react to this regime? There is no doubt that Uzbekistan occupies a vital geo-strategic position... Uzbekistan is a member of "The coalition of the willing". It provides the United States with an airbase... But it is absolutely essential as the easternmost of the ring of so-called lily pads, US airbases surrounding the "Wider Middle East". It is also a projection of US military force into the centre of a region which will become increasing essential in the next fifty years in satisfying Western demand for oil and gas. In the eyes of a Pentagon hawk, there is every reason to cosy up to [president] Karimov.

"There should be no doubt just how cosy this relationship is. Let me quote more from the current State Department briefing paper:

"US/Uzbek relations have flourished in recent years and were given an additional boost by the March 2002 meeting between President Bush and President Karimov in Washington, DC....High-level visits to Uzbekistan have increased since September 11 2001 `including that of the US Secretary of Defense Donald Rumsfeld, US Secretary of State Colin Powell and numerous congressional delegations...."

"The US has consulted closely with Uzbekistan on regional security issues, and Uzbekistan has been a close ally of the United States at the United Nations...on foreign policy and security issues ranging from Iraq to Cuba, from nuclear proliferation to drugs trafficking...Uzbekistan is a strong supporter of US military reactions in Afghanistan and Iraq and of the global war on terror..."

"The United States, in turn, values Uzbekistan as a stable, moderate force in a turbulent region."[14]

Craig Murray was UK Ambassador to Tashkent when he accused the Uzbekistani government of boiling prisoners to death. Since Mr Blair had just given Uzbekistan a licence to import British arms, this did not go down well in Whitehall, nor with the US ambassador. At the same time as Bush and Blair were defending the invasion of Iraq on the grounds of regime change of an evil dictator, Mr Murray was 'diagnosed' as suffering from nervous exhaustion and asked to resign. He was sacked by Blair and the Foreign Office for drawing attention to human rights abuses in Uzbekistan

The UK and the US have been dealing favourably with other countries in Central Asia, including Turkmenistan, Kyrgyzstan and Azerbaijan – all run by dictators who were once communist leaders. In 2004 British Petroleum signed an agreement to construct an oil pipeline linking Azerbaijan to Turkey. Halliburton is also involved. It seems some dictators are evil, and others lucrative.[15]

CONCLUSION: It seems that there is very little that will stop Mr Blair once he decides on a policy. Nor do the above cases tally with his oft repeated question, "Why can't people learn to accept my sincerity in going to war, just as I accept their good faith in opposing it?"[16]

---

[1] Michael Smith, Toby Helm, Andrew Sparrow and Ben Brogan, *Telegraph*, 19 July 2003.
[2] Ibid.
[3] *Independent*, 9 February 2005.
[4] Letter from the Prime Minister to the Director General of the BBC, 19 March 2003.
[5] Greg Dyke, *Inside Story*, London: HarperCollins, 2004.
[6] Michael Smith, 'Secret papers show Blair was warned of Iraq chaos' and 'Failure is not an option, but it doesn't mean they will avoid it', *Telegraph*, 18 September 2004.
[7] Paul Waugh and Kim Sengupta, *Independent*, 26 February 2004.
[8] Clare Rudebeck, *Independent*, 3 January 2005.
[9] Richard Norton-Taylor, *Guardian*, 23 February 2005.
[10] George Galloway, *I'm not the only* one, London: p149.
[11] Clare Short, *An Honourable Deception*, London: Free Press, 2004, p180.
[12] Ibid, p229.
[13] Colin Brown and Marie Woolf, *Independent*, 14 October 2004.

[14] Speech by Craig Murray, 'The Trouble with Uzbekistan', Chatham House, 8 November 2004.
[15] Rory Bremner, John Bird, and John Fortune, *You are Here. A Dossier*, London: Weidenfeld and Nicolson, 2004.
[16] Adrian Hamilton, *Independent*, 4 January 2005.

CHAPTER 7
CASE STUDIES.

These case studies show where the author claims there have been breaches in the Laws and Customs of War, and that these *prima facie* breaches warrant investigation by the Prosecutor of the International Criminal Court at The Hague.

It is not possible to classify these breaches because they overlap the various Conventions and Protocols. For instance, while the use of cable ties can come under the Statute of the ICC, Article 8, (*prisoners shall be treated humanely*); the November 2004 attack on Fallujah would appear to be in breach of many Conventions.

Some crimes do not come under the jurisdiction of the ICC and legislation does need to change to rectify omissions and the introduction of new weaponry and practices of war. For instance, the laws governing the use of private mercenaries to guard private companies within a sovereign state are not properly defined and need urgent consideration. The *conspiracy to make war by deceit* would be described as a *crime against peace* by the Nuremberg Charter of 1945, but is not as yet covered by the Statute of the ICC. Nevertheless, it must be regarded as one of the greatest crimes of mankind. Similarly the use of depleted uranium is not specifically banned by the Geneva Conventions or the ICC Statute, but if it is actually proven that one of its consequences is long term DNA damage over millions of years, it must then be banned as an act of genocide. While the use of old-fashioned dum-dum bullets is prohibited by the Hague Conventions of 1907, the use of fine steel spicule shrapnel in modern cluster bombs is not considered. The latter may be far more deadly, especially to children. Nor are unexploded cluster bombs properly defined yet as very unstable land mines without warning markings.

The house arrest of Augusto Pinochet in 1998 and the January 2005 trial in Spain of Adolfo Scilingo (the Argentine ex-naval officer who threw torture victims out of aeroplanes in the 1970s) show how the use of extradition has broken down state sovereign immunity without any statute of limitation. This must be the one of the ways forward for eventually bringing members of the UK Government to account.

7A. BREAKDOWN OF CIVIL ADMINISTRATION & POLITICAL PERSECUTION.

The disbandment of the Iraqi army and the police force, the persecution of members of the Ba'ath Party – which included most of the civil administrators – and the destruction of the civilian administrative buildings and records in May-June 2003, immediately after the initial invasion. These actions are the source of the anarchy that reigns in Iraq to this day [early 2005]; with failure of services, unemployment and increasing violence, including looting, kidnapping, car bombings, fires and theft. Doctors, professionals and middle class businessmen (most of whom are Sunnis and nominally – if not actually – Ba'athist) have been leaving Iraq in droves this year to settle in Jordan and Syria where there is security. This bleeding of the middle class will have a devastating effect upon Iraq, as had the 'disappearance' of 30,000 intellectuals during Argentina's dirty war in the late '70s. In December 2004 the interim government of Alawi was already carrying out repressive measures against any opposition to his continuance in power after the January 2005 elections.

RELEVANT LAWS AND CONVENTIONS: The Hague Convention (IV) Respecting the Laws and Customs of War on Land, 18 Oct 1907. Annex, Art.43 *The authority of the legitimate power having in fact passed into the hands of the occupant, the latter shall take all the measures in his power to restore, and ensure as far as possible, public order and safety, while respecting, unless absolutely prevented, the laws in force in the country.* The Rome Statute of the International Criminal Court, Article 7, *Crimes against humanity*, (h) *Persecution against any identifiable group or collectively on political...or other grounds...* Article 8, *War crimes* (a) *Grave breaches of the Geneva Convention of 12 August 1949, namely* (iv) *Extensive destruction and appropriation of property, not justified by military necessity and carried out unlawfully and wantonly;* (b) *Other*

> *serious violations of the laws and customs applicable in international armed conflict... (xiii) Destroying or seizing the enemy's property unless such destruction or seizure be imperatively demanded by the necessities of war.*

EVIDENCE OF VIOLATIONS: The Duke of Pirajno, who in 1943 was the Italian Governor of Tripoli, describes their surrender to Montgomery, "Thus with his back to the radiator of his car and his head drawn down... the British commander spoke in an abrupt nasal voice, emphasising his short sharp sentences with brief gestures of the hand...To avoid looking at us, he kept his eyes on the ground; the bone structure of his lean face was clearly visible... While Montgomery was speaking , I kept my eyes on his face – and the face of the enemy is never beautiful... 'Troops were to abstain from acts of violence,' he said, 'and to respect private property; the population was to refrain from provoking disturbances and from hostile acts; the Italian colonial officials were to remain at their posts because, in conformity with the laws of war, the functions of the local administration must go on; no political collaboration would be requested but, in the interests of the population, the normal administrative activities must continue under the control of the occupation authorities. If they carried out these instructions loyally, the Italian civilian officials would have nothing to fear.' The British Commander's car moved off and disappeared from sight."[1]

This surrender must be taken as a model of conformity with the laws of war.

In contrast, in the Iraq war of 2003 the USA, supported by the UK, has broken this Hague Convention resulting in widespread chaos. The immediate action of the US and UK forces on occupation was to disband the army, disband the Ba'athist police, open the prisons and dismiss the Ba'athist civil servants and professionals. Since an Iraqi citizen had almost certainly to be a member of the Ba'ath party even to work as a university professor, this political purge meant that many functions of the state ceased to operate. The 400,000 members of the Iraqi army were thrown into dire poverty. This is illustrated by the fate of Ali al-Meyahi, whose children were both injured by insurgent rockets fired at the military camp taken over by Polish soldiers. He said that he has since had to sell his bedroom furniture and his wife's jewellery. "We thought the coalition would come to liberate us, but what we have seen until now leaves us without hope."[2]

Since the policy of the US and UK forces had been to rely on high-tech weapons, with few troops or *boots on the ground* once the Iraqi police and soldiers had been summarily dismissed, there was no one to draw on to protect property against looting and arson. Subsequent attempts to bring soldiers and police back under the control of the US-dominated provisional administration were fraught with difficulties because by then these were seen as collaborators with the occupation and proper targets for suicide bombers and attack. Furthermore, in the first twenty four hours of victory, the US and UK armies stood by and encouraged looting and arson. This resulted in the destruction of all civil ministry buildings of the centralised Ba'athist government in Baghdad and Basra. Also destroyed in a blaze of arson and looting were Government records – except for those of the Oil Ministry buildings in Baghdad, which were immediately guarded by US troops and tanks. The normal functions of Government collapsed. To replace the Ba'athist civil administration, the US depended on the installation of a Provisional Administration. This was headed by a retired US General, Jay Garner who (among other qualifications) had been an arms trader and all of a sudden was expected to run a country the size of France with a staff of 600 foreigners.

A senior British official in Baghdad later said of the provisional authority. "The operation is chronically under resourced ... with a complete absence of strategic direction. This is the single most chaotic organisation I have ever worked for... Salaries, electricity, and security are not being delivered." April 2003 salaries remained unpaid.[3]

Neither the UK nor the USA had paid much attention to the problems of running a country this size during the run up to a war which, in contrast, was planned in meticulous detail. There was an element of political vindictiveness in all of this. Saddam had to be held up as the ultimate evil dictator who could do nothing right; therefore, any one associated with his Ba'ath party also had to be purged. Unfortunately this included just about every civil servant and professional – who were also predominantly Sunni middle class. This move against the political ruling class is considered a *crime against humanity* under the Statute of the International Criminal Court (ICC) Article 7 (h). It was also an act of unimaginable folly which has probably contributed more than anything else to the Sunni resistance movement against the occupation, with the resulting chaos and death that has followed. The undoubted initial relief (felt by the majority of Iraqis that Saddam Hussein's regime was no more) was quickly replaced by a growing anger towards the occupation, which has proved so incompetent at restoring peace and civil functions. This rapid disillusion was fuelled by the realisation that the US aim appeared to be primarily to secure Iraq's oil and that treatment of Iraqis by the occupiers was not civilised.

The new Mayor of Mohawil, Wasil al-Shameli said, "It's true it was a horrible regime, but there were government departments and offices working. But after the war and the looting, all the government institutions were destroyed. It happened suddenly. It left the Iraqis feeling naked. This was also complicated by the fact that we had an entirely military way of change. So of course we have a jungle now. It will not be a society of institutions because the Americans are allowing tribalism and religious extremism. If the forces of modernism retreat in the face of tribalism, it will create another dictator, another Saddam."[4]

On 3 May 2004 at a public discussion in Brighton, Rageh Omaar, a distinguished BBC television journalist, said that the behaviour of the occupying powers in respect of infrastructure provision and security had been irresponsible to a degree he could not understand. He said that the British and US government must have been aware of the delicate state of the Iraqi infrastructure, and especially Iraqi hospitals, as a result of 12 years of UN sanctions. Yet they appeared not to have planned for the post-invasion period at all. Sheik Yawar, head of a powerful tribe, said: "We blame the United Sates 100% for the security in Iraq. They occupied the country, disbanded the security agencies and for ten months left Iraq's borders open for anyone to come in without visas or even a passport."[5]

In June 2004, Mr Kamil, a shopkeeper in Baghdad, commented that his business had been cut by a half, "I used to keep it open until after midnight." He looked back to the Saddam era "when I was not worried when I left my house. I don't care about democracy any more... the main thing is security. The terrorists and the occupation force make life hell."[6]

The Amnesty International report on 2003 said of Iraq, "Hundreds of civilians were killed and thousands injured. Many civilians were killed as a result of excessive use of force by coalition forces. Scores of women were abducted, raped and killed as law and order broke down after the war. Torture and ill treatment by coalition forces were widespread." The report says the US and UK, "failed to live up to their responsibilities under international humanitarian law as occupying powers, including their duty to restore and maintain public order and safety, and to provide food, medical care and relief assistance."[7]

A Mujahideen commander said: "We do not hate the Americans and British, we hate the ideas they have brought here. We do not want their capitalism, we do not want communism. We have our own ideas about how we want our country to be run in a Muslim way."[8]

This state of affairs has continued up to February 2005. In a speech in September 2004 Mr Alawi, the interim Prime Minister, declared that fifteen of Iraq's eighteen provinces were "completely safe". Maithan Maki, an Iraqi lorry driver, said, "This speech was ridiculous... when Alawi became Prime Minister I was in favour of him but things have got worse and worse."[9] The roads are very dangerous; bandits not only steal lorries but also kidnap the drivers for ransom.

On 28 November 2004, the British Embassy in Baghdad issued the following note, "With effect from the 28th November, the British Embassy ceased all movement on the Baghdad International Airport road." This vital link to the outside world was considered too dangerous because of attacks by freedom fighters.[10]

By mid December it was uncertain whether elections would take place in the Sunni districts of Iraq in January. Iyad Allawi was already beginning to lump together various Shia factions (including the United Iraq Alliance) as being too clerical and close to Iran. In almost the same breath, Mr Shaalan, the interim Defence Minister, said that Jaish Mohammed, commander of a resistance group, had confessed (presumably under torture) that "the key to terrorism is in Iran."[11] Cynics will say that the manoeuvring of the US-appointed Alawi government was replaying out the act of 1920 and the appointment of Faisal as King. The last thing the US would want is a fundamental Shia-dominated government with close links to Iran.

Demographically, this would be inevitable with a one man-one vote system. Having persecuted the Sunnis, the Americans are now, in January 2005, faced with a different problem: a Shia government.

Critics of this commentary will claim that, in two or three years time the problem of security and administration in Iraq will be resolved. I would argue that that does not excuse the damage done during the occupation. The crimes against humanity with all their misery and deaths and chaos have been committed, but would not have been committed if the example set by Montgomery in 1943 had been scrupulously followed. The fact that the occupation of France by Nazi Germany, from 1939 to 1944, was only a brief period historically does not detract from war crimes committed in that period, nor from the heroism of those who resisted them.

CLAIM: I am of the opinion that members of the UK Government and military, together with their US allies, are responsible for the collapse of the civil and professional administration of Iraq, by effectively causing the destruction of its civil ministries and records as a consequence of the looting and arson which they initially allowed and encouraged. Therefore they are in breach of The Hague Convention IV 1907 and the Geneva Convention of 12 August 1949 viz (iv), (xiii). That they are also in breach of ICC Statute Article 7 (h) because of their political persecution (initially of members of the Ba'ath party and latterly of vocal opponents of the Alawi Interim Government); and Article 8, 2 (a).

UNEMPLOYMENT CAUSED BY WAR: Breakdown of civil administration leading to unemployment of main breadwinners is sited in Rageh Omaar's book, *Revolution Day*. Omaar met a young man in Basra who said: "We went through war! We were ready for this suffering because Bush and Blair said they would help us with everything after Saddam is gone. They made this promise and we believed them, that they will change Iraq, change our lives. And what has happened? Nothing! Just soldiers and occupation... I am a pharmacist... who used to work for the Red Crescent... and yet I am doing nothing now... there are no jobs for even educated people here in Basra. What is this occupation that brings nothing? Do they expect us to just be like dogs, to wait until each time they choose to feed us with small plates of old food?" Other men joined in, offering their condemnations in Arabic. "We want them out," said one of them, "They are doing nothing but stealing our oil. Let them go to the Kuwaiti rulers who are the servants of America and who give them their oil for free. This oil is for Iraqis."[12]

IRAQI WOMEN: Some doubts were at least expressed by a member of the UK Government that not all things would be better under a new regime. One of the Cabinet Ministers, Patricia Hewitt, expressed concern that there could be fewer women in Iraq's reconstructed parliament than under Saddam Hussein. Under Saddam Hussein, Iraqi women were better represented than in any other country in the Middle East. They held one in five seats in Iraq's parliament, compared with one in 30 in the rest of the region. Ms Hewitt said: "Unlike the situation in Afghanistan, Iraqi women already participated economically and politically in the, albeit politically-restricted, civil society under Saddam Hussein. They score highest of all Arab women on the United Nation's league table of gender empowerment.[13]

---

[1] The Duke of Pirajno, *Cure for Serpents*, London: Eland, 1955, p251.
[2] *Guardian*, 4 October 2003.
[3] Peter Foster, *Daily Telegraph*, 17 June 2003.
[4] *Guardian*, 4 October 2003.
[5] Justin Huggler, *Independent*, 1 June 2004.
[6] Patrick Cockburn, *Independent*, 27 June 2004.
[7] AI Report 2004, *Iraq Covering events from January - December 2003*;
http://web.amnesty.org/report2004/irq-summary-eng
[8] Lee Gordon, *Camden Journal*, 15 April 2004.
[9] Patrick Cockburn, *Independent*, 25 September 2004.
[10] Patrick Cockburn, *Independent*, 20 November 2004.
[11] Patrick Cockburn, *Independent*, 16 December 2004.
[12] Rageh Omaar, *Revolution Day*, London: Viking, 2004, p217.
[13] Marie Woolf, *Independent*, 22 May 2003.

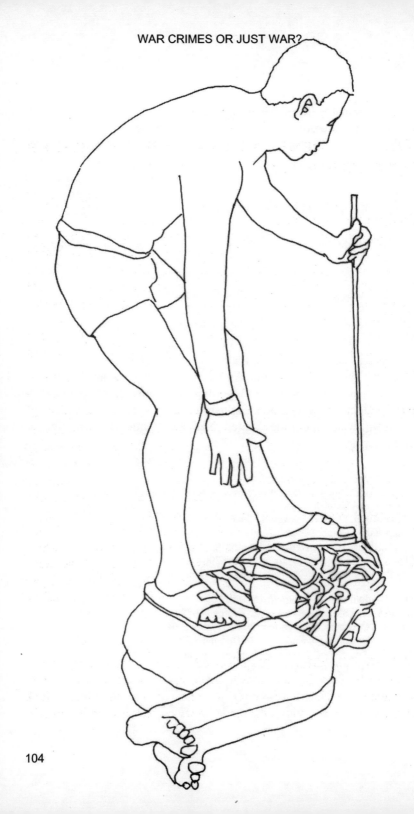

7B. DESTRUCTION OF SERVICES INFRASTRUCTURE.

The UK and US recklessly – and sometimes deliberately – damaged and destroyed Iraqi infrastructure (electricity, water supply, telecommunications, sewerage and drainage systems). They also allowed the civil administration to collapse; ministries were looted and destroyed with the resulting anarchy and lack of security. These factors endangered the lives of the inhabitants, especially sick and vulnerable children. These infrastructure systems are being repaired only slowly, if at all, and after nearly two years of occupation are still in a dire state. A new vital sewerage drain for Sadr City only commenced construction in December 2004. In the streets, families have to splash around in puddles of sewage.

RELEVANT LAWS AND CONVENTIONS: For the purpose of the Rome Statute of the International Criminal Court, Article 8 *war crime* means, 2(a)(iv) *Extensive destruction and appropriation of property, not justified by military necessity and carried out unlawfully and wantonly;* 2(b) (v) *Attacking or bombarding by whatever means, towns villages, dwellings or buildings which are undefended and which are not military objectives;* The Hague Convention IV Respecting the Laws and Customs of War on Land, 18 October 1907, Article 43 states: *The authority of the legitimate power having in fact passed into the hands of the occupant, the latter shall take all the measures in his power to restore, and ensure as far as possible, public order and safety, while respecting, unless absolutely prevented, the laws in force in the country.*

EVIDENCE OF VIOLATIONS: The British army were involved by bombing and rocket attack in the destruction of water, telephone and electricity supply to Basra. In the combined initial *Shock and Awe* bombing of Baghdad – which included cruise missile launches from British warships – electrical and telecommunications systems were targeted. Drainage systems were inevitably smashed. The result was a breakdown of lighting, electric power, water supply and sewage pumping machinery. This loss of services had an adverse effect on hospitals, public health and general living standards, as well as security. Streets were plunged into darkness. Homes, relying on power for air conditioning in very high temperatures, were left without cooling systems.

Baghdad is a very low-lying city with mechanically pumped water and sewage drainage systems. When these broke down from direct damage or lack of power, water became contaminated and sewage even ran out of taps in some peoples' homes. Iraqis who could afford it purchased bottled water. The poor drank the contaminated water. Gas supplies for cooking failed. The inhabitants resorted to oil lamps for lighting. Hospital operating theatres were in total darkness. Sewage leaked into the wards.

This situation has only slightly improved because of very poor security, which means that, in many cases, infrastructure reconstruction has not taken place. The following extracts from press reports give a chronological account of some of the problems caused during the occupation:

7 MAY 2003. Seven cases of cholera were reported in Baghdad. The city's water treatment shut down after American-led air strikes damaged the electric grid, leaving large parts of the city without clean water for several weeks.[1]

11 MAY 2003. A fire in the telephone exchange went unattended. The single fire engine ran out of water. As US Lieutenant Lance Tomlinson said, "We've got no water, no fire department."[2]

12 MAY 2003. Rubbish is piling up in the streets of Baghdad.[3]

No electricity means no water, means disease. Dr Ridha in a hospital north of Baghdad said of Ayham Mortadha (a child whose mother had to rely on river water for drinking and cooking since the war) that he would grow up stunted and with some damage to the brain. The taps in their home ran dry and mineral water is too expensive at £1 per bottle. "There was no other water available. It was dirty but I had no choice." There is no gas for cooking in the hospital kitchen. One of the main sewage plants in Kahlis was bombed, and then looted.

The network of cast iron water pipes is leaking. When the power cuts out, the negative pressure sucks in sewage and delivers it into people's homes. Staff at the water treatment plant have not been paid so they don't turn up. Majeed Waleed, Care aid agency worker said "There was a system before. It didn't work very well, but it worked... What the authorities are doing now is dismantling it and starting from zero... this is now an emergency."[4]

14 JUNE 2003. 13 people were killed in a car bomb attack. These included contractors for General Electric and security guards working for Olive Security, UK. There is a continuing shortage of electricity in Baghdad. Demand in the city is 2,200 megawatts and supply is 1,400.[5]

2 JUNE 2004. Mr Iyad Allawi, the Interim Prime Minister, said his government's priority would be sewage. At Iraq's main children's hospital, children are dying because basic repairs have not been carried out. The toilets are in such disrepair that they frequently overflow into the leukaemia ward.[6]

16 JUNE 2004. A year after the initial invasion, Baghdadis were sweltering in the heat with only eight hours electricity a day. The temperature rises to 120F. Even the poorest have air conditioners, but if they are not working a poorly insulated house turns into an oven. Fridges are not working, which means food cannot be stored. Computers and televisions are switched off. Children die of overheating. The situation is made worse by the sabotage of electricity supplies and the killing and kidnapping of foreign workers trying to mend power stations. Before the war Baghdad received twenty hours of electricity a day; now sometimes it only has eight. Raad al-Haref, the Deputy Electricity Minister, commented on electricity supplies, "The Americans tried to do everything themselves and they failed. We had to renegotiate with all our foreign suppliers through American companies and this took about eight months."[7]

30 JULY 2004. In their report on Iraq, the UK Foreign Affairs Committee warned there were insufficient troops on the ground. "The provision of basic services in Iraq is still not satisfactory." Britain's credibility was therefore damaged. The break up of the Iraqi army and the removal of former Ba'ath party officials from government "was contributing to instability and insecurity."[8]

31 JULY 2004. Of the $18 billion reconstruction budget approved by the US Congress for 2003, only $458 million had been spent by 31 July 2004. Cuts in power supply affecting refrigeration in temperatures over 50°C remain critical. Untreated sewage is still flowing in Baghdad streets. Mr Powell, US Secretary of State, acknowledged that there had been long delays in drawing up contracts for reconstruction.[9] Public health has not improved since the invasion last year, mainly due to unclean water. Dr Bashar, a senior house surgeon at al-Kindi said, "look around you. Baghdad is the dirtiest city in the world."

The US diverted $3.4 billion funds intended for water and electricity projects to security and the oil industry. Many Iraqi businessmen and doctors have fled to Amman and Damascus because of the fear of being taken hostage. (This haemorrhage of the intellectual and professional elite will severely affect Iraq for years to come, just as Argentina – where an estimated 30,000 intellectuals *disappeared* between 1976 and 1983 – suffers from poor professional leadership one generation later.) It is reported that the US and Allawi are having doctors and clerics who speak out against the interim government disposed of. [10]

13 NOVEMBER 2004. Commenting on the US attack on Fallujah, the Iraqi Red Crescent Society described conditions as a "big disaster". The IRCS urged the US to allow them to deliver food medicine and water into Fallujah. "Anyone who gets injured is likely to die because there is no medicine and they can't get to doctors. There are snipers everywhere. Go outside and you're going to get shot." Rasoul Ibrahim, who fled from Fallujah with his family said, "There's no water. People are drinking dirty water. Children are dying. People are eating flour because there's no food."[11]

CLAIM: That the UK and US Government acted with great recklessness in damaging the already fragile services infrastructure of Iraq and are therefore guilty of war crimes and crimes against humanity in breach of the Rome Statute of the International Criminal Court, Article 8 2(b) (v) (iv). And failure to abide by The Hague Convention IV Respecting the Laws and Customs of War, 18 October 1907.

[1] Donald Macintyre, *Independent*, 8 May 2003.
[2] Donald Macintyre, *Independent*, 12 May 2003.
[3] Jayne Atherton, *Metro*, 12 May 2003.
[4] Rory McCarthy, *Guardian*, 29 May 2003.
[5] Patrick Cockburn, 'Foreign contractors are being targeted by insurgents', *Independent*, 5 June 2004.
[6] *The Independent*, 2 June 2004.
[7] Patrick Cockburn, *Independent*, 16 June 2004.
[8] Ben Russell, *Independent*, 30 July 2004.
[9] Donald Macintyre, *Independent*, 31 July 2004.
[10] Naomi Klein, 'You asked for my evidence, Mr Ambassador. Here it is.', *Guardian*, 4 December 2004.
[11] Patrick Cockburn, *Independent*, 11 September 2004.

7C. DAMAGE TO HOSPITALS & ATTACKS ON MEDICAL FACILITIES

In 2003, after twelve years of sanctions, Iraqi Hospitals – once the pride of the Middle East – had fallen into a chronic state of neglect. It is asserted that 500,000 Iraqi children died unnecessarily during that period. (Madeleine Albright, ex US Secretary of State, and Envoy to the Middle East, when asked about the deaths of 500,000 Iraqi children, said that in order to restrain Saddam, "I think this is a very hard choice, but the price – we think the price is worth it." TV Interview May 12 1996.)

Inevitably the war, waged by the Coalition against Iraq, has made this situation even more dire. The damage to water, electricity and sewage systems – plus overcrowding on account of the war casualties – has meant that thousands more children and adults have died. To exacerbate this situation, the US army has targeted hospitals, clinics and ambulances contrary to the laws of war.

RELEVANT LAWS AND CONVENTIONS: There is a large body of laws and conventions relating to the protection of hospitals, the sick, and the wounded. The Rome Statute of the ICC, Article 8: *War crimes* 2(b)(ix) *Intentionally directing attacks against... hospitals and places where the sick and wounded are collected, provided they are not military objectives.* Hague Convention IV Respecting the Laws and Customs of War, 18 Oct 1907: Article 23: *In addition... it is especially forbidden* (c) *To kill or wound an enemy who... has surrendered.* Article 27: *...steps must be taken to spare... hospitals.* Article 43: *to restore, and ensure... public order and safety.* Charter of the Nuremberg Provisions, Article 6: (b) *War crimes,* (c) *Crimes against humanity.* Geneva Convention I, August 12 1949 Articles 3: (2) *The wounded and sick shall be collected and cared for.* Article 9: *... no obstacle to the humanitarian activities... of the Red Cross.* Article 12: *Members of the armed forces... who are wounded or sick, shall be respected and protected.* Article 15: ...

search for and collect the wounded and sick, to protect them... and to search for the dead and prevent their being despoiled. Article 19: Fixed... and mobile medical units... may in no circumstances be attacked. Article 24: Medical personnel... shall be protected. Article 25: Members... specially trained... as hospital orderlies... shall likewise be respected. Article 35: Transports of wounded and sick or of medical equipment shall be respected and protected. Article 46: Reprisals against the wounded, sick, personnel, buildings or equipment protected by the Convention are prohibited. Geneva Convention IV, August 1949 relative to the protection of civilian persons in time of war; Article 16: *The wounded and sick... and expectant mothers, shall be the object of particular protection and respect.* Article 17: *The Parties... shall endeavour to conclude... agreements for the removal from besieged or encircled areas, of wounded, sick, infirm... persons.* Article18: *... hospitals... may in no circumstances be the object of attack.* Article 20: *Persons... engaged in the operation and administration of civilian hospitals... shall be respected and protected*; Article 21: *... vehicles or hospital trains... shall be protected.* Article 23: *Each... Party shall allow the free passage of all* [medical] *consignments... for civilians... likewise... consignments of essentials.* Article 55: *... the Occupying Power has the duty of ensuring the food and medical supplies of the population.*

According to a report published in October 2004 by the Iraqi interim government's Ministry of Health, after eighteen months of occupation disease rates were soaring. In the aftermath of the invasion, one third of all health centres and one in every eight hospitals had been looted of furniture, fridges, air conditioners, and their equipment had been broken. Damage to water supplies and sanitation had lead to 5,460 cases of typhoid. One in five urban, and three in five rural, households did not have access to drinking water. Poverty had risen, with 27 percent of the population living on less than $2 a day. One in three children was chronically malnourished, and exposed to measles, mumps and jaundice. Between 1990 and 1998 the number of babies dying before their first birthday rose from 40 to 103 per 1,000. Maternal mortality was 279 per 100,000 births. Life expectancy has fallen below 60. The country's state of health was rated on a par with that of impoverished countries such as Sudan. Cancer, diabetes, heart conditions and infectious diseases were increasing.[1]

As we have seen in Chapter 7b: *Destruction of Service Infrastructure*, the British army and the RAF were involved in bombings and rocket attacks that destroyed the water, sewage drainage, telephone and electricity supply to Basra. Coalition forces in the initial *Shock and Awe* attack on Baghdad also damaged services. Special bombs were used to disrupt the electricity supply. In the November 2004 attack on Fallujah, the water supply to the city was shut down with the intention of staving out the freedom fighters. This was executed by the US army and supported by the British army and government.

Hospital security was also at stake. Looting of buildings associated with the Ba'ath socialist party in Basra was initially encouraged by the British government. When, after twenty four hours, they realised this was a mistake, it was too late to stop the orgy of looting by a deprived population. Even hospitals were looted of their equipment and drugs and doctors kidnapped for ransom. Many doctors could not stand the pressure and left for Jordan and Syria.

The consequence in these hospitals (by now in chronically-decayed conditions, now being denied proper electricity, clean water, and sanitation) was the death of a large number of children and adults. Children were already suffering from malnutrition as a result of UN sanctions. Many soon died unnecessarily victims of water-related diseases, especially diarrhoea and dehydration. Some parents were forced to take their children out of hospital because of the lack of drugs, the absence of beds, filthy conditions and the risk of cross-infection of highly infectious diseases. These parents attempted to nurse the children and the wounded themselves, but were hampered by the conditions in their homes; the water supply cut off and absence of power to cook meals. Many resorted to drinking river water or tap water, both heavily contaminated with sewage.

It is asserted that the damage to the attending infrastructure – caused by the Coalition – is so closely linked to the satisfactory running of a particular hospital, that it is for practical purposes an attack on that hospital. There were numerous records of hospital operations being plunged into darkness and equipment breaking down causing death. This at a time when already overstretched hospitals were trying to deal with causalities of war as well. The damage was prolonged because government engineers had not been paid and were refusing to repair the systems.

On 3 May 2004, at a public discussion in Brighton, Rageh Omaar, a BBC television journalist who had worked in Iraq up until the end of the invasion period, said that the behaviour of the occupying powers, in respect of infrastructure provision and security, had been irresponsible to a degree he could not understand. After 12 years of UN sanctions, the UK and US governments must have been aware of the delicate state of the Iraqis and the Iraqi infrastructure, especially hospitals. Yet they appeared not to have planned at all for the post-invasion period, specifically in relation to public health. The US has excluded those NGOs with the necessary expertise.

After seven months occupation, the US were actually aggravating the situation by strafing hospitals in gun battles with insurgents. Dr Salam el Obaidi phoned from the Baghdad Shahid Adnan hospital saying: "We have no oxygen supplies. We are finished... We are sending patients away... I have not slept for three days, I am so desperate... A man is dying in front of me. I can do nothing... We cannot pay the doctors wages..." The line went dead... "There is shooting above me, there are helicopters. There is shooting... I have to hide. For God's sake, the shooting is all over us. Some one has been shot I can hear them." A nurse and a clerk were killed.

The previous month the hospital had been without water after US tanks fractured the water pipes. Iraqi student doctors waiting to take their exams in Syria were prevented from obtaining passports by the US because of the diplomatic war between Washington and Damascus.[2]

In February 2004, after almost one year of occupation, at least one hospital in Baghdad, the Al-Iskan Premier Children's Hospital, was still in an appalling state. Children were dying because of shockingly poor sanitation and shortage of medical equipment. Lavatories were overflowing in the leukaemia ward, sewage dripped from the roof of the premature babies ward; blankets were still clotted with blood from Iraqi soldiers' wounds. There was shortage of oxygen cylinders, disinfectants, soap, water, intravenous sets, chemotherapy drugs, asthma treating equipment. Beds were overcrowded; sterilisation impossible; taps broken; air conditioning non-existent. As a result, patients were being turned away. Diarrhoea, septicaemia and chest infections were rampant. Death was present everywhere.

At Al-Iskan Hospital, five or six patients with leukaemia died every week. Iraq has a high incidence of leukaemia – blamed on the use of depleted uranium by the US and UK in the first Gulf War. There is an 80% rate of secondary infection. Dr Egab said: "We cannot keep different types of cases apart; often a patient arrives with a chest infection and ends up getting a stomach infection as well." One of the patients said: "The doctors are good to us, but we are suffering because of the water... there is only one tap and it is broken." Due to the stress of war there are many premature births. The shortage of oxygen is so great that babies have to be turned away knowing they will die. Outside Baghdad hospital conditions were worse. A report on southern Iraq, by Physicians for Human Rights, found that at local maternity clinics caesarean sections were being performed with unsterilised scalpels, needles were being reused and staff did not have clean water to wash the mother before she gave birth.[3]

The record of US army actions in Fallujah, in relation to the Geneva Conventions – respecting and protecting hospitals, hospital staff and hospital transport – is not good. In the April 2004 assault on Fallujah, ambulances were shot up on the grounds that they may have been harbouring terrorists in disguise. Doctors reported ambulances riddled with bullet holes. Lee Gordon a journalist said. "In fact US snipers were targeting ambulances. I saw the burning wreck of one, destroyed in a hail of bullets while evacuating casualties from an underfire hospital. What do you say when doctors turn to you for anaesthetics to operate on a volunteer nurse shot through the stomach by a sniper during a cease fire?"[4]

In November 2004, the US army made direct attacks on a health clinic in Fallujah, killing 20 doctors. The main Fallujah hospital on the West bank of the Euphrates was seized by American and Iraqi forces and journalists were forbidden entrance; the Americans did not want adverse publicity about civilian casualties in the siege of Fallujah. The Red Crescent were prevented from crossing the Euphrates and entering the city to rescue casualties. Residents who were too old, sick or poor to leave the city had been left without water or food. One pregnant woman had her seven month foetus ripped out by shrapnel. The Red Crescent aid convoy returned to Baghdad with empty ambulances. Commenting on the number of dead in Fallujah, US Marine Captain PJ Batty said of the body pick up: "This exemplifies the horrors of war. We don't wish this upon anyone, but every one needs to understand there are consequences for not following the Iraqi government."[5]

CLAIM: That through their recklessness in attacking Iraq while knowing the fragile state of the Iraqi children's health and the abysmal state of hospitals; and by the destruction of services infrastructure and their attacks on hospitals, ambulances and medical personnel; members of the United Kingdom government and military, and their allies the United States government and military, are in grave breach of the Rome Statute of the ICC, Article 8, 2 (b)(ix); The Hague Convention IV Respecting the Laws and Customs of War, 18 Oct 1907, Articles 23, 27 and 43; Nuremberg Charter Provisions, Article 6 (b) and (c); Geneva Convention I, August 12 1949 Articles 2, 3, 9, 12, 15, 19, 24, 25, 35 and 46; Geneva Convention IV, August 1949, 16, 17, 18, 20, 21, 23 and 55, in respect of the protection of hospitals, medical transport, medical personnel, the wounded, the sick and dying.

---

[1] Jeremy Lawrence, *Independent*, 13 October 2004.
[2] Lee Gordon, *Camden New Journal*, 2 October 2003.
[3] Justin Huggler, *Independent*, 21 February 2004.
[4] Lee Gordon, *Camden New Journal*, 29 April, 2004.
[5] Andrew Buncombe, *Independent*, 17 November 2004.

7D. DESPOLIATION OF MUSEUMS, LIBRARIES & ARCHAEOLOGICAL SITES.

Because at the end of the invasion period, the Iraqi army and police were immediately disbanded and any professional or bureaucrat who was a member of the Ba'ath party was sacked, and because of the initial encouragement of looting; there was a complete breakdown of law and order in Iraq. All prisoners were released from Iraqi jails, even though many were criminals. As a result there was widespread pillage of museums and archaeological sites. Artefacts were stolen to be sold on the international antiquities market. There was also wanton destruction of museums, including the use of bulldozers. There was widespread arson of very important Koranic libraries containing priceless and irreplaceable books and manuscripts. The arson of archives may have had a political motive: to destroy evidence of the relationship of the West with Saddam Hussein's regime. The National Archive in Baghdad was systematically destroyed, with petrol poured to ignite each floor of the building.

RELEVANT LAWS AND CONVENTIONS: The Rome Statute of The ICC Article 8: War crimes (2)(a) *Grave breaches of the Geneva Conventions of 12 August 1949...* and (b) *Other serious violations of the laws and customs applicable in international armed conflict, within the established framework of international law, namely, any of the following acts:*(ix) *Intentionally directing attacks against buildings dedicated to religion, education, art, science or charitable purposes, historic monuments, hospitals and places where the sick and wounded are collected, provided they are not military objectives.* The Hague Convention (IV) respecting the Laws and Customs of War on Land, 1907 Article 43: *The authority of the legitimate power having in fact passed into the hands of the occupant, the latter shall take all the measures in his power to restore, and ensure, as far as possible, public order and safety, while respecting, unless absolutely prevented, the laws in force in that country.* Article

47: *Pillage is formally forbidden.* The Hague Convention for the Protection of Cultural Property in the Event of Armed Conflict, 1954 Article 4: (1) *The High Contracting Parties undertake to respect cultural property... by refraining from any use of the property... and... from any act of hostility directed against such property.* (3) *The... Parties further undertake to prohibit, prevent and, if necessary, put a stop to any form of theft, pillage ... and any acts of vandalism directed against cultural property.* Article 28: *The High Contracting Parties undertake to prosecute and impose penal or disciplinary sanctions upon those... who commit or order to be committed a breach of the present Convention.*

EVIDENCE OF VIOLATIONS: At a press conference soon after the invasion, Donald Rumsfeld, the US Secretary of Defense, was challenged about the destruction of museums and archaeological sites. He replied flippantly, "Stuff happens. Free people are free to make mistakes and commit crimes and do bad things." He then moved on to the next question.[1]

Initially, the British army arriving in Basra actively encouraged the looting of Ba'ath Party property. These buildings were ransacked by local Iraqis. Geoffrey Hoon, the UK Secretary of Defence, said that the people of Basra were merely *liberating* their property from the Ba'ath party. A Lieutenant Colonel of the Royal Scots Dragoon Guards told the BBC that, "It is absolutely not in my business to get in the way [of looters]." The next day instructions were given from Whitehall and the army was told to stop the looting. By then the situation had got out of hand. The Americans, who had adopted a similar outlook, also failed to prevent anarchy. Hospitals, houses, shops, all were looted. People were afraid to leave their premises. US forces intervened only for an hour in the looting of the Iraq National Museum in Baghdad.

The Coalition governments must have known that they were invading a country where writing was first invented, where Baghdad had been a centre for Muslim culture and religion for a thousand years. And that there was a wealth of archaeological sites, priceless museum collections, and historic libraries of great importance to Islam and civilisation. UK scholars of Mesopotamia had tried to tell the UK Government of its great obligation to protect these structures and objects; yet the Government took no notice of these scholars, and even refused to meet with them. The initial encouragement of looting had disastrous effects on this irreplaceable heritage. Several libraries were set on fire and destroyed. The National Library and Archives of Baghdad contained historical records, such as letters of the Ottoman rulers of Baghdad and the letters from Sharif Hussein of Mecca, who fought with Lawrence of Arabia.

The Library of the Korans at the Ministry of Religious Endowment containing records of the formation of modern Iraq and beautiful hand written Korans was also set on fire. The Muslim community found this deeply offensive to Islam. Suspiciously, state archives were systematically destroyed by fire with the help of petrol. Was this an act of vandalism attempting to destroy incriminating records of Saddam's period, when the British and Americans were selling arms and chemical and biological agents to Iraq? And when Rumsfeld was shaking hands with Saddam after he had gassed the Kurds. Flames leapt a hundred feet in the air but the Americans made no attempt to put the fire out. The libraries of Basra and Mosul were also destroyed in April 2003.

Priceless museums were allowed to be looted and damaged. The Museum of Archaeology in Baghdad, established by Gertrude Bell, contained ancient Sumerian treasures: a sculptured head from Uruk, a *Ram in the Thicket* statue from Ur, early legal texts in clay tablets, the epic of Gilgamesh on tablets, a clay goddess of 5,800 BC, and mathematical tablets. This museum was smashed up. The display cases broken; the floors littered with broken glass and pots. Patty Gertenblith, a Chicago law professor, said the looting was completely inexcusable and avoidable. "The American military had been told of the importance of these museums and the danger of looting." Professor Giovanni Bergamini, curator of the Egyptian museum of Turin. said "I don't know... perhaps it was only fathomless ignorance, but that is quite bad enough in itself."[2] The Natural History Library (under British control in Basra) was also destroyed by fire.

Leading museums around the world are horrified at this wanton destruction as the Mesopotamian basin is regarded by this community as *the cradle of civilisation*. The first priority of the relatively small force of highly-armed British troops was securing and defending the oil fields near Basra. This – together with the disbanding of the Iraqi army and police – meant that there was no one left to guard historic monuments, many of which are in the desert in South Western Iraq. Failure to provide satisfactory administration is contrary to The Hague Convention of 1907, which makes it clear that the functions of the local administration must go on. These immensely important archaeological sites were damaged beyond repair. Robert Fisk writes: "The Sumerian palaces, the temple walls, the great pillars, oil lamps and giant pots, and delicately patterned plates and dishes, all have been smashed to bits.[3] Thieves searched for Sumerian artefacts to sell on international markets by digging holes and ripping down walls. Famous sites such as Nimrud and Ninevah Hatra have been smashed. Eqbal Qazem, deputy director of the Museum of Antiquities in Nasiriyah, surveying the scene of pillage at Um Alkarab and Umma was in tears. "How can I do anything but cry," she said. These cities were among the most important in Sumerian civilisation. Now they are gone.

Saddam Hussein, who realised the importance of these archaeological sites, had guarded them with ruthless severity. Raid Abdul Ridhar Muhamad an Iraqi Archaeologist said, "If a country's civilisation is looted... its history ends. Please tell President Bush... he promised to liberate the Iraqi people... this is not a liberation this is a humiliation."[4]

John Curtis, keeper of the British Museum's Near East department, said in a report in January 2005, that the US army had (incredibly) used the archaeological site of Babylon as a military base.[5] This is one of the most important sites of our civilization, where some of the first laws – dating back to between 1792 and 1750 BC – were found. Written by Hammurabi in cuneiform script, they describe women's' rights to own property, to carry our business, and to divorce. Babylon's massive awe-inspiring walls are decorated with dragon-headed beasts; each brick imprinted with Nebuchadnezzar's stamp (604-562 BC). One of the Seven Wonders of the World – the hanging gardens of Babylon – stands by the swift flowing River Euphrates. All around there are mounds of earth full of pottery, lapis lazuli, and priceless artefacts. The site of the biblical tower of Babel is found in a lake full of papyrus and bull frogs.

l-Marshal Viscount Allenby of Jerusalem and Feisal I, King of Iraq and ruler of ldad circa 1921.

The founders of Iraq on camels. Winston Churchill, Colonial Secretary, Gertrude E
archaeologist, T.E. Shaw (Lawrence of Arabia) at the Cairo Conference of 15 Febr
ary 1921.

C (RAF) plane crash in the dessert circa 1917. 20 lb bombs were lobbed out of the kpit by the pilot.

roup of US F-16 'Fighting Falcons' of the type that swept over Fallujah in April)3, strafing the population with laser guided missiles, and GPS guided bombs. t NW. photo AP)

Iraq "The Cradle of Civilisation"
Bricks stamped in cuneiform
script by Nebuchadnezzar,
650BC, at Babylon. Used by
US army to defend their camp.

Golden treasures from UR.
Many such priceless treasures
have been destroyed by looters
in the 2003-2005 Iraq war.

ch 31 2003, the US show kindness to a hooded Iraqi, and allow his son to stay
him.   (Text NW. photo AP)

soldiers after an aggressive patrol in Latifiyah in support of US assault on Fallujah
Nov. 2004. Note blindfolding after Whitehall had banned it early in 2004.
t NW   photo AP)

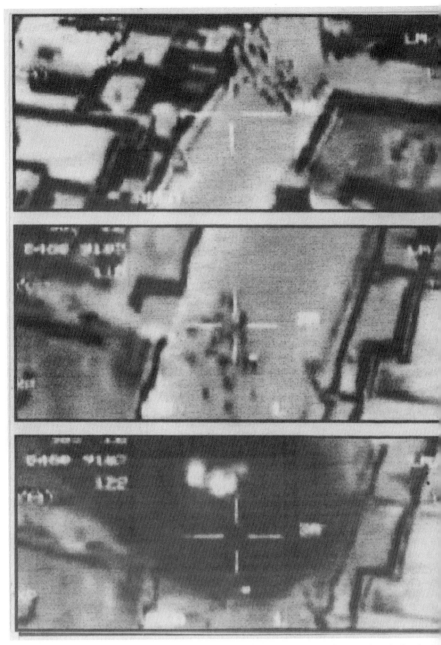

'Gun film footage', leaked from the Pentagon, showing the pilot's visual display
of a guided missile attack on a group of Iraqis in Fallujah. The dots in the top two
pictures are humans fleeing,   The bottom picture shows the missile strike.

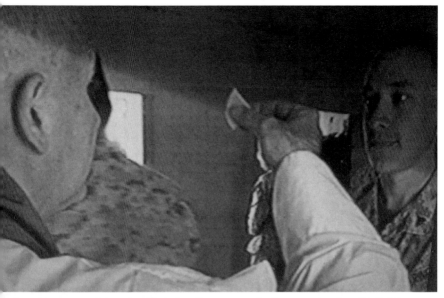

erican forces receiving the Christian Sacrament, before moving into Fallujah,
vember 2004   (BBC TV)

eli Defence Force methods in Fallujah: send in the tanks. (BBC TV)

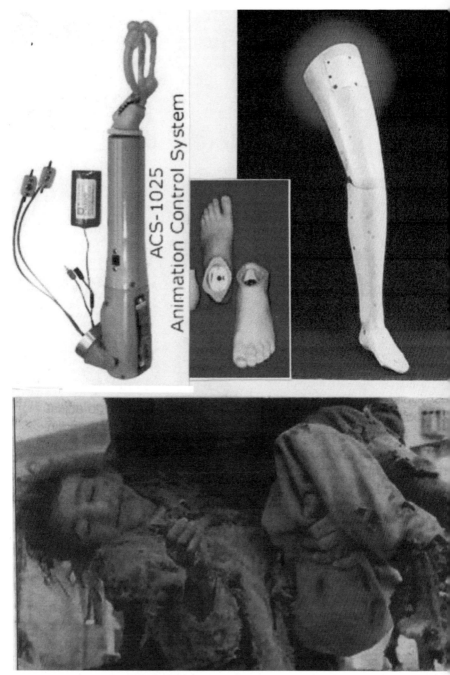

ACS-1025
Animation Control System

The madness of war: Iraqi children have the freedom to go on crutches........ that's
they've got any arms. The UK will deliver cluster bombs to the children from the a
but steadfastly refuses to give them artificial limbs.   Are we all monsters?

This famous archaeological site has been trashed by the American army who, in their blind ignorance and arrogance, found the high walls standing alone in the dessert ideal for a military base. The 2,600 year-old brick paving crushed by tanks, brick walls torn down to fill sand bags and the ground covered in gravel and chemicals for helicopter landing pads and dumps of oil tanks. This archaeological pollution beggars belief. Prior to the war, the British School of Archaeology in Iraq had provided Coalition Forces with a list of all the important archaeological sites in Iraq, to ensure they would be absolutely protected from any war damage or looting. The UK Government (led by Blair, Straw, Hoon, and Ingrams), who moved troops to the nearby Camp Dogwood base in support of the Americans, have not reacted with an iota of protest at this destruction. Silence can also be construed as a war crime.

When a secure civil administration is restored to Iraq, as an appropriate act of contrition, the British Government could return some of the artefacts from the British Museum that were "acquired" from Iraq in the late nineteenth and early twentieth centuries.

CLAIM: That the UK failed to protect the historic sites, museums and libraries of Iraq. Also, the UK initially encouraged looting in the Basra region, which resulted in widespread theft and destruction. The US (as allies of the UK) also failed to provide protection for sites, libraries and museums in their theatre of war. That these acts are in breach of The Rome Statute of The ICC Article 8, 2(a) and (b)(ix); The Hague Convention (IV) respecting the Laws and Customs of War on Land, 1907 Articles 43 and 47; and The Hague Convention for the Protection of Cultural Property in the Event of Armed Conflict, 1954 Article 4 (1) and (3), and Article 28.

---

[1] George Monbiot, *Guardian*, 20 May, 2003.
[2] Andrew Gumbel and David Keys, 'US blamed for failure to stop sacking of museum', *Independent*, 14 April 2003.
[3] Robert Fisk, *Independent*, 15 April 2003 and 3 June 2003.
[4] Andrew Gumbel and David Keys, 'US blamed for failure to stop sacking of museum', *Independent*, 14 April 2003.

---

[5] Sue Leeman, 'British Museum says US-led troops damaged ancient Iraqi city of Babylon', *Associated Press*, 15 January 2005.

7E. SEIZING THE ASSETS.

As we have seen in Chapter 1: *Brief history of Iraq & its Oil*, Iraq has the second largest oil reserves in the world, totalling 115 billion barrels of oil. In 1904 Anglo-Persian Oil (later BP) began pumping oil from Persia (Iran) down pipes to an oil terminal in Basra.

During the 2003 war, the first non-military objectives of the Coalition were to secure the oil fields and the Oil Ministry buildings in Baghdad. The provisional administration, installed by the USA immediately after the invasion, abolished the existing Iraqi economic laws and, on 19 September 2003, passed Order 39 privatising 200 state companies. Reconstruction projects were handed to US companies with close ties to the Bush Administration. All Iraqi companies were excluded. British interests were not served well – save in the provision of mercenaries and expenditure on armaments.

Privatisation and democratisation are virtually synonymous terms to the American Administration. Thus there is no dichotomy between *bringing freedom and democracy to the Iraqi people* and seizing their assets. Such privatisation, and sequestration, of Iraqi assets is contrary to international laws and customs of war.

RELEVANT LAWS AND CONVENTIONS: Charter of the Nuremberg Tribunal 1945 Article 6: (a) *Crimes against peace and* (b) *War crimes*. The Rome Statute of the ICC, Article 8: *War crimes* (2) *For the purpose of this Statute "war crimes" means:* (b) *Other serious violations of the laws and customs applicable in international armed conflict, within the established framework of international law, namely any of the following acts:* (xiii) *Destroying or seizing the enemy's property unless such destruction or seizure be imperatively demanded by the necessities of war.* The Hague Convention (IV) respecting the Laws and Customs of War on Land and its annex, 1907 Article 43: ... *the occupant... shall... restore... public order, while respecting unless absolutely prevented, the laws in force in the country.* Article 55: *The occupying State shall be regarded only as* *administrator and usufructuary of public buildings, real estate, forests, and agricultural estates belonging to the hostile State, and situated in the occupied country. It must safeguard the capital of these properties, and administer them in accordance with the rules of usufruct.*

The US army's *Law of Land Warfare,* states in Article 402 that *The occupant does not have the right of sale or unqualified use of [non-military] property.*

EVIDENCE OF VIOLATIONS: The pattern for free market capitalism and the seizure of Iraqi assets was set in America a hundred years ago. President Theodore Roosevelt said at the end of the 19th century that Red Indians should be brought "thoroughly and efficiently under the control of our civilisation. For under the Anglo Saxons' commercial necessities, progress has been solely due to the power of the mighty civilised races which have not lost the fighting instinct, and which by their expansion are gradually bringing peace to the red wastes where barbarian peoples of the world hold sway. On the border between civilisation and barbarism war is generally normal."

On 21 April 1898 Senator Beveridge declared "Fate has written our policy for us: the trade of the world must and can be ours. And we shall get it, as our Mother England has told us how... We will cover the ocean with our merchant marine. We will build a navy to the measure of our greatness... Our institutes will follow our trade... American law, American order, American civilisation, and the American flag will plant themselves on shores hitherto bloody and benighted, but by those agencies of God henceforth be made beautiful, and bright."

The economist Charles A. Conant wrote in September 1898, "The United States shall assert their right to free markets in all the old countries which are being opened to the surplus resources of the capitalist countries and thereby be given the benefits of modern civilisation."

In 1907 President Woodrow Wilson wrote: "Since trade ignores no boundaries and the manufacturer insists on having the world as a market, the flag of the nation must follow him, and the doors of the nations which are closed against him must be battered down. Concessions obtained by financiers must be safeguarded by ministers of state, even if the sovereignty of unwilling nations be outraged in the process."[1]

In the last throws of the Red Indian resistance in America in 1885, the chief of the Sioux, Sitting Bull, told Annie Oakley at the Wild West Show, that he couldn't understand how the white man could be so unmindful of their own poor. "The white man knows how to make everything, but he does not know how to distribute it."[2] He could have added that the white man regards the world as his oyster. This blindness might account for the fact that Americans (5% of the world population) consume 25% of world resources.

One of Hitler's objectives in the Second World War was to push his armies past Stalingrad into the oil rich area of the Caspian Sea to secure oil supplies for the Third Reich. In order to exploit these oil fields and the Russian economy, his Minister of Economics, Walther Funk, was appointed president of Continental Oil. Continental Oil planned this operation and Funk participated in conferences with Hitler to finance the war and make secret preparations for war. Funk was also responsible for the exploitation of the gold reserves in occupied Europe. These actions were considered *crimes against peace* and *war crimes* at the Nuremberg trials in 1946, where Funk was found guilty and imprisoned for life.[3]

There are parallels with the actions of the occupying powers in Iraq in 2003-2005. The Bush Administration is dominated by connections with the oil and arms industries. As a young man, President Bush started an oil exploration firm, *Arbusto*, partly bankrolled by the Saudi Royal Family and the Saudi Bin Ladens, of whom Osama is its most famous member.[4] President Bush's father is a spokesman for the Carlyle Group which has oil and arms interests. Vice President Cheney was Chief Executive of Halliburton, an oil and construction conglomerate. Condoleezza Rice, former National Security Advisor and current Secretary of State, was previously a director of Chevron, another oil company.

Guaranteeing future oil supplies for the massive American consumption would therefore inevitably be in the minds of the

American Administration when going to war with Iraq, since Iraq has the second largest oil reserves in the world. (The US Deputy Secretary of Defense, Paul Wolfowitz, said in April 2003: "We are dealing with a country that can really finance its own reconstruction and relatively soon".[5] There is also increasing competition with China, who has increased its consumption of oil by 400% in three years.

In 1973, without any pretext of *causa belli*, the US had secret plans to invade Middle Eastern states to secure oil supplies. At the time OPEC were raising the price of oil and cutting production in retaliation against American support for Israel in the Yom Kippur war against Egypt. This was causing a world wide recession. In a secret Joint Intelligence Committee report, MI6 warned the then Prime Minister Edward Heath that America had plans to seize oil fields in Saudi Arabia, Abu Dhabi or Kuwait. "This might be executed without any prior consultation of allies. The object would presumably be to teach the Arabs a lesson, to assure by physical control an adequate supplementary supply of oil for US domestic needs, with a good quantity over for the needs of selected friends and to enable the US to rid itself of restraints on its policies arising from the oil embargo… As regards Kuwait in particular, they [the US] could hardly afford to wait long because of the risk of Iraqi or other intervention."[6]

Prophetically the European reaction to this operation also worried JIC. "They (the EEC) would feel US pressures should be applied to Israel rather than the Arabs. Since the US would probably claim to be acting for the benefit of the West and would expect the support of allies, deep US/European rifts could ensue." The US was also thought to have an alternative strategy of regime change in Saudi Arabia, Kuwait and Abu Dhabi with "more amenable men." It was also feared that the Pentagon might ask the UK to assist, but "the situation following the US intervention in the Gulf would be highly volatile and difficult to predict. The greatest risk of such confrontation in the Gulf would probably arise in Kuwait, where the Iraqis, with Soviet backing, might be tempted to intervene."[7] It would lead to a general war in the region. The plan was abandoned when OPEC resumed production and prices fell.

US obsession with OPEC has continued to this day. Prior to the war of 2003, in a candid moment, President Bush declared that one of the US war aims in Iraq was to break the OPEC cartel. Almost as if OPEC was part of the *axis of evil*. It should be remembered that this was not the first US-planned intervention in a Muslim State. Between 1801 and 1805 the fledgling American Government, flexing it muscles, had tried unsuccessfully to install a puppet government in Tripoli, to protect American ships entering the Mediterranean.

How important oil was to the US became blatantly clear during the early stages of the invasion. While other administrative buildings were bombed – and allowed to be looted – the Ministry of Oil buildings in Baghdad were heavily protected by American troops and the oil fields of Southern Iraq were seized by the British Army. By contrast, at the same time, electricity, telecommunications, sanitation and administrative infrastructures were all destroyed or damaged as part of *Shock and Awe* tactics. After eighteen months of occupation, these infrastructures are still in a calamitous state.

The introduction of *democracy* and a capitalist economy in Iraq was another aim of this war (ostensibly to free the Iraqi people). Democracy has a special meaning in the United States, not necessarily shared by other nations. The word not only describes a system of government where representatives are elected by all eligible members of the population; it has also become inextricably linked to privatisation of nationalised assets – and a liberal freedom to allow private global companies to acquire those assets. (As well as a suppression of trade unionism in order to obtain maximum advantage and profit from those assets.) The concept that a democratically-elected Iraqi government might actually be inclined towards nationalisation rather than privatisation was not a concept that conformed to the American Republican philosophy or its war aims.

A provisional US/Iraqi administration was set up in the immediate aftermath of the invasion to facilitate this *democracy*, with Jay Garner at its head. A retired US Army general, Jay Garner – a former arms trader – was replaced after only one month by Paul Bremer, but during that period there was widespread looting and a total breakdown of order in Iraq. The Garner Administration had not been helped by the fact that several hundred of the British and US personnel in the headquarters compound in Baghdad had been struck down by a virus causing vomiting.[8]

Under Saddam Hussein, Iraq's constitution banned the privatisation of important state assets and foreign ownership of Iraqi companies. Nevertheless, in breach of The Hague Convention of 1907 and the US army's *Law of Land Warfare* (and contrary to existing Iraqi economic laws), on 19 September 2003 Paul Bremer enacted Order 39. Order 39 sanctioned the privatisation of 200 state companies and allowed 100% foreign ownership of Iraqi banks, mines and factories. It also allowed 100% of profits to be taken out of the country.

In a private memo sent to the Prime Minister on 26 March 2003, the Attorney General said, "The imposition of major structural economic reforms would not be authorised by international law." The only way to legalise this position so that the assets can not be returned to Iraq without compensation, is for the new government to ratify the contracts quickly, but even this is open to question. Order 39 is theft on a monumental scale in defiance of international law. Nor is it in accordance with the May 2003 UN resolution confirming the Coalition as the occupying power which stated that "it must comply fully with their obligations under international law including in particular the Geneva Conventions of 1949 and the Hague regulations of 1907."[9]

Under the guise of *Reconstruction* Bremer implemented programmes for wholesale privatisation, training Iraqis in capitalist methods and introducing new tax systems favourable to foreign companies. Lucrative reconstruction contracts were handed out primarily to American companies. The oil fields were taken over and oil futures sold on the international markets.[10] The excuse given for this sale of infrastructure and other assets to foreign companies was that Iraqi companies did not have sufficient finance to bid – even though Iraqis complained to the Provisional Authority that they had made lower bids than foreign firms but had still not won the contracts. The excuse for excluding countries such as France from bidding was that they had made no contribution to the war effort. In the words of Paul Wolfowitz, the US Deputy Secretary of Defense, the contracts should only be given to Coalition countries, "for the protection of the essential security interests of the United States."[11] British companies were somewhat annoyed that they did not receive many crumbs from the table. On 24 April 2003 Amec, a British company, entered a 49-51% joint venture with Fluor, an American construction and engineering group, in the hope of obtaining contracts from the US Army Corps of Engineers for rebuilding Iraq's oil industry. However, the successful bids were made by Halliburton and Bechtel. The Bush Administration had initially planned to give the job to Halliburton without a proper tender – on the grounds of avoiding delay – but was forced into tendering. A year later, these contracts are being investigated by the FBI for criminal malpractice.[12]

A report published by Christian Aid says that of the £20 million in oil revenues and funds handed to the Coalition Provisional Authority (CPA) a large amount has disappeared due to incompetence and corruption. Huge contracts have been handed to American companies, some charging ten times the price of local ones. Iraqi companies began receiving contracts in April 2004, but only for sums under $500,000. Contracts worth $2 billion were signed before the handover in June 2004. The terms make them uneconomical to revoke.[13]

Baghdad is full of stories of corruption and incompetence of the US-led CPA. Ahmed al-Rikaby, a Baghdadi television worker, said that three Iraqi Americans, on vast salaries, were appointed in charge of re-establishing Iraqi television. But, he said, they "had no expertise and never helped me or anybody else." He believed they got the jobs because they had influential friends in the Pentagon. The CPA might also, given its ideological commitment to private enterprise, be expected to have encouraged the reopening of the Baghdad stock exchange, which used to employ 5,000 people, but it remained shut for more than a year. An Iraqi stockbroker, Hussain Kubba, said: "There was no reason it should not have opened soon after the war." One of the reasons could be that the CPA appointed a 24-year-old Republican to oversee it. He had, so far as the Iraqis who dealt with him could see, very limited knowledge of stock exchanges.[14]

To a certain extent, this bonanza of reconstruction and privatisation has not materialised due to the ensuing insurgency. In December 2003 the US Congress authorised $18 billion for reconstruction but by September 2004, funds had to be diverted from reconstruction to security. In September 2004 the State Department diverted $3.4 billion funds from water and power projects to boost security and oil output.[15]

At least one British Army officer considered the capitalist democracy programme detrimental to Iraqis. Soon after the invasion of southern Iraq (and after appealing for three weeks), Lt Colonel Pete Jones, British military governor of Umm Qasr, was told by the British HQ there was no money to pay the local Iraqis for work. Lt Colonel Jones said he was tired of giving promissory notes and was now worried that his bluff would be called and there was no money to cover them. "Six weeks ago before the war these people had a job, food and water. Now they haven't and we are supposed to have liberated them," he complained. Lt Colonel Jones said he was depressed at the idea of introducing democracy to Iraq, the oldest civilisation in the world, which had developed its own democratic systems of local government where representatives were chosen by elders. He also dreaded the first Macdonald's. He said American building contractors had come with plans to restart the grain silos which had employed 750 Iraqis before the war and were proposing to cut costs by only employing 230 men. "I told them they can't do that. We can't liberate a country and throw its people out of work."[16]

The fact that there are very high temperatures in Iraq (which means people can only work for brief periods) did not even enter into the capitalist equation. Nor were all Iraqis impressed by these moves towards a capitalist economy. A young Iraqi in Basra met Rageh Omaar of the BBC and said, "We went through war! We were ready for this suffering because Bush and Blair said they would help us with everything after Saddam is gone. They make this promise and we believed them, that they will change Iraq, change our lives. And what has happened? Nothing! Just soldiers and occupation. I am a pharmacist and yet I am doing nothing now. But there are no jobs for even educated people here in Basra. Do they expect us to just be like dogs, to wait until each time they choose to feed us with small plates of old food?"[17]

In April 2004 in Fallujah, a Mujahideen commander said, "We do not hate the Americans and British, we hate the ideas they have brought here. We do not want their capitalism, we do not want communism. We have our own ideas about how we want our country to be run in a Muslim way."[18]

Here is an example of the close links between the US Administration and the companies awarded contracts: On 23 May 2003, soon after the invasion, a seminar organised by Bechtel for European and Asian firms was held in London. The aim of the seminar was to discuss contract opportunities in Iraq, where 90% of the work was to be subcontracted. Iraqi firms were largely excluded on the grounds that they had insufficient funds to operate. Prior to the seminar, Bechtel had already been awarded the biggest reconstruction contract (worth $680 million) by Andrew Nasios of the US Agency for International Development. Andrew Nasios had previously worked for Bechtel. George Schultz, Chairman of the Committee to Liberate Iraq, was also a member of the board of Bechtel.

A further example is found in Halliburton, the Texan oil services company formerly run by US vice-president, Dick Cheney. It has already received contracts related to Iraq (worth $500 million) from the US army. The Democratic congressman Henry Waxman called for an inquiry into the relation between Halliburton and the Bush Administration. Halliburton has completed works worth approximately £71 million to extinguish oil well fires lit during the conflict. It has also earned $425 million in Iraq-related projects in 2003. "It is simply remarkable that a single company could earn so much money from the war in Iraq." said Waxman in a letter to Les Brownlee, acting Secretary of the US army.[19]

Owing to the secrecy surrounding the award of contracts, much of the evidence is circumstantial, but it is estimated that 60% of the contracts were awarded to American firms who donated to the Bush Administration or who had ties with the military.[20]

A year later, Mike O'Brien, the UK Trade Minister, speaking at a conference in Westminster to promote investment opportunities in Iraq, insisted that British companies had a fair share of the 17,000 contracts and subcontracts for reconstruction work in Iraq. Twenty British companies (including De La Rue, Standard Chartered and Amec) won contracts in Iraq.[21] These involve primarily water, electricity and security services. The conference was also addressed by Tom Foley, the director of private sector development for the CPA (the country's de facto government) and the Iraqi Trade Minister, Iyad Allawi. Mr Foley said "There's great long term potential for UK companies in the private sector."

On 10 April 2003 Clare Short, at the time UK Secretary of State for International Development, went to a Ministerial meeting chaired by Jack Straw. The Foreign Secretary said, regarding the Office of Reconstruction and Humanitarian Assistance (ORHA) – organised by the Pentagon – and the legal limits of its powers, "We must not let word get out that we had any differences with the US." He went on to argue that we must secure contracts for UK firms. "We took the risks and bore the costs, we cannot let the French and Germans get their noses in the trough."[22] This attitude was reinforced by the Prime Minister's special Envoy for Iraq, Sir Jeremy Greenstock, who said on a television interview at the time that British firms "should have a slice of the action." The representation of Iraq as a piece of cake was anticipated in the 1915 Administration of Asquith. (cf Chapter 1: *Brief History of Iraq & its Oil.*)

One particular piece of the cake that British companies have profited from is the supply of mercenaries armed with light machine guns to guard foreign contractors. Mercenaries often include former members from British elite SAS units. There is evidence of personal financial benefit to at least one UK politician.[23] While he was not in office on 18 March 2003 and therefore had no vote on the war, Sir Malcolm Rifkind, former Foreign Secretary and candidate for Kensington and Chelsea, accepted the post of chairman of Armorgroup, a security firm protecting contractors in Iraq. Such security firms often employ semi mercenaries who do not appear to be governed by the rules of war. (cf Chapter 7t: *Mercenaries.*)

In November 2004 the rich nations of the world, including Britain, agreed to cancel 80% of Iraq's debt, with the proviso that the Iraqi economy would be run by the IMF for a ten-year period. This incorporated strict rules allowing multinational corporations unbridled freedom, free neoliberal economics including privatisation of services, non-competitive contracts and 15% flat rate tax. Irrespective of what the elected Iraqi government might want.[24] These moves are not going to help the Iraqi youth, 80% of whom already are unemployed.

Iraqis, whether they want it or not, are being tied into the capitalist dream, and their primary assets placed in the hands of foreigners. To many Arabs, privatising Iraqi state assets, to be grabbed by American companies, is seen as part of the Fourth Crusade.

CLAIM: That the UK and US governments have, by the theft of Iraq's assets and by order 39 of the Coalition Provisional Authority, breached the provisions of The Rome Statute of the International Criminal Court Article 8, 2, (b) (xiii). That they have also breached the provisions of The Hague Convention (IV) of 1907, the Geneva Conventions of 1949, the US army's Laws of Land Warfare, and the principles enshrined in the Charter of Nuremberg of 1945.

---

[1] Ziauddin Sardar and Merryl Wyn Davies, *American Dream Global Nightmare*, London: Icon Books, 2004 p99 et seq,

[2] Dee Brown, *Bury my Heart at Wounded Knee*, London: Vintage, 1991, p427.

[3] Uncovered Editions, *The World War II Collection*, The Stationery Office, 2001.

[4] Michael Moore, *Dude Where's My Country*, London: Penguin Books Ltd., 2003,p8.

[5] Rupert Cornwell, *Independent*, 6 Oct 2003.

[6] UK National Archives Documents, State Papers 1973.

[7] Ibid.

[8] Phil Reeves, *Independent*, 13 May 2003.

[9] Naomi Klein, *Guardian*, 7 November 2003.

[10] David Teather, *Guardian*, 31 May 2004.

[11] Andrew Buncombe, *Independent*, 11 Dec 2003.

[12] Michael Harrison, *Independent*, 25 April 2003.

[13] Kim Sengupta, *Independent*, 28 June 2004.

[14] Patrick Cockburn, *Independent*, 30 June 2004.

[15] Colin Brown and Patrick Cockburn, *Independent*, 16 September 2004.

[16] Rupert Cornwell, Independent, 2 May 2003.

[17] Rageh Omaar, *Revolution Day*, London: Viking, 2004, p217.

[18] Lee Gordon, *Camden New Journal*, 15 April 2004.

[19] Saeed Shah, *Independent*, 25 Feb 2004.

[20] Bill Condie, *Evening Standard*, 31 October 2003.

[21] Andrew Buncombe, *Independent*, 11 Dec 2003.

[22] Clare Short. *An Honourable Deception?*, London: Free Press, 2004, p205.

[23] Mark Scodie, *Jewish Chronicle*, 16 April 2004.

[24] Johann Hari, *Independent*, 22 December 2004.

WAR CRIMES OR JUST WAR?

7F. STEALING THEIR PLANTS.

The US has ensured that Iraqi agriculture falls into the hands of American companies through the passing of Provisional Authority Order 81.

RELEVANT LAWS AND CONVENTIONS: Charter of the Nuremberg Tribunal 1945 Article 6: (a) *Crimes against peace and* (b) *War crimes.* The Rome Statute of the ICC, Article 8: *War crimes (2) For the purpose of this Statute "war crimes" means:* (b) *Other serious violations of the laws and customs applicable in international armed conflict, within the established framework of international law, namely any of the following acts:* (xiii) *Destroying or seizing the enemy's property unless such destruction or seizure be imperatively demanded by the necessities of war.* The Hague Convention (IV) respecting the Laws and Customs of War on Land and its annex, 1907 Article 43: *... the occupant... shall... restore... public order, while respecting unless absolutely prevented, the laws in force in the country.* Article 55: *The occupying State shall be regarded only as administrator and usufructuary of public buildings, real estate, forests, and agricultural estates belonging to the hostile State, and situated in the occupied country. It must safeguard the capital of these properties, and administer them in accordance with the rules of usufruct.*
The US army's *Law of Land Warfare,* states in Article 402 that *The occupant does not have the right of sale or unqualified use of [non-military] property.*

According to the archaeologist, Colin Renfrew, samples of seeds, found in pre-pottery Neolithic strata in the Euphrates valley, both in Syria and Mesopotamia, show that cereals and legumes were beginning to be cultivated even at 10,000 BC when hunter gathering was still the main source of food. Very rapidly, in a period of a thousand years these cultivated plants became the main source of food in the region.[1]

The ancestors of Iraqi farmers started carefully selecting and planting their seeds in the very fertile yellow silt by the Tigris and Euphrates Rivers twelve thousand years ago. The superb fertility of the soil, irrigated by little ditches each side of the fields under the palm groves, has enabled multi-cropping and the rapid growth of an urban class who invented writing, among other things. All was going well with the Iraqi farmer, who regarded such plants as his birthright, and who was used to holding back ten percent of his seeds to sow the following season – until, that is, the arrival of the Americans in force, supported by the obsequious Mr Blair (another Monsanto fan), on 19 March 2003. Within a year the work of twelve thousand years was undone. Mr Paul Bremer, head of the Coalition Provisional Administration, had passed Order 81: *Patent, Industrial Design, Undisclosed Information, Integrated Circuits and Plant Variety.* This order amends Iraq's Patent Law of 1970, and is therefore contrary to the Geneva and Hague Conventions.

The CPA's Order 81 has made it illegal for Iraqi farmers to save their seed for replanting. It abolishes the prohibition against private ownership of biological resources and introduces monopoly rights over seeds. Guess who owns those rights? Yes, our multinational friends Monsanto, Syngenta, Bayer, and Dow Chemical (of Agent Orange fame). Iraqi farmers cannot sow, or save seeds for replanting, from any plant protected by largely American patents. Many (if not all) of the seeds promoted by these companies will be genetically modified, irrespective of their long term effects on the environment. Such planting will be part of the bribery involved in WTO and IMF negotiations with Iraq – along with the other packages requiring restriction of unions, foreign investors' rights etc.

And so, in just one year, the Iraqis have been robbed of 12,000 years of plant development; including Iraq's very own scientific botanical germ plasm research material. All in the name of ridding Saddam Hussein of weapons of mass destruction. Even the very plants are ripped out of the Iraqis hands in the name of freedom.[2]

CLAIM: That the UK and US governments, through the Coalition Provisional Authority, by enacting order 81, have organised the theft of Iraq's botanical assets and have thereby breached the provisions of The Rome Statute of the International Criminal Court Article 8, 2, (b) (xiii). That they have also breached the provisions of The Hague Convention (IV) of 1907, the Geneva Conventions of 1949, the US army's Laws of Land Warfare, and the principles enshrined in the Charter of Nuremberg of 1945.

---

[1] Colin Renfrew, 'Archaeology, Theories, Methods and Practice', London: Thames and Hudson, 1996, p280.

[2] World Food Day: Iraqi farmers aren't celebrating, report by *Grain* and *Focus on the Global South*, 15 October 2004, http://www.grain.org/nfg/?id=253

WAR CRIMES OR JUST WAR?

7G.   A   CRUSADE.   RELIGIOUS PERSECUTION.

To an Iraqi, a dog is an unclean animal. Mohamed is reputed to have cut his robe rather than disturb a cat that was asleep on it. But a dog is a different matter. An Iraqi would consider it a very grave insult to allow a dog to sniff in his wife's bedroom. Sniffer dogs were used by UK soldiers during *aggressive patrols*.

Since both Coalition leaders, Bush and Blair, come from fundamental Christian backgrounds, and the majority of the US and UK soldiers also are nominally Christian, a religious element has inevitably entered into the campaign, with God being brought in on the Coalition side (even though Rowan Williams (the Archbishop of Canterbury), the Pope, and representatives of US Churches condemned the war). This religious element has stigmatised the Iraqis as enemies; it has been used in torture; it has been used as a means of providing UK and US soldiers with a feeling of moral worth; and it has blinded the Coalition to the religious beliefs of Iraqis – even to the fact that 700,000 Iraqis are Christians who are now, as never before, being subject to persecution by fellow Iraqis as a result of the war.

RELEVANT LAWS AND CONVENTIONS: Rome Statute of the International Criminal Court Article 7: *Crimes against humanity.* (1) *For the purpose of this Statute, "crime against humanity" means any of the following acts when committed as part of a widespread or systematic attack directed against any civilian population, with knowledge of the attack:* (e) *Imprisonment or other severe deprivation of physical liberty in violation of fundamental rules of international law;* (f) *Torture;* (g) *Rape, sexual slavery... or any other form of sexual violence of comparable gravity;* (h) *Persecution against any identifiable group or collectivity on political, racial, national, ethnic, cultural, religious, gender as defined in*

paragraph 3, or other grounds that are universally recognised as impermissible under international law, in connection with any act referred to in this paragraph or any crime within the jurisdiction of the Court.
The United Nations Convention against Torture, ratified by the US in 1994.

EVIDENCE OF VIOLATIONS: The contradiction between American military action and the teachings of Christ has a long tradition. On 27 December 1890 the American cavalry made their last major assault on the remnants of the Indian population, demanding the arrest of Big Foot of the Sioux tribe as "a fomenter of disturbances". Three hundred and fifty of his tribe were forced to camp in the snow-bound valley of Wounded Knee. Big Foot was dying of pneumonia, and coughing up blood. On the following morning the tribe was fed with a breakfast of tack, disarmed, and their tepees raked with machine gun fire from the two ridges each side of the valley. The wagon load of wounded survivors, four men and forty seven women and children were carried into a church. Above the pulpit was a crudely lettered banner, *PEACE ON EARTH, GOOD WILL TO MEN.*[1] Lewis Lapham comments on the myth of moral righteousness of American expansionism. "The West was won less by the force of independent mind than by the lying government contract, the crooked lawsuit, and the worthless Indian treaty."[2]

Bush's and Blair's failure to grasp the fundamental dichotomy between military action and the Christian Commandment, *thou shalt not kill*, remains a mystery to the atheist.

In the run up to the Iraq war, Mr Bush declared that the *war against terror* was a *crusade*. This was an unfortunate turn of phrase and it was quickly rectified. But the damage was done; the underlying anti-Muslim sentiment remained. Mr Blair's wife, Cherie, a strict Catholic, made a similar unthinking mistake a year earlier when she compared and attacked Muslim women's dress code, not realising that a Muslim's view of semi naked Western women is that they are sisters of Satan. Incidentally, the Third Crusade had shown that Saladin's magnanimity in battle compares very favourably with modern Coalition behaviour in Iraq. When Richard Coeur de Lion lost his horse, Saladin chivalrously sent him a replacement. (In a society based on oral tradition, Richard Coeur de Lion is still the bogeyman of the stories Arab grandmothers tell their children).

That the Coalition forces are imbued with Christianity can be gauged by pictures of the Black Watch marching on parade to a Christian service of blessing, in October 2004. (Soldiers whose Christian observance during peace time would probably be minimal.) The atheist anthropologist will regard this preparation of the troops for battle as a normal occurrence for young soldiers, be they Roman, Greek, Maori, or Stone Age. In a BBC news report filmed during and just prior to the American assault on Fallujah in November 2004, soldiers are seen praying and receiving the communion biscuits symbolising *the Body of Christ*. Several chaplains were embedded with the troops. Lieutenant Commander Denis Cox, a Naval Chaplin used biblical language in answer to questions about the morality of the war. He said that the marines were "agents of wrath (of God) to bring justice to wrong doers or evil doers, and that's what marines are doing. Bringing wrath of a just government against an unjust group of individuals, terrorists. "The Marines Battalion Commander, Colonel Gareth Brandt said this was "the right fight: the good fight... The enemy has got a face and he's in Fallujah. He is called Satan."[3]

Many US military strategists are religiously motivated. The officer responsible for tracking Osama Bin Laden, Lieutenant-General William Boykin, said Islamists hated the US "because we're a Christian nation, because our foundation and our roots are Judeo-Christian and the enemy is a guy called Satan." The Reverend Franklin Graham said in a speech at the Pentagon that Islam was "a very evil and wicked religion".[4] Strangely, this extreme fundamentalist Christian viewpoint has allied itself with the predominantly-Jewish neocon lobby responsible for the 1997 *Project for the New American Century*. Islam has now replaced communism as the bogey of American fears, to be defeated by American might. Ironically in a mirror image, Osama Bin Laden has said President Bush is in league with Satan.

US and UK soldiers ape their leaders and approach war from a Christian perspective. Though the war aim was to liberate the Iraqi people, Iraqis are identified as different, and in the heat of battle as the "enemy" allied to Satan. There are other unfortunate consequences to a Christian crusade. The war inevitably becomes racial as well as having religious undertones.

There are very strict Koranic codes of religious behaviour which, if abused, can cause the violated or humiliated person to be so ashamed than he might want to kill himself, or others, or feel forced to seek exile away from those he knows, even if they are his wife and children. Humiliation can also cause a Muslim to seek to become a martyr as a suicide bomber. Muslims take Koranic codes very seriously indeed. Thus, interrogation techniques which are designed to make a Muslim break the Koranic code, is deeply despicable. The following methods of torture, specifically designed to humiliate Muslims, were approved by Donald Rumsfeld on 2 December 2002:

(8)   *Removal of all comfort items (including religious items).*
(10)   *Removal of clothing.*
(11)   *Forced grooming (shaving of facial hair, etc...)*[5]

These methods have been used in US-run jails in Iraq, notoriously at Abu Ghraib. The Rumsfeld memo was interpreted by US guards in Iraq to go beyond the first steps of humiliation. What more tempting with a totally naked prisoner cowering in fear than to do something far worse – and then take photographs of the naked prisoners to show them images of their total humiliation in every sexual posture and action imaginable? That is what happened. Bored, hot, sexually-frustrated US foot soldiers – seeking revenge for their fallen comrades, in an atmosphere that regards the foreigner (and particularly the Muslim) as *the enemy* – need some stern discipline coming from their superiors to respect international conventions. That discipline has been totally lacking. The Geneva Conventions, the Statute of the ICC and the Principles of Nuremberg were formulated against the background of the Holocaust, but they must also apply to the persecution of Muslims.

Methods employed by the British Army also break the Koranic code. This code lays down very strict rules of privacy for the home. A stranger must not look into the windows of a house. A stranger must not enter the women's quarters, nor look upon the women of the house. In some strict sects a stranger must not look at a woman's face unveiled. All of these codes are broken when a British soldier enters an Iraqi home unannounced. British soldiers were instructed by the Prime Minister and the Secretary of Defence to enter houses unannounced by *aggressive patrolling*.

Not surprisingly the Christian aspect of the war has resulted in a backlash against the 700,000 Iraqi Christians. Iraq under Saddam Hussein, perhaps because of his ruthlessness, had been in fact a model of religious tolerance. Jews, Christians and Muslims had been able to live side by side on account of Saddam's policies aimed at creating a secular state. This was not understood by Bush and Blair. This tolerance has now disappeared and Christians are now living in fear. In August 2004, four Christian churches in Baghdad and one in Mosul were blown up, killing twelve people and injuring 61[6]. A further five churches were bombed in Baghdad in the second week of October 2004. Seven Christians were shot up in Baghdad on 13 October 2004. Since the invasion, 110 Christians have been killed, many in the southern sector of British-run Iraq. There have been mortar attacks on community centres, shooting of Christian shopkeepers, and kidnapping of businessmen for extortion. Thousands of Christian Iraqis have fled the country.[7] In northern Iraq Assyrian Christians live in fear.

In December 2004, when things started to go really wrong with the occupation of Iraq, God was invoked once again. Briefly visiting Iraq on 21 December 2004, the Prime Minister stood on a table in Basra and addressed a thousand British troops. "I know you are going to be away from your family and loved ones over Christmas. I am sorry about that but, my God, it's a job worth doing.[8] This may have been using God's name in vain, but more probably it was not. On the same day in another part of Iraq, in Mosul, in a mess tent that had been blown up by a suicide bomber killing 19 US troops and injuring many more, US Chaplain Eddie Barnett prayed, "help us now, God, in this time of very tragic circumstances."[9] After two years of war, Blair is deeply unsure of himself when he says desperately: "Why can't people learn to accept my sincerity in going to war, just as I accept their good faith in opposing it."[10]

If we add to this Mr Blair's oft repeated mantra, *I firmly believe what I am doing is right* and then we hear him again saying, with a mind-blowing lack of humility, "I am prepared to meet my Maker" we realise we are entering a dangerous psychological world. One that can justify children's limbs being torn off 2,500 miles away.

Colonel Tim Collins, British army commander of the 1st Battalion, the Royal Irish Regiment in the Southern Sector of Iraq, on retirement said on the BBC *Today* programme that abuses against Iraqi civilians was partly the result of the leaders referring to them as the enemy instead of treating them as a people. "Either it was a war to liberate the people of Iraq, in which case there was gross incompetence, or it was simply a cynical war that was going to happen anyway to vent some anger on Saddam Hussein's regime with no regard to the consequences on the Iraqi people, In that case it is a form of common assault- and the evidence would point to the latter." While he felt that the liberation of Iraq was the right thing to do. "The evidence would show, in hindsight, that the preparations for a free and fair Iraq were not made and therefore one must question the motivation of the powers that went to attack it. It is fair to say that the United States and its ally the UK are living the consequences having removed the Ba'athist regime without any thought about what would replace it. The abuse of any individual is to be condemned without qualification. However I would observe that if the leaders of a country, or the leaders of an alliance talk in terms of "them", "the enemy" rather than treating them as people, how can they expect the lowest common denominator, the basic soldiery, to interpret it in any other way."[11]

On 11 January, at the court-martial of US army specialist Charles Graner, a victim at Abu Ghraib, Amin al-Sheik said Graner forced him to violate his Muslim faith by making him eat pork and drink alcohol. He also told him to thank Jesus for keeping him alive. Another US soldier from Abu Ghraib quoted Graner as saying: "The Christian in me says it's wrong, but the corrections officer in me says I love to make a grown man piss himself."[12]

At the same trial Guy Womack, Graner's attorney, said of the pile of naked Iraqis, "Don't cheerleaders all over America form pyramids six to eight times a year?" And of the photograph of Lindie England holding a naked Iraqi by a dog lead: "You're keeping control of them. A tether is a valid control to be used in corrections." Of Sergeant

144

Graner he said: "He was doing his job. Following orders and being praised for it."[13]

CLAIM: That members of the UK Government and Military have carried out, and supported, acts of religious persecution; especially in relation to aggressive patrols and torture of detainees and PoWs; and that these acts are in breach of the Rome Statute of the International Criminal Court Article 7: (1)(e), (f), (g) and (h), and are in breach of the UN Convention against Torture ratified by the US in 1994.

---

[1] Dee Brown, *Bury My Heart at Wounded Knee*, London: Vintage, 1991.

[2] Ziauddin Sardar, Meryl Wyn Davies, *American Dream Global Nightmare*, Cambridge: Icon Books, 2004.

[3] BBC 2, *Newsnight*, 24 November 2004.

[4] Robert Fisk, *Independent*, 24 October 2003.

[5] Pentagon action memo (unclassified), *Counter-Resistance Techniques*, approved by SECDEF on 2 December 2002

[6] Donald Macintyre, *Independent*, 2 August 2004.

[7] Kim Sengupta, *Independent*, 12 October 2004.

[8] Donald Macintyre and Colin Brown, *Independent*, 22 December 2004.

[9] Patric Cockburn and Jeremy Redmond, *Independent*, 22 December 2004.

[10] Adrian Hamilton, *Independent*, 4 January 2005.

[11] Kim Sengupta, *Independent*, 17 September 2004.

[12] Roland Watson, *Times*, 12 January 2005.

[13] Adam Tanner, *Independent*, 11 January 2005.

WAR CRIMES OR JUST WAR?

7H. CABLE TIES.

Plastic ties (normally used to tie pipes together) are used by the US and UK armies to restrain detainees. These ties may be pulled very tight and cause injury.

RELEVANT LAWS AND CONVENTIONS: Geneva Convention IV relative to the Protection of Civilian Persons, 1949, Article 37: *Protected Persons who are confined pending proceedings or subject to a sentence involving loss of liberty shall during their confinement be humanely treated.*
The Rome Statute of the ICC Article 8: *War crimes,* (2)(a) *Grave breaches of the Geneva Conventions of 12 August 1949...* (iii) *Wilfully causing great suffering, or serious injury to body or health.*
Charter of the Nuremberg Tribunal, 1945.

EVIDENCE OF VIOLATIONS: On 28 July 2003, Robert Fisk described a night raid in Sadr City, the shanty suburb of Baghdad. The Iraqis were woken up by US troops. "They tied up all the men with plastic and steel cuffs around their wrists and took all our guns... A soldier pointed his rifle at this child here and said in Arabic they would count to ten to be told where our guns were. Yes of course we have guns: we have to defend ourselves from thieves who come here at night. Everyone in Baghdad has a gun now because there is so much robbery and killing." The guns were taken, but the men were left handcuffed. "We had to find knives to cut them free," said a woman in a black abaya.[1]

Cable ties are narrow plastic bands with a ratchet indentation passing through a square hole used for securing bundles of cable. The only limit on how tight they can be drawn is dependant on the resistance of the cables. To undo them there is only one method: to cut them off. These cable ties, initially designed for the construction industry, have been used for numerous other purposes including tying trees to posts, notices to lampposts, and cycle baskets to handle bars.

They are also used by the military as an alternative to heavy and expensive metal handcuffs. Prisoners in Iraq are invariably restrained with these plastic ties. Because there is no limit on how tight they can be pulled, they are inevitably often pulled too tight. This results in injury. Eleven civilians arrested by the British military in Hilla were restrained by these clips. On British television they showed their scarred wrists.[2]

The British Army apologised in writing for their detention. The Iraqis did not accept this apology as they considered there had been absolutely no grounds for being detained plus they had been injured. This represents a minute proportion of Iraqis who have been subjected to this treatment. Detainees are not only PoWs in Iraq, but ordinary citizens, some of them reported to be women. Nor are the handcuffs necessarily removed in custody, but – for the convenience of the guards – kept on for long periods and even used as part of a torture process. The plastic ties are standard issue to British and American soldiers.

There is a military reason for there use. Owing to the high-tech warfare waged by the invaders, there are few soldiers in relation to captives. Therefore it is seen to be necessary to restrain detainees immediately so they can be removed from the combat area without danger to their guards. Instead of the expensive and cumbersome metal handcuffs used by UK police (which have limitations regarding tightness, but are wider and therefore do not dig into the flesh), they use these plastic ties which they carry in bundles.

The fact remains that they frequently cause wrists to bleed. At Nuremberg in 1949, it was argued successfully that military expediency did not override humane considerations towards those invaded.[3] The question is, should we as invaders condone a system of detention that inevitably causes injury? If we do, we are opening Pandora's box to the use of cable ties as standard practice by the civilian police, border controls, and private contractors acting as bodyguards or security to commercial companies. Is this what we want?

During the Second World War it is noticeable that photographs of prisoners, from whatever theatre of war, are shown (at initial surrender) with their hands held above their heads and subsequently in columns – either with their hands on their heads or walking normally. Significantly they are often guarded by more soldiers than in Iraq, but there is no question of them being restrained by handcuffs.

If it is considered impossible to conduct modern warfare without wrist restraint of prisoners (and this may be perfectly reasonable), it must be possible to design plastic handcuffs with broad bands and stepped ratchets; with limits on how far they can be tightened. Of course this will double the cost, but it will tend to be more humane. At the moment, we can only conclude that the use of cable tie type handcuffs is contrary to the Geneva Conventions and, therefore, a war crime.

CLAIM: That members of the UK Government and Military by authorising and using cable ties to restrain detainees are in breach of the Geneva Convention IV relative to the Protection of Civilian Persons, 1949 Article 37; The Rome Statute of the ICC Article 8 (2)(a)(iii); and The Charter of the Nuremberg Tribunal 1945.

---

[1] Robert Fisk, *Independent*, 28 July 2003.
[2] Channel 4 documentary, *Iraq: Journey into Madness*, 19 October 2003.
[3] Nuremberg judgement on Goering, 1946.

71. Hoods.

A very high proportion of Iraqis detained by UK and US military are restrained with handcuffs and blindfolded with hoods or bindings. There are recorded instances where these blindfolds are not removed for very long periods, and also where the Iraqis are subject to beatings or rough handling while hooded. Hooding is also used as a means of torture. After a year of the use of hoods by UK soldiers, the practice was (allegedly) ended following protests in Parliament but, until that point, it had been regarded as standard practice by the Ministry of Defence. However in November 2004, a raid on a village on the east bank of the Euphrates by the British Army Black Watch appeared to have ignored the change in rules, as all the prisoners rounded up in the night raid were seen being taken away with blankets over their heads.[1]

RELEVANT LAWS AND CONVENTIONS: The Rome Statute of the International Criminal Court, Article 7: *Crimes against Humanity* (e) *Imprisonment or other severe deprivation of physical liberty in violation of fundamental rules of international law.* International Covenant on Civil and Political Rights, Article .10: *All persons deprived of their liberty shall be treated with humanity and with respect for inherent dignity of the human person.* The Hague Convention (IV) Respecting the Laws and Customs of War on Land, 1907, Annex, Article 4: *Prisoners of war ... must be humanely treated.* Charter of the Nuremberg Tribunal 1945, Article 6: (b) *War crimes... which include... ill treatment of prisoners of war.* Geneva Convention (III) relative to the Treatment of Prisoners of War, 1949, Article 3 (1) ... *members of armed forces who have laid down their arms... shall in all circumstances be treated humanely.* Protocol (1) Additional to the Geneva Conventions of 1949 and relating to the Protection of Victims of International Armed Conflicts, 1977, Article 75: (2)(a)(ii) *Torture of all kinds, whether physical or mental;* (b) *Outrages upon personal dignity, in particular humiliating and degrading treatment, enforced prostitution and any form of indecent* *assault;* Article 86: (1) *Failure to act when under a duty to do so.*

EVIDENCE OF VIOLATIONS: Ironically when the *Daily Mirror* published fake photographs to illustrate stories of the abuse of Iraqi prisoners by British soldiers, it was not the soldiers' stories which were discredited by the Ministry of Defence, but the fact that the photographs were faked. One of the reasons given by the MoD for knowing the photographs to be fake was the state of the hood on the alleged prisoner. According to the *Mirror*, the MoD claimed that "The sandbag on the Iraqi's head is too clean and looks almost ironed. Sand bags used as hoods by troops were kept crumpled up, in their pockets or pouches for quick use as necessary."[2] This was in fact an admission that it was standard practice to hood prisoners. Colonel Mike Dewar said soon after in the *Officer* magazine: "Hooding is a perfectly standard procedure to disorientate people when they are arrested. Every single person who is arrested is hooded. Does it surprise you? Sometimes robust methods are required. We are dealing with counter insurgency. There is no story. It goes on every single day of the week."[3]

Many Ba'ath party members and PoWs rounded up by the British Army were sent to one or another of the 17 American-run prison camps in Iraq (and possibly elsewhere). These are all largely secret. However, Amnesty International and the Red Cross have indicated that there have been various violations of the international laws governing war. One violation is the use of torture. Pictures of prisoners on capture being gagged, hooded, handcuffed with tight plastic bands and bundled into trucks are frequent. This method of treating prisoners appears to be different from that used by both sides in the Second World War. Then The Hague Conventions of 1907 were applied and prisoners were merely required to hold their hands up and display a white flag to surrender. There are many photographs of German, French, Italian, and British prisoners surrendering in this way.

In contrast, in the Channel 4 documentary *Iraq: a Journey into Madness*, Iraqi prisoners are seen being bundled into a military lorry by British soldiers. One British soldier punches a hooded Iraqi on the side of the head to get him into the lorry. This might seem to be a minor assault but, if we stop to think about it, to have a sack put over you head and then be assaulted – while negotiating your way into the back of a lorry – without knowing when, or why, or from which direction the blow is coming, must be terrifying.[4]

AT LEAST TWO IRAQIS DIED WHILE HOODED.

In November 2003, in Abu Ghraib prison, specialist Sabrina Harman posed smiling with her head close to the face of Manadel al-Jamadi, a dead Iraqi prisoner. A post mortem showed he had broken ribs and was badly beaten. He had collapsed in the prison showers while being interrogated and had died. The CIA interrogators only saw he had untreated head wounds after they had removed his hood.[5]

On 14 December the UK High Court ruled that the European Convention on Human Rights (ECHR) extended to "outposts of the state's authority" in foreign lands (including Iraq), and that an inquiry could be conducted into the case of Baha Mousa, an Iraqi hotelier from Basra who was hooded, deprived of water and kicked across the prison room by UK soldiers in Iraq.[6]

Photographs taken inside the US-run Abu Ghraib prison show hooded Iraqis. Some are being tormented by Lindie England (a US army prison guard) and piled on top of each other naked save for the hoods. One prisoner is shown wearing a conical hood and standing on a box with electrodes attached to toes, fingers and genitals. The prisoner had been informed that if he stepped off the box he would be electrocuted.

Carlos Mauricio, a Salvadorean who had been tortured in El Salvador in 1983 said, "I had flashbacks when I saw the guy with the hood. What happened at Abu Ghraib was torture by the book; they were implementing US policy."[7]

Writing in the Toronto Globe and Mail, Miles Schuman, a physician who documented torture for the Canadian Centre for Victims of Torture, said "the black hood covering the faces of naked prisoners in Abu Ghraib was known as *la capucha* in Guatemalan and Salvadorean torture chambers. The metal bed frame to which the naked and hooded detainee was bound in a crucifix position at Abu Ghraib was *la cama* for a former Chilean patient."

Many Latin American dictators (including Viola, Galtieri, Velasco Alvarado and Noriega) graduated from the US Army School of the

Americas (SOA). Based in Panama since 1946, the school was relocated to Fort Benning, Georgia in 1977. It was closed due to international criticism at the end of 2000, but reopened under another name just one month later. It is now known as the Western Hemisphere Institute for Security Co-operation (WHINSEC). Two declassified CIA training manuals, *Human Resource Exploitation Training Manual* and *KUBARK Counterintelligence Interrogation*, seem to confirm the allegations made by torture victims that what is happening in Abu Ghraib is consistent with US military intelligence teaching.[8]

In spite of the UK government's moratorium on the use of hoods in early 2004, a BBC News report of a Black Watch night assault on a small village east of the Euphrates, in November 2004, showed some of the 260 male detainees being marched from their homes with their heads covered in blankets. These blankets were all different, so one assumes that they were taken from the individual homes. Nevertheless, they performed the same function as hoods, save that it would be possible for them to see the rough ground as they walked.[9]

In the siege of Fallujah that same month, a wounded Iraqi was shown being operated on by US military surgeons for severe leg wounds caused by shrapnel. The photograph showed him in agony but blindfolded. This would indicate a dearth of anaesthetics on the one hand and the fact that blindfolds were left on longer than purely during transportation.[10] We cannot see any possible justification for blindfolding a prisoner while he is being operated on, and can only imagine the process to be terrifying. Nor do we assume this to be an isolated incident, but rather standard procedure.

There is mounting evidence from information provided by the Red Cross and Amnesty International[11] (as well as from the court-martials of British soldiers and the revelations of the US-run prisons) that the hoods are not necessarily removed once the captives have been taken into custody. They are in fact used as a method of torture. Again, we abhor this method of treating prisoners not only from a moral point of view – as a disgraceful action against Iraqis whom we are supposed to be liberating from Saddam's terror – but also from the long term view that, if we do not discontinue it, it will become standard practice in civilian life before long. We have to ask ourselves if we want this to be a generally accepted method of detention, especially as more and more state prisons are being privatised, all in the name of military expediency.

After a whole year of war, in May 2004, the MoD was forced to abandon the use of hoods by public and parliamentary pressure. However the damage had already been done. In the view of one British officer, Colonel Tim Collins, abuses against Iraqi civilians were partly the result of "leaders of an alliance" constantly referring to them as the "enemy" rather than treating them as people.[12] Nor is the argument of military expediency satisfactory if we follow the Judgements of Nuremberg, when Goering's defence on those grounds was not accepted.

It is noticeable that individual British soldiers are now being prosecuted for causing injury and death to Iraqi prisoners. We might cynically say that this is to divert real blame from UK parliamentary and military leaders. But at Nuremberg it was leaders such as Goering who were tried. These leaders often had never personally hurt anyone and some were conspicuously sentimental about animals and children. Nonetheless, they were held to be responsible for what went on in the theatre of war.

CLAIM: By authorising prisoners to be hooded by UK soldiers, following a common policy with the US Government and Military, members of the UK Government and armed forces are in breach the Rome Statute of the ICC , Article 7 (e); ICCPR ,Article 10; The Hague Convention IV, 1907, Annex to convention Article 4; Charter of the Nuremberg Tribunal, 1945, Article 6 (b), Geneva Convention (III) 1949, Article 3 (1); Protocol (1) Additional to the Geneva Conventions 1977, Article 75 (2)(a)(ii), (b), and Article 86 (1).

---

[1] BBC 1 News film, 28 November 2004.
[2] Paul Byrne and Stephen White, *Daily Mirror*, 3 May 2004.
[3] Colin Brown, *Independent*, 8 May 2004.
[4] Channel 4 documentary, *Iraq: Journey into Madness*, 19 October 2003.
[5] Andrew Buncombe, 'New Abu Ghraib photos show guards posing with body of dead detainee', *Independent*, 21 May 2004.
[6] Robert Veraik and Nigel Morris, *Independent*, 15 December 2004.
[7] Andrew McLeod, *Sunday Herald*, 12 December 2004.
[8] Ibid.
[9] BBC *Newsnight*, November 2004.

[10] cf. Photograph, *Independent*, 15 November 2004.
[11] Amnesty International report, AI Index : MDE 14/157/2003, July 2003.
[12] Kim Sengupta, *Independent*, 17 Sep 2004.

7J. SETTING THE DOGS ON IRAQIS.

As we saw in Chapter 7g: *A Crusade. Religious Persecution*, to an Iraqi, a dog is an unclean animal. Where cats are encouraged to enter homes – usually across flat roofs from the adjoining houses or through holes in the front doors – dogs are not welcome and are even feared. They are primarily used for guarding farms and flocks.

There have been several known instances of large dogs being used to intimidate and bite Iraqi PoWs; as a punishment, as a means of extracting information during interrogations, or just as wanton acts of sadism by individual soldiers. Large dogs have also been used on *Aggressive Patrols* by UK and US troops.

RELEVANT LAWS AND CONVENTIONS: The Rome Statute of the International Criminal Court, Article 7: *Crimes against Humanity* (e) *Imprisonment or other severe deprivation of physical liberty in violation of fundamental rules of international law.*
International Covenant On Civil and Political Rights, Article 10: (1) *All persons deprived of their liberty shall be treated with humanity and with respect for inherent dignity of the human person.*
Hague Convention IV, 1907, Annex to convention, Article 4: *Prisoners of war... must be humanely treated.*
Charter of the Nuremberg Tribunal, 1945, Article 6: (b) *War crimes... shall include... ill-treatment of prisoners of war.*
Protocol I Additional to Geneva Conventions 1949, Article 75: (2) *The following acts are and shall remain prohibited at any time and in any place whatsoever, whether committed by civilian or by military agents:* (a)(ii) *torture of all kinds, whether physical or mental;* (b) *outrages upon personal dignity.* Article 86 *Failure to act* (1) *The High Contracting Parties and the Parties to the conflict shall repress grave breaches, and take measures necessary to suppress all other breaches... which result from a failure to act when under a duty to do so.*
Geneva Convention III, 1949, Article 3: *... members of armed forces*

who have laid down their arms ... shall in all circumstances be treated humanely.

EVIDENCE OF VIOLATIONS: In 1513 Bartolomé de las Casas commented on the cruelties of the Spanish Conquistadors: "They taught their hounds, fierce dogs, to tear them to pieces at the first view, and in the space that one may say a Credo, assailed and devoured an Indian as if it had been a swine." The modern European would hope that there had been some advance in methods used in warfare in the 500 year period to 2004. Such optimism may be misplaced.

On 2 December 2002 Donald Rumsfeld US Secretary of State for Defense approved a list of interrogation methods to be used on prisoners in Guantanamo Bay. These methods were tacitly accepted by the Prime Minister when, on 4 June 2003 at Prime Minister's Question Time and in answer to Charles Kennedy's concern about British nationals held at Guantanamo Bay, he said: "... obviously that situation [failure to comply with principles of international justice] cannot continue indefinitely, although it is complicated by the fact that the information is still coming from the people detained there. I cannot say any more than that. The information is important."[1]

Of the nine methods approved by Donald Rumsfeld, two stand out: (8) removal of all comfort items (including religious items), and (12) using detainee's individual phobias (such as fear of dogs) to induce stress.[2] The following year these methods were adopted in the seventeen Iraqi jails run by the US Army. The commander of Guantanamo Bay, Major General Geoffrey Miller, was transferred to run the jails in Iraq. By February 2004 the conditions in these jails were well known to the UK government and military. (During the invasion period, Donald Rumsfeld had declared that the Geneva Conventions did not apply to Ba'ath party members, people carrying white flags as a cover for attack, suicide bombers, and terrorists.) Prison guards were often private contractors not held to be governed by Geneva Conventions.

Brigadier Karpinski, the US commander of Abu Ghraib, said Miller visited her in Baghdad. "He said they are like dogs and if you allow them to believe at any point that they are more than a dog then you have lost control of them."[3]

Photographs of several prisoners being intimidated by large dogs were shown in newspapers on 22 May 2004. In at least one incident, an Iraqi was shown standing naked in front of snarling dogs. (Interesting that the genitals are pixilated, that part of the photograph being considered too obscene to be viewed by the public.) Another picture shows a clothed Iraqi kneeling in front of a snarling dog.

There is evidence that the dogs were in fact allowed to bite the Iraqi prisoners. On 24 August 2004, a panel led by James Schlesinger, a former defence secretary, published an official report into violations at Abu Ghraib. The report said that abuses were not limited to a few individuals; there were 300 cases of mistreatment under investigation. There was "sadism on the nightshift" he said, and added, "It was a kind of Animal House on the night shift." An Internal US army investigation headed by Major General George Fay said that military guards used dogs on prisoners as young as 15 in a game to make them urinate on themselves.[4]

Aggressive patrols carried out by British soldiers included the use of large sniffer dogs ostensibly to sniff out hidden arms caches but, in fact, since they inevitably bark, they would also frighten women and children in the houses ransacked. It is well known that in the Second World War the Gestapo, SS and SD used attack dogs (mostly Alsatians), for patrols, searches and guard duty.

A Court in Majar received complaints from 24 families in the week of 17 June 2004 and recommended further post-mortems of the bodies. The case involved troops from the Argyll and Sutherland Highlanders who were alleged to have mutilated and then killed 20 Iraqi prisoners after running battles on 14 May 2004. "The bodies were returned to local hospitals the following day with injuries, including castration, gouged eyes, partially severed hands and dog bites."[5]

Anyone who suffers from a phobia of dogs (and this is quite common in countries that have a high incidence of rabies) will understand the terror of standing naked before dogs straining on their leashes.

Huda Alazawi, aged 39, a wealthy Baghdad business woman, received a demand from a blackmailer that unless she gave him $10,000 he would inform the Americans that she was working for the Iraqi resistance. Her brothers were arrested. On 3 December, she went to protest to the US base at Adhamiya. She was arrested herself. "They handcuffed me and blindfolded me. They bundled me into a humvee... I was dumped in a room with a single wooden chair. It was extremely cold. After five hours they brought my sister in. I couldn't see anything but I could recognise her from her crying." Alazawi said that the US guards left her sitting on the chair overnight, and the next day they took her to a room known by detainees as "the torture place". The US officer told us, "If you don't confess we will torture you. So you have to confess." My hands were handcuffed. They took off my boots and stood me in the mud with my face against the wall. I could hear women and men shouting and weeping." She said her brother Mu'taz was brutally sexually assaulted. She said the American guards then made her stand with her face to the wall for twelve hours, then her dead brother Ayad was dumped at her sister's feet. She was told, "Nobody is going to sleep tonight." She was subjected to loud noises to keep her awake. "It was Christmas. They kept us there for three days. Many of the US soldiers were drunk."

On 4 January 2004 she was transferred to Abu Ghraib prison, where she spent 156 days in solitary confinement. She said that the guards used wild dogs. "I saw one of the guards allow his dog to bite a 14-year-old boy on the leg. The boys name was Ali. Other guards frequently beat the men." She was released after eight months. The US military continue to detain 2,400 prisoners without charge or legal access.[6]

UNCLASSIFIED

GENERAL COUNSEL OF THE DEPARTMENT OF DEFENSE
1600 DEFENSE PENTAGON
WASHINGTON, D. C. 20301-1600

2002 DEC -2 AM 11: 03

OFFICE OF THE
SECRETARY OF DEFENSE

ACTION MEMO

November 27, 2002 (1:00 PM)

DEPSEC_____

FOR: SECRETARY OF DEFENSE

FROM: William J. Haynes II, General Counsel

SUBJECT: Counter-Resistance Techniques

RECOMMENDATION: That SECDEF approve the USSOUTHCOM Commander's use of those counter-resistance techniques listed in Categories I and II and the fourth technique listed in Category III during the interrogation of detainees at Guantanamo Bay.

SECDEF DECISION:

Approved _____ Disapproved _____ Other _____

Attachments
As stated

However, I stand for 8-10 hours
A day. Why is standing limited to 4 hours?

D.R DEC 0 2 2002

cc: CJCS, USD(P)

Under Authority of Executive Order 12958
Secretary, Office of the Secretary of Defense
Marriott, CAPT, USN

UNCLASSIFIED

X04030-02

(7) The use of 20-hour interrogations.

(8) Removal of all comfort items (including religious items).

(9) Switching the detainee from hot rations to MREs.

(10) Removal of clothing.

(11) Forced-grooming (shaving of facial hair etc..)

(12) Using detainees individual phobias (such as fear of dogs) to induce stress.

Memo listing methods of investigation of detainees authorised by Rumsfeld on 2 December 2002, three months before Iraq War. cf also Chapter 7k: Standing for hours & other Tortures.

CLAIM: That members of the UK Government and Military by the misuse of dogs in aggressive patrols and prisons, and by being in alliance with the US Administration and Army, are in breach of the Rome Statute of the ICC, Article 7, (e); International Covenant On Civil and Political Rights, Article 10, (1); Hague Convention IV, 1907, Annex to convention, Article 4; Charter of the Nuremberg Tribunal, 1945, Article 6: (b); Protocol (I) Additional to Geneva Conventions 1949, Article 75, (ii) (b), Article 86 (1); and Geneva Convention III, 1949, Article 3.

---

[1] Hansard, column 164, 4 June 2003
[2] Unclassified DEFSEC approved Action Memo, 2 December 2002.
[3] BBC News, 15 June 2004.
[4] Julian Borger, *Guardian*, 25 August 2004.
[5] Lee Gordon, *Camden Journal*, 24 June 2004.
[6] Luke Harding, *Guardian*, 20 September 2004.

7K. STANDING FOR HOURS & OTHER TORTURES.

Frequently Iraqi PoWs and detainees are made to stand still and upright for several hours. This treatment is designed as a punishment and as a means of producing information at interrogations. In more bizarre forms, it is reported that at least one Iraqi prisoner was told that if he stepped down off a box, he would be electrocuted.

RELEVANT LAWS AND CONVENTIONS: The Rome Statute of the International Criminal Court, Article 8: *For the purpose of this Statute, 'war crimes' means:* (a) *Grave breaches of the Geneva Convention of 12 August 1949, namely, any of the following acts against persons or property protected under the provisions of the relevant Geneva Convention:* (ii) *Torture or inhuman treatment;* (iii) *Wilfully causing great suffering or serious injury to body or health.* The Convention against Torture (ratified by the US in 1994) Article 2: (2) *No exceptional circumstances whatsoever, whether a state of war or a threat of war, internal political in stability or any other public emergency, may be invoked as a justification of torture.* (3) *An order from a superior officer or a public authority may not be invoked as a justification of torture.*

EVIDENCE OF VIOLATIONS: Since June 2003 Amnesty International and the Red Cross have made serious allegations of the use of torture on PoWs, including by British military in southern Iraq and, in areas nominally administered by the British Army, by Iraqi personnel settling old scores with members of the Ba'ath party. While the *Mirror* was castigated in May 2004 for running a series of articles with fake photographs of abuse by UK soldiers, it was the faking of the photographs which was discussed by the Ministry of Defence, not the substance of the soldiers' stories, which talked of widespread abuse. Subsequently soldiers have been charged with offences ranging from abuse to wanton killing. However, the atmosphere that allows such instances to take place was described by Colonel Tim Collins, Commander of the 1st Battalion, the Royal Irish Regiment in the southern sector of Iraq. In September 2004, after retirement, Collins said that if the leaders talk of Iraqis as "the enemy" the ordinary soldiers are going to think of them in the same way.[1] At Nuremberg the emphasis was on trying the leaders who inspired violence, not individual soldiers, even though the leaders had not necessarily been personally violent.

This conduct towards Iraqis, and Muslims in general, was established by the United States, the main coalition partner who, in a war allegedly to liberate Iraq from a foul dictatorship, should have scrupulously followed International law. But clearly there was an anti-Muslim agenda in the forms of torture used, to fulfil the American and British wish to make an impact on Al Qa'ida and to demonstrate that Arab terrorism would not succeed. It should be remembered also that Iraqis captured by British soldiers were sent to US-run prison camps, and that these camps were inspected by British personnel.

In Argentina between 1976 and 1980, under the ruthless rule of a military junta supported by the USA, some 30,000 citizens *disappeared*. Among many other similar cases recorded, Liliana Pereyra, a 21 year-old pregnant law student, was allowed to give birth and then shot in the head. In their trial, Generals Videla's and Galtieri's defence that the battle against terrorism necessitated "unconventional methods" was not accepted.[2] These generals (like most of the top brass in that country) had graduated from the US military School of the Americas (SOA).

Four months after the 11 September attacks, President Bush said prisoners at Guantanamo Bay who belonged to Al-Qa'ida or the Taliban were not protected by the Geneva Conventions on prisoners of war. In a White House memo, the President said "I have the authority to suspend Geneva [conventions] as between the United States and Afghanistan. I reserve the right to exercise this authority in this or future conflicts". This authority was given to him by a team of lawyers advising the President. In early 2003 President Bush was told by Air Force Counsel Mary Walker that no international law was more important than "obtaining intelligence vital to the protection of untold thousands of American citizens."

The document said that "the prohibition against torture must be construed as inappropriate to interrogation undertaken pursuant to commander-in-chief authority... The Justice Department has concluded that it could not bring a criminal prosecution against a defendant who had acted pursuant to an exercise of the President's constitutional power." The same code was extended to the conduct of guards in the US-run prisons in Iraq. General Miller, commander at Guantanamo, was sent to Baghdad in 2003 "with the mission of making interrogations of suspected Iraqi insurgents at Abu Ghraib more productive." Brigadier Karpinski the US commander of Abu Ghraib said Miller told her that "they are like dogs. If you allow them to believe they are more than dogs you have lost control."[3]

On 2 December 2002 a memo regarding the methods allowed for the treatment of prisoners for interrogation purposes was passed to Donald Rumsfeld for his signature. These recommendations included:

A. CATEGORY I TECHNIQUES:
(1) Yelling at the detainee.
B. CATEGORY II TECHNIQUES:
(1) The use of stress positions (like standing), for a maximum of four hours.
(4) Use of isolation facility for up to 30 days.
(5) Deprivation of light and auditory stimuli.
(6) The detainee may also have a hood placed over his head during transportation and questioning.
(7) The use of 28-hour interrogations.
(10) Removal of clothing.
(11) Forced grooming (shaving of facial hair, etc.)
(12) Using detainees individual phobias (such as fear of dogs) to induce stress.

Approving them, Mr Rumsfeld added a hand written note saying: "I stand for
8-10 hours a day. Why is standing limited to four hours?"[4]

This form of sadistic joke is what one expects of a public school gym master of the first half of the twentieth century. But it wasn't a joke, because it set the tone for abuse against predominantly Muslim prisoners. Such sadism was condemned in Nazi leaders such as Himmler and Heidrich and contributed to their eventual downfall. Mr Blair however, is prepared to stand *shoulder to shoulder* with an administration that includes such a character.

In light of this, it is not so surprising to find out that young female US troops have been holding dog leads around the necks of naked Iraqis covered in their own excrement, or have been putting their laughing faces next to the heads of Iraqi corpses. Such images are now lodged firmly in the Muslim mind and are going to be very detrimental to the dialogue between the West and the Muslim world for a very long time. This was a grotesquely irresponsible memo.

The description given by Huda Alazawi, the Iraqi business woman arrested on the word of a blackmailer, illustrates these methods of torture. "The US officer told us: 'If you don't confess we will torture you. So you have to confess.' My hands were handcuffed. They took off my boots and stood me in the mud with my face against the wall. I could hear women and men shouting and weeping."[5] This makes it clear that standing is a routine method of detention. If the prisoner needed to use a lavatory, that was the prisoner's problem.

Presumably in Mr Rumsfeld's school of logic, there must be some things worse than standing for hours on end, to induce the prisoners to stay upright. Are they beaten with sticks? Threatened with death? Punched? Sexually abused? We are not told the full details of what is being done in our name in this effort to impose democracy on Iraq. One guide to possible methods employed to establish the four hour (or is it ten hour?) standing rule is given by a picture released showing a hooded prisoner standing on a box. Sabrina Harman of US 372 Military Police Company stated in a sworn statement that the detainee was made to stand on a box with wires attached to fingers, toes and penis, and a bag over his head. The prisoner was told if he touched the ground he would be electrocuted. Harman said that her job "was to keep detainees awake. Military Intelligence wanted to get them to talk."[6]

In response to a parliamentary question on Guantanamo Bay methods, Mr Blair said that they were providing useful information.[7]

One unfortunate British citizen, released after spending time in Guantanamo and Bagram, has a different view of his custody. "My torture was even less than they did to others. A broomstick was inserted in my backside and I was beaten severely and water was thrown on me before facing an air conditioner."[8]

At the 1946 Nuremberg trials, the responsibility for sadistic acts, committed between 1939 and 1945 by Wehrmacht soldiers, was considered to be driven by the leadership of the High Command and the Nazi Party. It was the leaders that were first punished, followed by a few lower ranks.

CLAIM: That the UK Government has condoned and participated in the use of torture against Iraqi PoWs and Iraqi civilians in breach of its obligations as a signatory of the 1994 Convention Against Torture, and has committed a war crime as defined by the Rome Statute of the International Criminal Court Article 2, (a)(ii).

NB. This breach of the 1994 Convention against Torture has also set the tone for British Justice. In 2004, The Law Lords ruled that evidence obtained under torture in another country was admissible in British Courts. The concept of the 1215 Magna Carta – that while it was inconvenient for the executive not to be able to lock someone up and throw away the key, also recognised it was very important that the executive could not do this – is being thrown out of the window. In the words of the solicitor Gareth Pierce, in *progressive experimental* stages.

---

[1] Kim Sengupta, *Independent*, 17 September 2004.
[2] Geoffrey Roberston QC, *Crimes against humanity*, London: Penguin, 2002. p 264.
[3] Robin Cook, *Independent*, 26 June 2004.
[4] Unclassified DEFSEC approved Action Memo, 2 December 2002.
[5] Luke Harding, *Guardian*, 20 September 2004.
[6] Patrick Sawer, *Evening Standard*, 5 May 2004.
[7] Hansard, 4 June 2003.
[8] Robert Fisk, *Independent*, 8 January 2005.

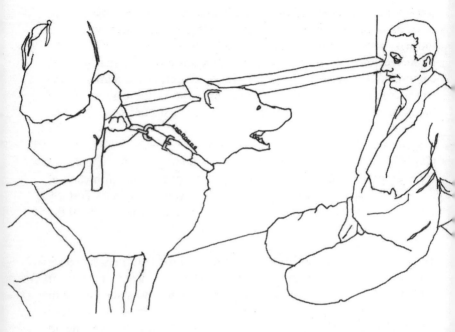

7L. AGGRESSIVE PATROLLING.

UK and US forces have been involved in house searches at night through whole districts, isolated farms and villages. The soldiers smash down front doors and internal doors, and enter brandishing guns. The occupants are often terrified, having been woken up in the night to the sound of shouts, dogs barking and wood and metal breaking. Iraqi males are handcuffed, blindfolded and taken away for interrogation – and in some cases imprisonment.

RELEVANT LAWS AND CONVENTIONS: The Rome Statute of the International Criminal Court, Article 8, *War crimes* (2) *For the purpose of this Statute "war crimes" means* (a) *Grave breaches of the Geneva Convention of 12 August 1949...* (b) *Other serious violations of the laws and customs applicable in international armed conflict, within the established framework of international law, namely, any of the following acts:* (ii) *Intentionally directing attacks against civilian objects, that is, objects which are not military objectives;* (xxi) *Committing outrages upon personal dignity, in particular humiliating and degrading treatment.*

EVIDENCE OF VIOLATIONS: At 2am in the morning, there are angry shouts in a foreign language out in the street. With a tremendous crash of splintering wood the front door is battered open. Five or six soldiers shouting and waving machine guns enter the front room. You struggle out of bed, already your wife and children are screaming. You beg the soldiers not to break any more doors. They don't understand you; they push you aside and smash their way into the other rooms with blows of their boots. Your howling wife and daughter have locked themselves in the lavatory, your old mother tries to stop the soldiers and she is flung so hard into a metal door that her head dents the steel. The rickety kitchen cupboard is broken open, pots and pans clatter off the stove. Your teenage son is roughly handcuffed. And so are you. You are hooded. You can no longer see anything. You can hear your wife screaming, terrified, pleading that you are innocent, wondering whether she will ever see you again.

It is mid summer in Tikrit in the year 2003. You have just been subjected to *aggressive patrolling* by a combined American and British Aggressive Patrol. The next day, the British Prime Minister announces in Parliament that, yes indeed the British army has been carrying out *aggressive patrolling*. The combined operation is necessary, he says, to flush out insurgents in the Sunni Triangle. Unexpectedly, after President Bush has announced the war has been won, in the area around Baghdad guerrilla tactics suggest that the occupiers are not welcome in all parts of Iraq. It is soon discovered that the nocturnal *aggressive patrols* are actually counterproductive. More and more incensed Iraqis join the resistance. Raids on these often ramshackle homes, made of mud bricks with a few sticks of furniture, were subsequently largely abandoned. Until the Fallujah offensive of November 2004 that is, when the tactics became dominated by the Israeli Defence Forces training. Then no longer did soldiers enter through the front door, instead they smashed a hole in the wall to get in.[1]

The British army adopted these night raids for two reasons: British soldiers had an advantage over the Iraqi insurgents because they could see in the dark with the night vision equipment on their helmets. The Iraqis had no such equipment. There was also the standard advantage of surprise, and the fact that Iraqi males would probably be sleeping at home.[2]

Robert Fisk described a night raid in Sadr City, a shanty suburb of Baghdad. They were woken up by US troops. "They tied up all the men with plastic and steel cuffs around their wrists and took all our guns ... a soldier pointed his rifle at this child here and said in Arabic they would count to ten to be told where our guns were. Yes of course we have guns: we have to defend ourselves from thieves who come here at night. Everyone in Baghdad has a gun now because there is so much robbery and killing." The guns were taken but the men were left handcuffed. "We had to find knives to cut them free," said a woman in a black abaya.[3]

A more aggressive form of house-to-house clearance was shown during the Fallujah assault of November 2004, as exposed by a news report for television. US soldiers are seen entering houses and other buildings, not through the front doors but through holes blown up on the external or intercommunicating walls. This is an Israeli technique adopted by the US Army, as the streets are considered too dangerous because of sniper fire. Soldiers engaged in this sort of street fighting are, understandably, in an extremely nervous condition; as well as on an adrenaline high, ready to shoot at anything that moves or even does not move. One soldier, Lance Corporal Bradley Faircloth, Alpha Company, US Marines, is shown emerging from a wrecked building saying "I went in there, there was a bunker. [sic] There was a guy sleeping. I shot him. As soon as I shot him, a frag [hand grenade] was thrown at us, so we threw two frags in there."[4]

A week later, the UK army were involved in further aggressive patrols in a sector south of Baghdad. On 25 November 2004 the Black Watch executed a night raid on the village of Al Latiffiyah, on the east bank of the Euphrates, opposite their base at Camp Dogwood. It was believed that rebels had fired rockets at Camp Dogwood from the village. Seven hundred UK soldiers took part in the raid. One sergeant said "It's payback time." A Black Watch officer said, "There are so many of the lads involved in this that there won't be a bayonet left in the camp. Everyone wants to be part of it because feelings are running high about the deaths of our colleagues." To the sound of loudspeaker music of bag pipe bands, armoured personnel carriers smashed through boundary walls.

Troops jumped out of vehicles, smashed down doors with sledge hammers and threw noise grenades. They broke into a mosque. They captured every male in the village over fourteen and took away to Camp Dogwood 100 blindfolded and handcuffed Iraqis. Ten Iraqis were detained as suspect insurgents, the rest were released. American Cobra assault helicopters, an AC 130 Hercules gunship and a Puma helicopter flew overhead while women and children screamed. An officer described the attack as "a surprise attack, bloodless and successful. We didn't go there this morning to pick a fight, we came here for peacekeeping, and I think we achieved that aim." A few AK 47 guns were found, but no rockets or bombs.[5]

In an area dominated by small farms, Black Watch soldiers broke into an isolated farm and took away a man and his 20-year-old son. His wife and eight daughters started sobbing and screaming. Lt Alf Ramsey the platoon commander took a risk and decided the farmer and son were not insurgents and released them.[6]

This area, south of Baghdad, on the east bank of the Euphrates was considered by the Coalition as a centre of Sunni insurgence determined to prevent the January 2005 elections for an interim government. The elections were arranged by the interim administration appointed on 30 June 2004 and set up by the Coalition Provisional Administration (CPA) appointed in June 2003. In early 2005 it is difficult to see an end to the guerrilla war. Further Coalition raids of this kind are expected. This operation took place 18 months after victory was declared, and twelve months after *aggressive patrolling* was tried and abandoned in the Tikrit and Basra areas. The British Ministry of Defence considers these night raids legitimate peacekeeping operations; but to the inhabitants (especially young children and mothers) they are extremely traumatic episodes, because every male Iraqi is considered a suspect. It is also an interesting insight into combat techniques taking place long after hostilities were supposed to have ended and when presumably the Iraqi people were being freed from dictatorship. Blindfolding was still in practice six months after the UK Parliament said it should no longer be used. The language employed by officers and soldiers showed signs of a revenge element. Guns had been fitted with bayonets. Terror tactics involving sound were being used, such as loud music and noise grenades. Sledge hammers were being employed to break holes in walls and break down doors in a more aggressive manner than twelve months previously.[7]

The question should be asked at this point in time, whether there would be any insurgents firing rockets if there were no British soldiers present, and thus no need for a reaction by the British forces? Why was there no attempt to have a truce between the parties in 2003? Was there confusion in the minds of the occupiers as to what the political objectives were? As Clausewitz observed, without a clear political aim a project is doomed.

Save for a paltry £550 standard payment, there is no compensation offered to the Iraqis for trashing their homes. No payment for broken doors, cupboards, bullet-scarred walls or traumatised children. No redress for the males of the family being carted off for interrogation without dignity or respect, their foreheads stained with indelible dye applied by foreign soldiers, showing the map grid reference of their homes. All this wanton intrusion in the specious name of ridding Saddam Hussein of weapons of mass destruction.

On 28 September 2004, the British Prime Minister finally admitted that "The evidence about Saddam having actual biological and chemical weapons, as opposed to the capability to develop them, has turned out to be wrong. I acknowledge that and accept it. I can apologise for the information that turned out to be wrong..."[8]

Koffi Annan, the UN Secretary General, has said that he believed the war was illegal. "I have stated clearly that it was not in conformity with the Security Council, with the UN charter."[9] There is still no contrition by the British Prime Minister for these acts of violence. The only people in Britain who can seriously imagine the terror of these night raids are those whose parents and relatives were hauled out of bed to be sent to Auschwitz.

CLAIM: That by authorising and carrying out aggressive patrols, members of the UK government and military are in breach of the Rome Statute of the ICC, Article 2 (ii) and (xxi).

---

[1] Channel 4 documentary, *Iraq: Journey into Madness*, 19 October 2003.
[2] Amnesty International report, AI Index : MDE 14/157/2003, July 2003.
[3] Robert Fisk, *Independent*, 28 July 2003.
[4] BBC 2, *Newsnight*, 24 November 2004.
[5] David Harrison, 'Mission accomplished for Black Watch', *Daily Telegraph*, 26 November 2004.
[6] Ibid.
[7] Ibid.
[8] Andrew Grice, *Independent*, 29 September 2004.
[9] Colin Brown and Patric Cockburn, *Independent*, 16 September 2004.

WAR CRIMES OR JUST WAR?

7M.   KILLING & WOUNDING TREACHEROUSLY.

While the UK army have probably behaved in a better manner, as compared to the US army, there have been a number of incidents (possibly in the order of one hundred cases) of wanton killing and wounding of Iraqis by UK soldiers. The UK has however been allied to the US army – which is trigger-happy and much more prone to unnecessary violence. There are many recorded instances of them shooting innocent civilians (for example at check points) or shooting people bearing white flags. Also many reports of deaths while in custody. I have been told by a group of distinguished Iraqis that you do not look US soldiers in the eye when motoring in Baghdad. This atmosphere of lawlessness emanates from the leadership of the Coalition.

RELEVANT LAWS AND CONVENTIONS: The Rome Statute of the International Criminal Court, 2002, Article 8: *War crimes*, 2b *Other serious violations of the laws and customs applicable in international armed conflict...* (xi) *Killing or wounding treacherously individuals belonging to the hostile nation or army.* The responsibility of leadership, over and above the acts of individual soldiers, is laid down in the Charter of the Nuremberg Tribunal, 1945.

EVIDENCE OF VIOLATIONS: In May 2004, the press reports indicated that UK soldiers had been involved in cases of homicide of Iraqis held in custody. One young Iraqi, who could not swim, was forced to swim across a river and subsequently drowned. A PoW was beaten up and dumped off the back of a vehicle and presumed dead.[1] In June 2004 seventy-five similar cases were being investigated by the UK military. Compensation was being sought in 12 cases where Iraqis were alleged to have been shot or beaten to death without reason by British soldiers. The standard compensation amount offered to Iraqi victims' families by the British Army is £540.

EXAMPLES: Abbas Kuhdayar Gatteh was killed while preparing for prayers during a house search where the front door was smashed down. Ahmed Jabbar Karim Ali, 17, was forced (after being beaten) to swim across the River Zubair; weakened by the beating, he drowned. Jaafer Hashim Majeed, 13, was killed by a cluster bomblet while he played outside his home. Hazim Jum'AA Gatteh al-Skeini, 23, was shot by British soldiers while at a funeral of another villager. Baha Ahmed al-Awari, 23, was a guard at the local school. He was standing by the building during a protest when the soldiers opened fire on the crowd. He died of chest and stomach wounds. Muhammad Abdul Ridha Salim, a 45-year-old teacher, was killed in a house search where the front door was smashed down. Hannan Shmailawi, 33, was shot dead as she sat down to supper with her husband and children. Her husband was the night guard at the Institute of Education in Basra. Waleed Fayayi Muzban, 43, was shot at while driving his van; he died the following day from wounds to his chest and stomach. Lafteh Ahmed Awdeh, 22, was working in fields with his father when he was hit by a truck from a column of British Army vehicles. He died instantly. Kasber Farhoud Jasim was fishing in a boat when he was shot in the head by a passing river patrol. Raid Hadi al-Musawi, a 29-year-old policeman, was shot by a British patrol while making a delivery to a judge's house. Riyadh Turki Taha Yaseen, 65, was fixing the water pump in his farm. Patrolling soldiers mistook the hammer in his hand for a weapon and shot him dead.[2]

"It seems that the British troops have not been instructed or trained in appropriate rules of engagement for the occupation of Iraq, bearing in mind there are real differences between Basra and Belfast" said Phil Shiner, of Public Interest Lawyers.[3] On 14 December 2004, in a landmark judgment, the High Court has now confirmed this: the UK's obligations under the European Convention of Human Rights and the Human Rights Act can extend to outposts of the State's authority, including UK-operated prisons in Iraq, and that the Government must conduct an effective investigation into the death of Baha Mousa, an Iraqi civilian who died in British custody in Iraq.[4]

Robert Fisk, reporting from Baghdad in July 2004, said the statistics of violent death were now beyond shame. There were 506 violent deaths in under three weeks in Baghdad alone. The American troops were reckless in their behaviour. One man was shot dead by a US soldier as he overtook their convoy on the way to his Baghdad wedding. A US tank collided with a bus north of Baghdad – seven civilians were killed. A US M1A1 Abrams tank, attempting to cross the motorway at Abu Ghraib, collided with a car killing a woman and her two daughters. Tony Blair says it is safer here. He is wrong. Every month is a massacre in Baghdad. No wonder the occupying powers refuse to reveal the statistics of Iraqi dead.[5]

Colonel Tim Collins, a British army commander in the 1st Battalion of the Royal Irish Regiment in the Southern Sector of Iraq, on his retirement said on the BBC *Today* programme, Either it was a war to liberate the people of Iraq, in which case there was gross incompetence, or it was simply a cynical war that was going to happen anyway to vent some anger on Saddam Hussein's regime with no regard to the consequences on the Iraqi people. In that case it is a form of common assault – and the evidence would point to the latter." On the abuse of Iraqi prisoners, he said that "if the leaders of a country, the leaders of an alliance talk in terms of 'them', 'the enemy' rather than treating them as people, how can they expect the.. basic soldiery to interpret it in any other way?"[6]

There have also been numerous accounts of American contraventions of the Geneva Convention in relation to random killing of civilians during the war period. In April 2003, US troops killed seven peaceful demonstrators in Mosul and 13 more at a demonstration in Fallujah, wounding 75 civilians. At Nassiriya they shot at any vehicle that approached their position; in one night alone they killed 12 people. On a bridge into Baghdad they killed 15 civilians in just two days. On several occasions US soldiers have fired on ambulances. They have shot at medical crews who came to retrieve the dead and wounded at Fallujah.[7] As explained in Chapter 3: *Allies in War as Partners*, the UK is party to these war crimes.

Americans have a reputation for indiscriminately shooting civilians at US road blocks and check points, all Iraqis being considered potential terrorists. Jimmy Massey, 33, a US staff sergeant said, "I was never clear on who the enemy was. We were shooting up people as they got out of their cars trying to put their hands up, I don't know if the Iraqis thought we were celebrating their new democracy. I do know that we killed innocent civilians." He thought his unit had killed more than 30 civilians in 48 hours in the Rashid district of Baghdad.[8]

On 4 January 2005 two American soldiers were court-martialled for forcing two Iraqis at gunpoint to swim in the Tigris River at Samarra. One 19 year-old could not swim and drowned. The Americans said the Iraqis had been out after curfew in a van carrying plumbing equipment that could be used to make bombs.[9]

CLAIM: That members of the UK and US governments and military, by creating an atmosphere in which Iraqis were treated as the enemy, have allowed wanton acts of violence towards individual Iraqi citizens and PoWs, in contravention with the Rome Statute of the International Criminal Court, Article 8, 2(b)(xi). Nor is it sufficient, under current international legislation, for individual soldiers to be court-martialled; the leadership should be accountable for allowing such acts to occur, as described in the Charter of the Nuremberg Tribunal, 1945.

---

[1] Robert Verkaik, Jonathan Brown, and Colin Brown, *Independent*, 6 May 2004.
[2] Terri Judd and Severin Carrell, *Independent*, 1st March 2004.
[3] PA News, *Times*, 5 May 2004.
[4] www.redress.org/news/Press%20Release%20Al%20Skeini%2014%20Dec%202004.pdf
[5] Robert Fisk, *Independent*, 28 July 2004.
[6] Kim Sengupta, *Independent*, 17 September 2004.
[7] George Monbiot, *Guardian*, 20 May 2003.
[8] Andrew Buncombe, *Independent*, 9 December 2004.
[9] Andrew Buncombe, *Independent*, 6 January 2005.

7N. MARKING THEIR BODIES.

There is evidence of UK and US soldiers placing their boots on prisoners' heads while posing for photographs. US soldiers, having stripped Iraqi detainees naked, are seen in full battle dress. A quarter of a million civilian refugees returning home to Fallujah at the end of December 2004 were required to wear identification tags on their outer garments at all times. There is also evidence that the American and British armies have used indelible magic markers to write identifications on the chests and heads of Iraqi detainees. Such acts can be considered degrading and humiliating.

RELEVANT LAWS AND CONVENTIONS: The Rome Statute of the International Criminal Court, Article 8: (2) *For the purpose of this Statute, 'war crimes' means:* (b) *Other serious violations of the laws and customs applicable in international armed conflict, within the established framework of international law, namely, any of the following acts:* (xxi) *committing outrages upon personal dignity, in particular humiliating and degrading treatment.*

EVIDENCE OF VIOLATIONS: Early in the conflict, on 26 April 2003, there was a photograph of Iraqi looters stripped naked in front of American soldiers in full battle dress. One Iraqi was shown close up with writing on his chest. The writing in indelible magic marker said Ali Baba (Arabic for thief).[1] The US officer in charge said that this method of making fun of looters was probably better than internment. However well intentioned this officer was, there is evidence that this practice of marking Iraqi detainees was more widespread and not particularly altruistic.

A year later, we see a blindfolded Iraqi having an operation to repair a broken leg in an American Field hospital in the Fallujah district. Close inspection of the photograph reveals that he too has writing on his chest.[2] The two incidents are nineteen months apart, under completely different circumstances. Was it therefore standard practice to mark detainees in this way? Militating against this was the fact that naked prisoners being tortured at Abu Ghraib were not marked. There is however uncorroborated hearsay evidence from a UK non-commissioned officer taking part in aggressive patrols in support of the US Army in Tikrit. This was in 2003, during the initial stages of the occupation. After rounding them up, Iraqi males were all marked on their foreheads with GPS (Global Positioning System) grid reference for identification purposes. The NCO carrying out this MoD order was reminded of Nazi Germany, and felt appalled.

A further sophistication of this identification, that has precedents in the use of Yellow Stars by the Third Reich, is the compulsory wearing of identification tags on outer garments. Refugees from Fallujah, who were allowed to return home at the end of December 2004, had to go through five checkpoints, have their finger prints taken, along with DNA samples and retinal scans. Each citizen was issued with a badge with their address on it, to be worn at all times. Major Francis Piccoli, of 1st Marine Expeditionary force said "Some may see this as a *Big Brother is watching over you* experiment. But in reality, it's a simple security measure to keep the insurgents from coming back."[3]

Another act which can be considered degrading is the one depicted by the triumphant UK soldier posing with his hand on the head of an Iraqi prisoner.[4] There are several photographs of US soldiers treating Iraqis in a similar way, some with their boots on the prisoners' heads. Having a boot placed on your head is deeply offensive to any human being. Ironically, in the British Museum there are Assyrian reliefs of 750 - 800 BC taken from the palaces of Nineveh and Nimrud near Mosul. These show prisoners being treated in humiliating ways, kneeling with their hands bound behind their backs.

CLAIM: That members of the UK Government and Military are guilty of war crimes by ordering and carrying out humiliating and degrading acts on Iraqi detainees, in breach of the Rome Statute of the ICC Article 8 (2)(b)(xxi).

---

[1] cf. Photograph, *Mail*, 26 April 2003.

[2] cf. Photograph, *Independent*, 15 November 2004.
[3] Patrick Cockburn and Ken Sengupta, *Independent*, 11 Dec 2004.
[4] cf. Photograph, *Independent*, April 2003.

70. THE HAMOODI FAMILY.

During the invasion, in April 2003, a house in a residential district of Basra was targeted by British war planes. This house was thought to belong to *Chemical Ali*. The bombs opened up a 5-metre deep crater where the house once stood. The houses on each side of the crater were demolished, killing 11 members of the Hamoodi family on one side, and 17 on the other. *Chemical Ali* was not in the targeted house.

RELEVANT LAWS AND CONVENTIONS: The Rome Statute of the International Criminal Court, Article 7: *Crimes against humanity.* (1)(a) *Murder.* [taken under the narrow definition of targeted assassinations.] Article 8: (2) *For the purpose of this Statute, "war crimes:" means:* (a) *Grave breaches of the Geneva Convention of 12 August 1949, namely any one of the following acts against persons or property protected under the provisions of the relevant Geneva Convention.* (b) *Other serious violations of the laws and customs applicable in international armed conflict, within the established framework of international law, namely any of the following acts:* (i) *Intentionally directing attacks against the civilian population as such or against individual civilians not taking direct part in hostilities.* (iv) *Intentionally launching an attack in the knowledge that such an attack will cause incidental loss of life or injury to civilians or damage to civilian objects...* (v) *Attacking or bombarding by whatever means, towns, villages, dwellings or buildings which are undefended and which are not military objectives...*

EVIDENCE OF VIOLATIONS: A televised news report showed how a house in Basra was targeted by British war planes in a residential district. This house was thought to belong to Ali Hassan al-Majid – Saddam Hussein's cousin, also known as *Chemical Ali* –

who featured on the playing card list of fifty most wanted Iraqis, dead or alive. Co-ordinates were provided from intelligence sources. The bombs left an enormous, 5 metre deep, crater. The houses on each side of the crater were demolished, killing 11 of the Hamoodi family on one side, and 17 on the other. A British Brigadier, regretted the deaths, but did not regret the targeting, saying that after seven hours deliberation the UK and US had decided to bomb this house with "carefully selected ordnance." *Chemical Ali* was not in the targeted house. [1]

The Hamoodi family were an upper middle class family, living in an expensive house. They were Sunnis, but had no connection with the Ba'ath Socialist Party. Abid Hassan Hamoodi, 72, the patriarch of the family has two sons who have lived in the UK for nearly thirty years. Ten members of his family were killed, including seven grandchildren. The house was badly damaged. Mr Hamoodi said he intended to sue Blair personally for this action. When his surviving daughter was asked what they were going to do, she replied, "we have nothing left to do but weep."

Looking in a mirror, as John Pilger would have us do, as a UK citizen living in a sovereign country, I would feel entitled to live in my residence without being bombed from the air by an illegally acting foreign country. I would not be sympathetic to the idea that this bombing was to eliminate WMDs, when no WMDs existed.

DEBATING ISSUE: If the original act of invasion was illegal, as declared by Kofi Annan, Secretary General of the United Nations, does it follow that all other acts, apart from withdrawal of forces, are also illegal? If so, are the Hamoodi family entitled to monetary compensation? If the act of bombing *Chemical Ali's* house in a built up residential district, where collateral damage is inevitable, is in itself declared illegal, is the Hamoodi family entitled to compensation from the UK Government and/ or Mr Blair personally? Will the Pinochet extradition case provide a future precedent for the extradition of Blair to face charges, where he might personally be liable to pay damages to the Hamoodi Family?

On 29 October 2003 three UK citizens, sons of Abid Hassan Hamoodi the family head commenced a legal action against the UK Government.

The MoD spokesman responded, "We recognise that this is a very difficult time for the Hamoodi family, and the Minister for the Armed Forces Adam Ingram has personally written to them to express sympathy... We deeply regret any loss of civilian life and we took great care to try to avoid civilian casualties at all times. Regrettably this is not always possible... We are confident our armed forces acted legally and properly on this occasion and we defend robustly any action arising from loss caused by the conflict."

One of the sons, Mazim Hamoodi, said, "I feel absolutely devastated even now. A third of my family was killed for a silly stupid reason... We never had any problem with Saddam's regime, none of the family ever interfered, and yet we got murdered by the British and the Americans... I am now a British citizen and I have nothing but admiration for the British army. But we have been deeply hurt by the complete non reaction from the UK government." His father said, "This was a big mistake committed here in Basra. Ali Hassan (*Chemical Ali*) was living 50 metres away. But they could have come to arrest him, instead of killing innocent people. This was stupidity."[2]

We believe it was also contrary to the laws and customs of war (see above); that the climate for this illegal act was set by the Prime Minister, Mr. Hoon, Mr Ingram, President Bush and Mr Rumsfeld with their so called *55 Most Wanted* deck of cards.

CLAIM: That members of the UK Government and Military, by authorising an air attack on *Chemical Ali's* house in a residential district of Basra were in breach of the Rome Statute of the International Criminal Court, Article 7 (a), and Article 8: (2)(a), 2(b)(i), (iv) and (v), and that full compensation should be awarded to what remains of the Iraqi family.

---

[1] BBC *Panorama,* 27 April 2003.
[2] Blaise Tapp and Don Frame, *Manchester News,* 29 October 2003.

7P. A WEDDING IN THE DESERT.

In May 2004, a wedding party asleep in a small village near the Syrian border was bombarded from the air by US forces (supported politically and logistically by the British government) resulting in the death of forty guests, including babies, but not the bride and groom, who were sleeping in a tent away from the main building.

RELEVANT LAWS AND CONVENTIONS: The Rome Statute of the International Criminal Court, Article 8: (2) *For the purpose of this Statute, 'war crimes' means:* (b) *Other serious violations of the laws and customs applicable in international armed conflict, within the established framework of international law, namely, any of the following acts:* (v) *Attacking or bombarding by whatever means, towns villages, dwellings or buildings which are undefended and which are not military objectives*

EVIDENCE OF VIOLATIONS: It was 2am on the night of 19 May 2004. Ten miles from the Syrian border, in Makradheeb, a desert village close to Ramadi, the wedding party was over. The guests were all asleep. They had been entertained by Hussein Ali (a well-known Iraqi wedding singer) and musicians. The wedding video footage shows women and children, elderly men with babies in their arms sitting round the walls of a room. An hour later 41 wedding guests – including Hussein Ali – were dead, killed by helicopter gunfire. The newly married couple survived because they were sleeping in a special honeymoon tent.

The US claimed this attack was legitimate in response to ground fire. Brigadier General Mark Kimmitt, deputy director of operations for the US in Iraq said the attack was within the military's rules of engagement. "We conducted an operation about 85 km south west of Qaim, against suspected foreign fighters in a safe house. We took ground fire and we returned fire."[1]

This killing exposes the arrogance and extreme ignorance of the American military. Major General James Mattis, Commander of the US 1st Marine Division asked, "How many people go to the middle of the desert 10 miles from the Syrian Border to hold a wedding 80 miles from the nearest civilisation?" When shown evidence of the casualties, General Mattis said, "There were more than two dozen military age males. Let's not be naïve. I have not seen the pictures but bad things happen in wars. I don't have to apologise for the conduct of my men." The fact that many of the 40 corpses were women and children did not seem to bother him.[2]

One man who saw the attack said, "At 3am they rained the air with bombs. One after another the bombs were falling." The attack had the hallmarks of a similar incident in Afghanistan two years ago in which a US jet fired at a wedding party in Uruzgan province, in the south, killing 48 Afghan civilians and wounding more than 100.[3]

Iraqis said that people in the area frequently marry neighbours from across the border and that the village was where they had lived all their lives. It is common for villagers to keep guns, as a protection from robbers and wild animals while they are guarding their flocks. This is an area of scattered villages, some consisting of no more than a few tents. At Iraqi weddings, it is customary to fire guns in the air to celebrate, though in this incident the surviving Iraqi guests said there had been no gunfire. Sheik Nasrallah Mikfil head of the Bani Fahd tribe said it would not be surprising for the US to find a satellite phone and Syrian passports in the wreckage. The village has no telephone line and no mobile coverage, satellite phones are comparatively cheap in Iraq. The village is near the border, people in the area frequently cross into Syria and vice versa.

The failure of the Coalition allies to take extreme care in identifying targets, and the ignorance of Iraq by the High Command, shows a reckless and callous indifference to the fate of civilian Iraqis in the war waged to disarm Saddam Hussein of WMDs.

CLAIM: That the air bombardment of the wedding party at Makradheeb by US forces (supported politically and logistically by the British government), which caused the death of over 40 civilians was indiscriminate, and therefore in breach of the Rome Statute of the International Criminal Court Article 8: (2)(b)(v).

---

[1] Justin Huggler, *Independent*, 20 May 2004.
[2] Justin Huggler, *Independent*, 21 May 2004.
[3] Rory McCarthy, *Guardian*, 20 May 2004

WAR CRIMES OR JUST WAR?

7Q. HAIFA STREET. MURDER MOST FOUL.

On 12 September 2004, Iraqis setting off for work in Haifa Street, Baghdad, were attracted to the site of an empty burning US vehicle in the street. Children and youths were also among the spectators. The vehicle had been blown up by a roadside bomb at approximately 4am. At around 8am, US helicopters flew over the area three times and strafed the bystanders, including a TV cameraman. Thirteen people were killed.

RELEVANT LAWS AND CONVENTIONS: The Rome Statute of the International Criminal Court, Article 8: (2) *For the purpose of this Statute, war crimes means.* (b) *Other serious violations of the laws and customs applicable in international armed conflict, within the established framework of international law, namely any of the following acts:* (i) *Intentionally directing attacks against civilian population as such or against individual civilians not taking direct part in hostilities.*
Geneva Convention IV Relative to the Protection of Civilian Persons in Time of War, 1949, Article 3: (1) *Persons taking no active part in the hostilities... the following acts are and shall remain prohibited at any time and in any place whatsoever with respect to the above-mentioned persons:* (a) *violence to life and persons.* Article 33: *No protected person may be punished for an offence he or she has not personally committed. Collective penalties and likewise all measures of intimidation or of terrorism are prohibited... Reprisals against protected persons and their property are prohibited.*
Protocol I Additional to the Geneva Conventions, 1977, Article 51: *Protection of civilian population.* (2) *The civilian population... shall not to be the object of attack. Acts or threats of violence... to spread terror among the civilian population are prohibited.*
Protocol II to the 1980 Convention as amended in 1996, Article 3: (7) *It is prohibited in all circumstances to direct weapons... either in offence, defence or by way of reprisals, against the civilian*

population as such or against individual civilians or civilian objects.

EVIDENCE OF VIOLATIONS: Early morning in Haifa Street. An Iraqi has just dropped the handbag fashionable to clerical staff in Baghdad. He slumps to his knees. One eye appears cut in half; the other is seeing but unseeing. He slowly slides to the ground and reaches out as if grasping for something. He dies.

I remember walking down Haifa Street in 1986. I was working close by on the restoration of some important buildings of the Ottoman and Colonial periods. The Hyundai Corporation was building a massive scheme of large concrete blocks of flats with arched balconies on Haifa Street. Palm trees were being planted each side of the road. The people I worked with also carried their money and notes, and sometimes their lunch, in small leather satchels.

The 13 Iraqis who were killed on a working Sunday in Haifa Street were not carrying guns. They had gathered curiously, like children, around an American armoured vehicle that was on fire. It had being blown up by an improvised explosive device four hours earlier. The US Kiowa light helicopters came to the scene and fired on the spectators. A film cameraman was taking pictures. The helicopters went away. A few minutes later the two helicopters returned and again fired rockets on the crowd. Ghaith Abdul Ahad, a *Guardian* journalist, crouched with others beside a wall. Again the helicopters went away only to return. The reporter retired to a stairway in a nearby building. One of the men lying in the street was Mazen al-Tumeizi, a Reuters TV cameraman. He was dead. But he had taken video footage which showed the helicopters firing on the crowd. Children had been swarming over the vehicle and had set it on fire again. Many of the dead were office workers whose families would wonder why they did not return home that day. "We are just ordinary workers. We are just trying to live," said Haidar Yahtiah one of the 61 wounded. They said they had been sleeping on the roofs and in the early hours the Bradley vehicle was blown up. Four lightly wounded US soldiers had been removed from the vehicle. At 8am the men went out onto the street to go to work. It was then that the US helicopters arrived.

Major Phil Smith of US 1st Cavalry Division said "The helicopter fired on the Bradley to destroy it after it had been hit earlier and it was on fire. It was for the safety of the people around it."[1]

The questions to be answered before a war crimes tribunal will be:
On what grounds did these US helicopter crews kill the Iraqis in Haifa Street?
Was it not quite clear visually from the helicopters what the situation was on the ground?
Why did the helicopters return three times?
Who gave the orders?
Who were the leaders of the Coalition that established the rules of engagement?
What was the political objective of those leaders?[2]

CLAIM: That the 19 May 2004 air bombardment of civilians in Haifa Street by the US forces (politically and logistically supported by the UK government) was a purposely targeted reprisal and in breach of the Rome Statute of the International Criminal Court Article 8 (2)(b) (i); Geneva Convention IV Relative to the Protection of Civilian Persons in Time of War, 1949, Article 3 (1) (a) and Article 33; Protocol I Additional to the Geneva Conventions, 1977, Article 51 (2); Protocol II to the 1980 Convention as amended in 1996, Article 3 (7).

---

[1] Ghaith Abdul-Ahad, *Guardian*, 14 September 2004.
[2] Patric Cockburn, *Independent*, 13 September 2004.

7R. CLUSTER BOMBS.

The US and UK forces have used (and continue using) cluster bombs. Cluster bombs are one of the most savage and inhumane weapons in the arsenal of the Coalition forces. They consist of a canister that opens in mid-air scattering the small explosive bomblets over a wide area. Each cluster bomb is composed of 140 to 700 bomblets. These bomblets are of three main types: incendiary, penetrational and shrapnel. When a shrapnel bomblet explodes it fragments into about 2000 pieces of jagged steel – sending out virtual blizzards of deadly shrapnel. Once released, they fall for a pre-set amount of time or distance before opening and spreading the bomblets. This makes the bombing thoroughly indiscriminate. Since twenty percent of the bomblets fail to explode, they act in the same way as land mines, causing death and injury long after the initial explosion. Another form of cluster munition is the artillery shell L20 made by Israel, each containing 47 bomblets. Two thousand of these shells were fired by the UK army in the first six weeks of the war in the Basra region.

RELEVANT LAWS AND CONVENTIONS: The Rome Statute of the International Criminal Court, Article 8: (2) *For the purpose of this Statute, "war crimes" means: (a) Grave breaches of the Geneva Convention of 12 August 1949, namely, any of the following acts against persons or property protected under the provisions of the relevant Geneva Convention: (iii) Wilfully causing great suffering or serious injury to body or health; (b) Other serious violations of the laws and customs applicable in international armed conflict, within the established framework of international law, namely, any of the following acts: (i) Intentionally directing attacks against the civilian population as such or against individual civilians not taking direct part in hostilities; (iv) Intentionally launching an attack in the knowledge that such attack will cause incidental loss of life or injury to civilians or damage to civilian objects; (v) Attacking* *or bombarding, by whatever means, towns villages, dwellings or buildings which are undefended and which are not military objectives;* (xx) *Employing weapons, projectiles and materials and methods of warfare which are of a nature to cause superfluous injury or unnecessary suffering.*

The Charter of the Nuremberg Tribunal, 1945: Article 6: (b) *War crimes: Violations of the laws and customs of war;* (c) *Crimes against humanity.*

Protocol I Additional to the Geneva Conventions 1977 Article 51 (4) *Indiscriminate attacks are prohibited. Indiscriminate attacks are:* (b) *those which employ a method or means of combat which cannot be directed at a specific military objective;* (5)(b) *an attack which may be expected to cause incidental loss of civilian life, injury to civilians, damage to civilian objects, or a combination thereof;* 52 (2) *Attacks shall be limited strictly to military objectives. In so far as objects are concerned, military objectives are limited to those objects which by their nature, location, purpose or use make an effective contribution to military action.*

The 1997 Ottawa Mine Ban Treaty. (Because the large number of duds among the bomblets effectively become land mines).

EVIDENCE OF VIOLATIONS: It is difficult to imagine the effect of cluster bombs. Some idea of their devastating power can be gained from looking at star bursts in a modern firework display, almost instantaneously spreading crackling stars over a large area. Often these cluster bombs are made by the selfsame UK firework manufacturers, but are much more powerful. These huge bombs are designed to explode above ground level, scattering hundreds of bomblets over an area the size of two football pitches. These bomblets are of three main types: A parachute type that has an incendiary effect in mid-air; a shrapnel type, each spreading 2,000 spicules of steel over a 20 metre radius (described by one surviving Iraqi as being in a rainstorm of steel); and a third type, a small depleted uranium cone which is designed to penetrate tanks. Eighty percent of humans found in the drop area will be killed by fire or shrapnel.[1] It is not surprising that the weakly-armed Iraqi army ran away and resorted to guerrilla tactics during and after the devastating invasion.

A press report prior to the November assault on Fallujah, described the weapons to be used. It also revealed that cluster bombs are routine munitions. Weapons to be used were heavy artillery, Abrams battle tanks, *Warthog* gunships, FA-18, F-16 and F-15E warplanes armed with laser and satellite-guided 500lb bombs, favoured over larger bombs to minimise, in the words of the US Command, "collateral damage".[2]

Warthogs are A-10 fixed-wing aircraft fitted with a GAU 8/A seven-barrel Gatling gun capable of firing 3,900 rounds a minute. In a further description of larger 1000/1500lb bombs carried by F-117A stealth bombers and F-16, F-15E and FA-18 warplanes, it is noticeable that cluster bombs are an integral part of the armoury. An AGM-154 JSOW cruise missile fired 17 miles from target at low level, uses GPS/INS (global positioning system/inertial navigation system) navigation, and IR (infrared) for final targeting against "soft targets", such as vehicles or troops (or civilians). It carries 145 BLU-97 A/B CEB (combined effects bomblets). Each CEB has a conical-shaped charge which can penetrate 5 to 7 inches of armour, a main charge which produces 300 high-velocity shrapnel fragments, and a zirconium sponge incendiary device. The bomblets are dispensed a few hundred feet above target.

Cluster bombs evidently kill civilians, especially children. Targeting the *dispenser* may prove difficult as, due to its wide range, it inevitably includes civilian areas. In addition, some twenty percent of the bomblets fail to explode, in effect becoming extremely sensitive land mines. They are even more dangerous than traditional land mines because sometimes the firing pin is a fraction of a millimetre from the detonator and held only by friction. The parachute-type bomblet, painted bright yellow and the size of a small milk bottle, is picked up by innocent children. It can also become buried up to 1 metre in soft ground and subsequently ploughed up. Maiming, amputation and death are its consequences. Since the conflict officially ended, there have been incidents such as that of Hanan Yusfieh who lost her foot when she poked a device with a stick while herding sheep. Ali Mahdi Katum lost his arm and shoulder when he and a friend found a bomb. Ali Mustapha and his brother played with a cluster bomb in their garden. They were both burnt. He is now blind, brain damaged and with chest injuries.

The British army dropped 1,200 cluster bombs and rockets during the thrust on Basra. Therefore, the number of bomblets coming from these *dispensers* totals hundreds of thousands. The British army has instructions to clear up unexploded bomblets only in areas and pathways used by the British military which are dangerous to British soldiers. There is no mandate for British soldiers to clear up unexploded bomblets in purely civilian areas and this is left to the Iraqis. Hamsa, a 23-year-old ex-soldier who lived on the outskirts of Kerbala, volunteered. He cleared 5,000 bomblets to allow children to go to school before being killed by one himself.[3]

It is estimated that more than 1,600 civilians (400 Iraqi and 1,200 Kuwaiti) were killed and over 2,500 injured in the first two years after the end of the Gulf war 1991 from accidents involving submunitions.[4]

During the conflict Geoffrey Hoon, the British Minister of Defence, stated that "cluster bombs are perfectly legal weapons with an entirely legitimate military role." He accepted that cluster bombs left a continuing problem, but balanced against this was the risk to coalition forces if this particular capability was not used. He said they were only used "when it was absolutely justified... because it is making the battlefield safer for our armed forces. That is something I am not prepared to compromise." When it was put to him that the Iraqi mother of a child killed by cluster bombs would not thank British forces for their actions, Mr Hoon replied: "One day they might."[5] It is argued by the MoD that the "proportionality" of the civilian casualties caused is not great enough to prohibit their use. But the MoD would have great difficulty in justifying proportionality when it is not UK policy to count Iraqi casualties, civilian or military. Estimates of Iraqi casualties run into tens of thousands, and they rise day by day.

Goering used the argument of military expediency at Nuremberg. "My point of view was decided by political and military reasons only." As a defence this was rejected, and he was condemned to death for war crimes. As far as is known, no major financial compensation has been offered by the UK to families killed or maimed as a result of the 2003 Iraq war.

EVIDENCE OF THE USE OF CLUSTER BOMBS AT HILLA:

Rageh Omaar, the famous BBC TV journalist, describes how the flimsy tin doors of the dwellings at Hilla were peppered with tiny little holes ringed in brown where the rust had begun to set in. The living and sleeping quarters were in a small brick block. There were just three interconnecting rooms, all without furniture, where the whole family slept and ate… At the back was a tiny grass patch. Virtually every wall was pockmarked with shrapnel holes. This is where Hussein, a young man just out of his teens, lived with his father and four siblings.

On 1 April coalition forces showered parts of Hilla and surrounding hamlets with anti personnel devices. Hussein said, "Everyone was outside as normal. I just heard a series of explosions, and blinding light and heat. I didn't know what the weapons were at the time. I saw my brothers and sisters covered in blood." I pressed him, asking if he was sure that there were no Iraqi forces in the area. He wagged his finger sternly, "No! They were not in our area. They were outside the area, on a road far from our village."

One man waved his burnt hand in front of my face. "Nothing has been done for us as a result of this war," he said "we have only experienced loss. There are no jobs, there is no electricity, there is no safety and security in our land. Is this the democracy we were promised? Is this the freedom we were told we would have? I tell you our lives have been destroyed." I walked… towards the edge of the village near an open field. The houses were much smaller and mostly made of mud rather than bricks. This was where Abdel Jawad Tamimi recalled the day of the attack... He'd heard the initial explosions at the end of the village and he and his wife Aliya, gathered their six children together. Deciding that staying inside was more dangerous, they opted to make a run for it. He described how he tried to lead his family out of the village. He kept looking behind him and up at the sky.

"At first I did not think it could be from planes, for why would British and Americans be bombing civilian areas?' Then suddenly he felt a devastating blast close to them. "It was ten o'clock in the morning when it happened. It was horrible. I... fell down an embankment into a small river." Wounded and bleeding he looked round to see what had happened to his six children. "My life ended that day. I crawled back up the embankment where I saw my children lying face down, blood everywhere, shrapnel all over their bodies. They are children! They are children! The bombs were very powerful. Adults could not have taken it let alone children."[6]

Lee Gordon, a freelance journalist who is trying to raise money for children who have lost their limbs in Iraq, describes the case of ten-year-old Zeynab. Zeynab, who lost her mother grandmother, brothers, sisters, uncles, nieces, and nephews in a cluster bomb raid on her village outside Basra, was brought to the UK by Baroness Helena Kennedy to have an orthopaedic limb paid for by Heather Mills McCartney. Unfortunately, when she arrived at the September 2003 Labour Conference she was bumped into by Mr Blair's motorcade. During her stay, she asked to see Hillary Benn, whose department is responsible for reconstruction in Basra, and Anne Clwyd, the Prime Minister's Special Humanitarian Envoy for Iraq, in order to ask the UK for help for child amputees. Neither minister was available to meet her. Presumably both thought it unwise to set a precedent of assisting the wounded of the Iraq war, as it might prove very costly.[7]

UK Government priorities are rather different. Sixty-six new *Storm Shadow* air-to-ground robot missiles were fired by the RAF in the first six weeks of the conflict. Each missile cost £750,000. Mr Hoon expressed himself pleased with their performance: "Early indications are that its use is highly effective." Total cost: £49 million.[8]

CLAIM: That members of the UK government and military, by using cluster bomb munitions in Iraq, are in breach of The Rome Statute of the International Criminal Court, Article 8: (2)(a)(iii). (b)(i), (iv), (v) and (xx); The Charter of the Nuremberg Tribunal, 1945: Article 6: (b) and (c); Protocol I Additional to the Geneva Conventions 1977 Article 51 (4)(b), (5)(b), 52 (2); and of the Mine Ban Treaty 1997.

FOOTNOTE: When we look out of the train window in North of London, some of the sheds alongside the track are not as innocent as they seem. At Ampthill in Bedfordshire, there is a major British manufacturer of cluster bombs. Hunter Engineering make the RBL-755, a 600lb bomb. It makes you wonder whether the British economy relies on continuous war. It is hardly likely that these weapons are piled on a rubbish dump by the car park. They must either be sold to some regime or used by the British forces.

---

[1] Richard Lloyd and David Taylor, expert presentation on cluster bombs, LSE, 18 November 2003.
[2] Kim Sengupta, *Independent*, 28 October 2004.
[3] Channel 4 documentary, *Iraq: Journey into Madness*, 19 October 2003.
[4] Human Rights Watch report, *Ticking Time Bombs*, June 1999.
[5] Paul Waugh and Ben Russell, *Independent*, 5 April 2003.
[6] Rageh Omaar, *Revolution Day*, London: Viking, 2004.
[7] Lee Gordon, *Camden New Journal*, 17 February 2005.
[8] BBC NEWS/UK/FACT FILE, news.bbc.co.uk/l/hi/uk/2882597.stm

WAR CRIMES OR JUST WAR?

7S. DEPLETED URANIUM.

Hard-tipped munitions using depleted uranium are standard issue ordnance for UK and US forces. The Ministry of Defence says there is no substitute for their armour-penetrating power. On impact they scatter fine particles of dust containing radioactive depleted uranium. After the first Gulf War, where large numbers of these projectiles were used, there have been dramatic increases in cancers, and birth defects. The MoD denies the link between DNA damage and depleted uranium, as claimed by Iraqi doctors working in the area. The munitions continue to be used even though a misjudgement by the MoD could have effects lasting millions of years.

RELEVANT LAWS AND CONVENTIONS: The Rome Statute of the International Criminal Court, Article 8: (2) *For the purpose of this Statute, "war crimes" means:* (b) *Other serious violations of the laws and customs applicable in international armed conflict, within the established framework of international law, namely, any of the following acts:* (iv) *Intentionally launching an attack in the knowledge that such attack will cause incidental loss of life or injury to civilians or damage to civilian objects or widespread, long-term and severe damage to the natural environment which would be clearly excessive in relation to the concrete and direct overall military advantage anticipated.*
Judgement of the Nuremberg Tribunal, 1946: Goering. (Purely military priorities were not regarded as an adequate defence with regard to the actions of Wermacht soldiers and the uses put to various weapons.)

EVIDENCE OF VIOLATIONS: "Women in Basra are afraid to become pregnant because there are so many deformed babies. We are leaving a deadly legacy for generations to come." Caroline Lucas, a Green Party Euro-MP visiting Basra.

At the Peacerights Inquiry into the alleged commission of war crimes by Coalition Forces in the 2003 Iraq War, held at the London School of Economics on 8-9 November 2003, when asked about clearing up dud depleted uranium shells which have not impacted any object, a Ministry of Defence scientist replied that MoD reports on what to do had not been completed, but that the munitions were too widely scattered for clearance to be practical; so it would probably be recommended to encourage Iraqis to pick up these weapons and carry them to *a communal collecting point.* (This does not refer to the more attractive looking cluster bomblets, which should not be disturbed). Some of these munitions look like 25mm thick metal pencils, others come in larger 4.5kg shells. According to the MoD specialist, they have a very low radiation level. Obviously, it is not possible to pick up the munitions that have hit their targets as they vaporise into fine dust. This dust then falls on earth and sand, is blown about by the wind and eventually reaches the water supply.

When asked if there was an alternative to these munitions, the same scientist replied there was none as they have the unique power – owing to their very high velocity (4-5 MACH) and high atomic weight in relation to steel – of penetrating heavy armour, such as tanks. The use of depleted uranium ordnance was justified by the British government as a means of ensuring a minimum loss of British soldiers' lives. This was seen as an absolute priority, overriding all other considerations. Maps and records of Iraq indicate the widespread use of depleted uranium shells.

The British government claims these weapons do not pose any environmental hazard. The same assertion is made in the Journal of Environmental Radioactivity by a member of the International Atomic Energy Authority.[1]

However, *Voices in the Wilderness* and the doctors of various Iraqi hospitals are adamant that the effects of these weapons have long-term consequences other than purely military. The incidence of cancers and birth defects in the southern region of Iraq has grown sevenfold since the Gulf War of 1991, when similar munitions were used. The radiation effects of these munitions which scatter radioactive dust on impact over a wide area are likely to persist. The half life of this radioactivity is measured not in millions but in billions of years.[2] Damage to human DNA is irreversible.

Photographs of affected babies can be found in various sites on the internet.

Doctor Jawad Al Ali, from Basra Talimi Teaching Hospital, said that "rates of cancer have multiplied 15 times since the Gulf War 1991. Thirteen doctors and nurses at Talimi have themselves contracted leukaemia since 1991." In 1990 the hospital was hit by a US missile strike killing four patients and burying a doctor. The doctor said it is estimated that 1,000 to 2,000 metric tons of depleted uranium have been used by US and UK forces in the Iraq War 2003-2005. *Voices in the Wilderness* say that it is highly toxic and destructive of human DNA It acts slowly and the worst effects appear after 4 years. The radioactive life is 4.5 billion years.

Dr Jawad said children in particular are susceptible to DU poisoning because they have a higher absorption rate than adults. Rare diseases such as bone cancer, lymphoma, and leukaemia are appearing in children more frequently. What dismays him is that double and triple cancers in different organs are occurring as never before. Dr Jawad said there was a spiralling emergency which should be investigated. During the sanctions period, World Health Organisation (WHO) teams were not allowed in the country to investigate. Monitoring equipment and hospital computers were removed in case they could be used for weapons programmes. The doctor said there were now many horrific birth defects; children born without heads, or limbs, or eyes.[3]

One of the strongest spokesmen against the use of DU is Dr. Ahmad Hardan, who stated, "Depleted Uranium has a half life of 4.7 billion years – that means thousands upon thousands of Iraqi children will suffer for tens of thousands of years to come. This is what I call terrorism."[4] Dr Hardan, scientific adviser to WHO, says that women as young as 35 are developing breast cancer. Sterility in men has increased tenfold since the Gulf War 1991. There is also an alarming occurrence of delayed growth in children.[5]

It has been argued that there could be other factors causing genetic defects in Iraq. However it is noticeable that leukaemia, cancer and birth deformity rates in Kuwait are not above normal. No depleted uranium weapons were used in Kuwait in the Gulf War, but Kuwait was subject to the same considerable pollution from burning oil fields as Basra.

Doug Rokke, former director of the Pentagon's depleted uranium project said, "We must do what is right for the citizens of the world: Ban DU."

It is estimated that 300 tons of depleted uranium was used in 1991 and five times as much in 2003. Child Victims of War say the number of Iraqi babies born with deformities has risen from 3.04/1000 in 1991 to 22.19/1000 in 2001. Babies born with Downs Syndrome have increased fivefold. Radiation levels in destroyed tanks are 2,500 times normal levels.[6]

Until it is absolutely certain that depleted uranium does not cause birth defects and cancers, it is utterly irresponsible to use these weapons when their effects cannot be reversed over millions of years. This is an extremely callous legacy to leave any population, especially as pregnancy and birth should be things of joy not of terror.

CLAIM: That the use of depleted uranium projectiles by the UK military, authorised by the UK Government is in breach of the Rome Statute of the International Criminal Court Article 8 (2)(b)(iv); and the Judgement of the Nuremberg Tribunal 1946.

---

[1] ELSEVIER SCIENCE ISSN 0265 - 931X, USA: Reed Business Information, 5 February 2002.
[2] Ewa Jasiewicz, 'Uranium in Your Koolaid: an interview with Cancer Specialist Dr Jawad Al Ali', *Voices in the Wilderness*, 26 January 2004.
[3] Nigel Morris, *Independent*, 13 May 2004.
[4] Brita May Rose, 'America's Radioactive', *Counterpunch.org*, 19 November 2004.
[5] Lawrence Smallman, 'Iraq's real WMD crime, *Aljazeera.net*, 30 October 2003.
[6] Nigel Morris, *Independent*, 13 May 2004.

7T. MERCENARIES.

Because of the policy by both the British and the Americans to employ the minimum number of expensive troops and rely on high technology to conduct this war, there has been a dearth of *boots on the ground*, to use the jargon of war. Since there are so few soldiers, in order to introduce some sort of security, a large number of private mercenaries have been employed by the Coalition armies, the CPA, the private companies and the contractors. Donald Rumsfeld has envisaged a more widespread use of mercenaries in future conflicts conducted by the USA. To take this logic to extremes, if future wars could be conducted entirely by robots and unmanned drones with massive firepower, there would be no need for soldiers at all. This use of mercenaries for security duties poses many moral and legal questions as mercenaries operate largely outside the rules of war.

RELEVANT LAWS AND CONVENTIONS: Since the widespread use of mercenaries, not enrolled as soldiers in recognisable regiments, (as for example in the Napoleonic wars) is largely a new phenomenon, their control has been hardly covered by Conventions. Their employment is frowned upon by regular soldiers, and they fall outside the scope of the laws and customs of war. Mercenaries are not given the same PoW protection as regular soldiers, but on the other hand their actions often fail to conform to the rules of war, and they act as brigands. It could be said that the reliance on mercenaries is in itself a breach of the Geneva Conventions, Hague Conventions, and Charter of the Nuremberg Tribunal.
International Convention against the Recruitment, Use, Financing and Training of Mercenaries, 1989, makes some attempt to cover the use of mercenaries, but has not yet entered into force.
Protocol (I) Additional to the Geneva Convention, 1977, Article 47:
(1) *A mercenary shall not have the right to be a combatant or a prisoner of war.* [However, being neither should not allow them

> unbridled licence to kill on the one hand, nor to be subjected to
> inhumane treatment on the other.]

EVIDENCE OF VIOLATIONS: It is difficult to consider the
violations of relevant laws when these are so limited in their scope.
However, this matter should be carefully considered. For instance,
mercenaries (or private security contractors) are used in the US-run
Abu Ghraib prison precisely because they are considered to be
operating outside the Geneva Conventions, and therefore immune
from prosecution for acts of torture of PoWs and detainees. This
clearly makes a mockery of the laws of war. We shall also examine
the moral and practical problems associated with the use of armed
mercenaries to guard private companies in a sovereign state. This
matter urgently needs to be settled by the United Nations.

There is one area in which British companies have done well in the
occupation of Iraq, that is in supplying mercenaries armed with light
machine guns to guard these exploitations. Mercenaries often include
elite British ex-SAS soldiers. There is evidence of personal financial
benefit to at least one UK politician. While he was not in office on 18
March 2003, and therefore had no vote on the war, Sir Malcolm
Rifkind a former Foreign Secretary and candidate for Kensington and
Chelsea, accepted the post of chairman of ArmorGroup, a security
firm protecting contractors in Iraq.[1]

This group was founded in 1988 by two ex-Scots Guards officers.
Profits in 2003 were $20 million dollars, 7,600 employees.
ArmorGroup, Aegis Defence Services, Olive Security, Global Risk
Strategies, Erinys, all these security companies have made large
profits in Iraq. Aegis Defence Services (previously Sandline), run by
the former British Army Colonel Tim Spicer, has a $293 million
Pentagon security contract in Iraq, with a staff of 20,000. While a
regular soldier will earn £300 a week, an ex-SAS man will earn £500
a day.[2]

In May 2004, Ahmet Ersavci, a Turkish Security Contractor said,
"There is still a huge competition for every contract that the Iraqi
Coalition Provisional Authority announces... I know because I am
bidding for them. It's dangerous but it is still very lucrative"[3] At the
time, the American group Bechtel employed two security staff for

every one of its Western employees in Baghdad and there was little sign of reconstruction or of road building. Electricity was only available for twelve hours a day and Baghdad' s sewer system was collapsing.[4]

It was estimated there were 17,000 private bodyguards operating in Iraq, 6,000 of which were armed. Following the deaths of a number of bodyguards in Iraq, private mercenaries demanded more powerful weapons.[5]

On 26 November 2004 a mortar attack on a " camp for Ghurkhas" in the *Green Zone* in Baghdad killed four former Ghurkhas and wounded 15 others. The Ghurkhas were working for the London-based security firm Global Risk Strategies. Ghurkhas are employed guarding the *Green Zone* and Baghdad airport. They are renowned for their fierceness as soldiers. The presence of foreign security firms adds to the danger. Many use four wheel drives with black glass windows, and drive at high speed.[6] They also wear no recognisable uniform. Some wear bandannas, dark glasses, leather jackets and jeans, others, to add to the confusion, quasi military uniforms. At what point does a security firm become a private mercenary army?

The distinction between military and bodyguards is blurred. Four men from Blackwater Security Consulting, a US company, were killed in Fallujah.

The killing of four *contractors* and their brutal deaths justified (in the eyes of the American and the British governments) the reprisals of April 2004 when 600 Iraqis were killed in Fullujah. In the same month, other Blackwater guards were involved in a firefight in Najaf. Because they were not considered military personnel, no military reports were kept. No records of Iraqi casualties were kept.

The use of mercenaries in war raises two important questions – not least because Donald Rumsfeld has said he can see an increasing need for their employment in future actions, and that 100,000 may be employed in Iraq during 2005.[7] The Pentagon says they may be used in Iraq for another ten years.

First, in a combat situation there should be no defence that anybody, in any way associated with an occupying party, is not governed by the Geneva Conventions. Without this caveat, mercenaries, bodyguards, contractors, etc. can do what they please in the field of rape, killing, theft, and destruction.

Second, we should be gravely concerned that armed men with no subjection to the laws of a sovereign state, but whose only loyalty is a contractual one, are allowed to operate all over the world. As from 28 June 2003, Iraq has been, nominally, a sovereign state. In Iraq, mercenaries are protecting private companies with machine guns and dogs and other unspecified devices. Are we to tolerate this to happen with no laws governing their actions? Can they be allowed to operate elsewhere, even in the UK? Again, are we all part of an experiment? What is to stop a large multinational oil company from having private security guards in Nigeria, for instance, with instructions to shoot on sight? What is to stop the private company British Nuclear Fuels from having armed security guards stationed at British power stations, with instructions to shoot at anyone who strays near the fence, or who *looks* like a terrorist?

These mercenaries can be hired on the internet. Peter Kilfoyle, a Former Minister of Defence said "I have asked endless questions to the Foreign Office on what is being done to regulate these mercenaries, but never get an answer. Nobody is responsible for these companies, they are not accountable and there is widespread abuse." The Foreign Office staff in Iraq are protected at the cost of £15 million. One British Army veteran said, "You see Americans, Serbians and South Africans strutting around with guns... like something out of Rambo. There is no shortage of alcohol here and at nights there are firefights involving some of these cowboys." Four Iraqi civilians were killed in a brawl in June 2003.[8]

CLAIM: That members of the UK Government and military, in collaboration with the US Administration and military, are in breach of the Geneva Conventions: by allowing mercenaries to operate in Iraq; by stating that the laws and customs of war are not applicable to mercenary combatants, private company security staff, or private prison security guards, therefore implying that they have carte blanche to do as they please. That the United Nations should urgently consider the role of mercenaries in combat situations and the responsibilities of those who employ them so that they are not outside the law.

---

[1] Marc Scodie, *Jewish Chronicle*, 16 April 2004.

[2] Peter Oborne, *Spectator*, 11 December 2004.

[3] Jamie Wilson, *Guardian*, 17 April 2004.

[4] Justin Huggler, *Independent*, 13 May 2004.

[5] *Independent*, 17 April 2004.

[6] Patrick Cockburn, *Independent*, 27 November 2004.

[7] Daniel McGrory, 'Dogs of war may be muzzled as safety fears grow', *Times*, 30 August 2004.

[8] Ibid.

WAR CRIMES OR JUST WAR?

7U. REVENGE KILLING: THE FIRST ASSAULT ON FALLUJAH.

In April 2004, in response to the killing of four American *contractors* (actually mercenaries), the US government demanded that the people of Fallujah hand over the killers; otherwise the US army would enter the city and seek them out. The people of Fallujah did not respond, so the US army entered and strafed Fallujah, leaving 600 fatalities among the population. A large number of the casualties were women and children. The American army left the city after two weeks. Both logistically and politically the British government continued to support their American allies during and after this attack.

RELEVANT LAWS AND CONVENTIONS: The Rome Statute of the International Criminal Court, Article 8: (2) *For the purpose of this Statute," war crimes" means:* (b) *Other serious violations of the laws and customs applicable in international armed conflict, within the established framework of international law, namely any of the following acts:* (i) *Intentionally directing attacks against civilian population as such or against individual civilians not taking direct part in hostilities.*

Geneva Convention IV Relative to the Protection of Civilian Persons in Time of War, 1949, Article 3: (1) *Persons taking no active part in the hostilities... shall in all circumstances be treated humanely... To this end the following acts are and shall remain prohibited at any time and in any place whatsoever with respect to the above-mentioned persons:* (a) *violence to life and person.* Article 33: *No protected person may be punished for an offence he or she has not personally committed. Collective penalties and likewise all measures of intimidation or of terror ism are prohibited... Reprisals against protected persons and their property are prohibited.*

Protocol I Additional to the Geneva Conventions, 1977, Article 51: *Protection of the civilian population* (2) *The civilian population... shall not be the object of attack.* (4) *Indiscriminate attacks are*

211

prohibited. Indiscriminate attacks are: (b) *those which... cannot be directed at a specific military objective;* (5) *Among others...* (b) *an attack which may be expected to cause incidental loss of civilian life, injury to civilians, damage to civilian objects, or a combination thereof, which would be excessive in relation to the concrete and direct military advantage anticipated.* (6) *Attacks against the civilian population or civilians by way of reprisals are prohibited.*
1978 Red Cross Fundamental Rules of International Humanitarian Law Applicable in Armed Conflicts, 6. *Parties to a conflict and members of their armed forces do not have an unlimited choice of methods and means of warfare; 7. Neither the civilian population as such nor civilian persons shall be the object of attack.*
Protocol II on Prohibitions or Restrictions on the Use of Mines, Booby-Traps and other Devices, 1980, Article 3: (2) *It is prohibited in all circumstances to direct weapons... either in offence, defence or by way of reprisals, against the civilian population as such or against individual civilians.* (3) *The indiscriminate use of weapons... is prohibited. Indiscriminate use is any placement...* (b) *... which employs a method or means of delivery which cannot be directed at a specific military objective; or* (c) *which may be expected to cause incidental loss of civilian life, injury to civilians, damage to civilian objects... excessive in relation to the concrete and direct military advantage anticipated.*
Protocol II on Prohibitions or Restrictions on the Use of Mines, Booby-Traps and Other Devices, amended 1996, Article 3: (7) *It is prohibited...to direct weapons... either in offence, defence or by way of reprisals, against the civilian population as such or against individual civilians or civilian objects.*

EVIDENCE OF VIOLATIONS: In April 2004, a tight group of six F-16 *Fighting Falcon* US planes descends towards Fallujah at 200 to 300 mph in a ground attack support mission. The acquisition and designation systems in the nose of the planes are scanning the ground for targets. One of the pilots sees, in one of the two multifunction display units in the cockpit, a group of fuzzy grey dots sweeping out from behind a building into a wide street. Might these be insurgent terrorists? Or a group of civilians, maybe children, running for cover?

As the flight continues hurtling towards Fallujah, the time to act is a matter of split seconds away. The pilot consults the Joint Attack Terminal Controller (JATC). "I've got numerous individuals on the road. Do you want me to take those out?" Almost without pause the JATC replies, "Take them out." Heavy regular breathing is heard in the pilot's mouthpiece. "Ten seconds." The cross hairs on the target display screen are gently aligned by the pilot with the moving centre of the group of dots. He squeezes the firing button. The laser controlled missile locks onto its target in a parabolic trajectory. The screen goes black with a large flash at the top of the cross hairs. "Impact... Oh, dude." exclaims the pilot ecstatically as the plane roars into a climb.[1]

Prior to firing the missile, at no point was it confirmed from the ground that these Iraqis posed a threat or were armed. Dr Salam Ismael, at the local hospital said the attack was in the afternoon of the fourth day of the assault on Fallujah. He had heard they were innocent civilians fleeing for safer ground. He said ten bodies were brought into the hospital. Among them were women and children. Close examination of the gun film shows about thirty individuals, some of them small, probably children. Most were killed. Rob Henson, Editor of *Jane's Air Launched Weapons* said that it was clear that sighting of the target was only from the air, not the ground, and that the decision to bomb was very rapid.

After screening the pilot's video, Channel 4 received the following e-mail overnight. "This video is indeed gun film footage from a US Air Force F-16 fighter… This was a close air support mission flown by an F-16 *Fighting Falcon* in the Fallujah vicinity and under the command of a Joint Terminal Attack Controller serving with ground forces in the area. The JTAC designated the target and confirmed the hit."[2]

From a technical point of view, this video poses a number of questions. The pictures on the screen are not high definition. It is very difficult to make out what is building, roof top or garden wall. The boundaries of Arabic houses are notoriously difficult to judge, as often the flat roofed houses share dividing walls, and marriage customs allow properties to be linked like jigsaws. Do all combat support missions obtain their targets by this means, or are some targets pre-designated by global positioning systems (GPS)? We hear that in the constant bombing raids against Fallujah the Americans are taking out *illegal* road blocks and *insurgent safe houses*.

How, in an attack aircraft flying at speed, with such fuzzy equipment, can the pilot gunner accurately decide what is happening on the ground? Are there different sized missiles fitted to the under side of the plane or bomb bay? If they are all the same size *proportional response* is an impossibility. If this cockpit video is typical (and we have no reason to doubt otherwise) precision targeting and proportional response is so much propaganda. The truth is that many non-combatant civilians are being shot to pieces among the so called terrorist insurgents.

The gun film footage taken on board the F-16 *Flying Falcon* showed a small part of a major American assault on Fallujah in April 2004. The April assault was in response to the brutal killing of four American mercenary contractors, whose bodies were hung from a bridge. President Bush declared that the killers would be found. Because the town did not hand over the killers, 600 civilians, including women and children, were indiscriminately killed by American forces. Ambulances trying to transfer the wounded to Baghdad were stopped at US checkpoints and prevented from doing so, contrary to the Geneva Conventions. At least one ambulance was destroyed by gunfire.

After three weeks of fighting, American casualties were high and a truce was made. The Americans withdrew. Two weeks later, Mr Blair showed his political solidarity with the US administration after international condemnation of the US assault on Fallujah by saying, "We stand shoulder to shoulder with the US." Militarily, the UK continues to protect the main supply line (MSL) from Kuwait to the US army in the north, and to occupy the southern theatre of war.

Two major revenge killings come to mind: In May 1942, during World War Two, Reinhard Heydrich was blown to pieces in a car in Prague. In response to the assassination, Himmler organised the burning of a small village called Lidice outside Prague. All 173 males were shot, and 198 women and 98 children were sent to concentration camps. This was regarded as one of the worst crimes of the Second World War. The number of civilians killed in Lidice was less than 469.

In March 1968, during the Vietnam War, a unit known for its violent tactics and psychologically prepared for a major attack entered the village of My Lai looking for Viet Cong. There were no Viet Cong in sight, so the soldiers started shooting the villagers. They killed hundreds of civilians – primarily old men, women, children, and babies. Some were tortured or raped. Dozens were herded into a ditch and executed with automatic weapons. As soon as the massacre ended the cover up began. When in November 1969 the American public began to hear about it, support for the war began to wane. By 1973 America had to pull out of Vietnam. Between 347 and 504 villagers were slaughtered in My Lai.

The 600 civilians killed in Fallujah in April 2003 are in excess of these numbers.[3]

The record of the US army's actions in Fallujah, in relation to the Geneva Conventions and the protection of hospitals, hospital staff and hospital transport, is not good. On 15 April, a British journalist in Fallujah reported, "There's slaughter going on here". He had seen a volunteer nurse yards from him killed by sniper fire. "The F-16s had been playing about for a while and flying low, but about half an hour ago they began to bomb the area... There was tank shelling... and heavy machine gun fire."[4] Ambulances were shot up on the grounds that they might have been harbouring terrorists in disguise. Doctors reported ambulances riddled with bullet holes. Our journalist was witness to one such ambulance. "In fact, US snipers were targeting ambulances. I saw the burning wreck of one, destroyed in a hail of bullets while evacuating casualties from an under-fire hospital. What do you say when doctors turn to you for anaesthetics to operate on a volunteer nurse shot through the stomach by a sniper during a cease fire?" He also visited a field hospital. "The walls were pockmarked with shrapnel holes, glass crunched underfoot, the result of a missile fired at the hospital less than 24 hours earlier. Four year old Ali was lying with a massive groin wound and a leg amputated above the knee in a blood stained cot. The doctor said Ali's mother, brother and sisters had been killed, probably by an F-I6 bomb attack."[5]

CLAIM: That the attacks by the US Army on Fallujah in April 2004, supported by the UK government and military logistically and politically, were not proportional, and were reprisal killings, therefore in breach of the Rome Statute of the International Criminal Court, Article 8 (2)(b)(i); the Geneva Convention IV Relative to the Protection of Civilian Persons in Time of War, 1949, Article 3 (1)(a) and Article 33; Protocol I Additional to the Geneva Conventions, 1977, Article 51(2), (4)(b), (5)(b) and (6); 1978 Red Cross Fundamental Rules of International Humanitarian Law Applicable in Armed Conflicts, 6 and 7; Protocol II on Prohibitions or Restrictions on the Use of Mines, Booby-Traps and other Devices, 1980, Article 3 (2), (3)(b) and (c); and Protocol II on Prohibitions or Restrictions on the Use of Mines, Booby-Traps and Other Devices, amended 1996, Article 3 (7).

---

[1] Channel 4 News, 5 October 2004.

[2] Ibid.

[3] Iraq Body Count, 7 November 2004.

[4] Lee Gordon, *Camden New Journal*, 15 April, 2004.

[5] Lee Gordon, *Camden New Journal*, 29 April, 2004.

7v. FALLUJAH REVISITED: NOVEMBER 2004.

In November 2004, a second major assault was carried out on the city of Fallujah. The US army was supported by a small contingent of Iraqi soldiers and by the UK army in reserve areas – ostensibly to eliminate a group of between 1,500 and 3,000 guerrilla fighters from a population of 250,000. The civilian population was advised to leave the city. Eighty percent did. The assault involved widespread destruction of property, the death of an uncounted number of non-combatants (including children), prevention of access to hospitals and clinics for the wounded, attacks on medical facilities and staff, killing of the wounded, blindfolding of the wounded while being treated for injuries, and overwhelming and indiscriminate firepower - including aerial bombardment with 500lb bombs. The aim of the attack was to eliminate a centre of resistance in order to pave the way for elections in January 2005. The attack was nominally ordered by the Prime Minister of the interim government, Iyad Allawi. However, the Sunni faction of the administration resigned in protest.

RELEVANT LAWS AND CONVENTIONS: The Rome Statute of the International Criminal Court Article 8: *War crimes (2)(a) Grave breaches of the Geneva Convention of 12 August 1949, namely, any of the following acts against persons or property protected under the provisions of the relevant Geneva Convention:* (i) *Wilful killing;* (iv) *Extensive destruction and appropriation of property, not justified by military necessity and carried out unlawfully and wantonly;* (b) *Other serious violations of the laws and customs applicable in international armed conflict, within the established framework of international law, namely, any of the following acts:* (ii) *Intentionally directing attacks against civilian objects, that is, objects which are not military objectives; (v) Attacking or bombarding by whatever means, towns, villages,*

dwellings or buildings which are undefended and which are not military objectives.
Protocol I Additional to the Geneva Conventions and relating to the Protection of victims of International Armed Conflicts, 1977, Article 12: *Protection of medical units* (1) *Medical units shall be respected and protected at all times and shall not be the object of attack*; Article 21: *Medical vehicles shall be respected and protected in the same way as mobile medical units under the conventions and this Protocol. The Geneva Convention also prohibits attacks that may cause "incidental loss of civilian life, injury to civilians, damage to civilian objects, or combination thereof, which would be excessive in relation to the concrete and direct military advantage anticipated*; Article 51: (1) *The civilian population... shall enjoy general protection against danger arising from military operations.* (2) *... Acts or threats of violence the primary purpose of which is to spread terror... are prohibited.* (4) *Indiscriminate attacks are prohibited*; Article 57: (1) *In the conduct of military operations, constant care shall be taken to spare the civilian population, civilians and civilian objects.*
Charter of the Nuremberg Tribunal, 1945.

EVIDENCE OF VIOLATIONS: RABBITING. Fifty years ago corn was cut, not with combine harvesters, but with binders which circled the tall crop until all the rabbits were concentrated in an ever diminishing rectangle of corn. When they saw the blades of the binder and heard the rattle of the canvas belts getting louder and louder, the rabbits would then start screaming in panic and rush out of the corn to be beaten to death with sticks by men and boys who had ranged round them. This is an analogy of the battle of Fallujah in November 2004.

Fallujah was a city with a quarter of a million inhabitants, mainly Sunni Iraqis, situated on a bend of the Euphrates River and approached by two long bridges, one of which had been built by the British in 1927. The other three sides of the rectangular city were bordered by desert. Some 1,000 to 3,000 freedom fighters had their base in Fallujah. In April of 2004 America had made an assault on Fallujah but had found the narrow street fighting very dangerous and after two weeks in which they killed some 600 Iraqis, including women and children, they retreated and made a truce.

The spectre of Vietnam entered the equation. During the summer the American troops received training in street fighting from the Israeli Defence Force (IDF). Their tactics essentially involve massive fire power; identifying guerrilla targets by drawing their fire; bringing in tanks and helicopters to fire on targets, demolishing buildings in the process; establishing snipers on roofs; smashing holes in party walls rather than using the streets for infantry (a tactic first used by the Greeks 2,500 years ago). To this the Americans added the tactic of shooting at anything that moved. Thus the US army prepared itself for the second assault in November 2004. The *causa belli* was provided by Iyad Allawi, the US-appointed Iraqi prime minister, who warned residents in Fallujah to give up the suspected militant Abu Musab al-Zarqawi or face an onslaught.[1] The likelihood of this request being fulfilled was as remote as Bin Laden successfully making a demand for Mr Blair. Zarqawi had probably fled the city anyway. Contrary to the rules of war, the Fallujah negotiator was held captive; he was released after protest. The *causa belli* had been established. All the inhabitants of Fallujah were advised to leave. Two weeks later, 80% of them had left the city. Some were encamped in dire conditions outside Fallujah, others fled to nearby towns as best they could, leaving their houses to the mercy of the Americans and the looters.

This, lest we forget, was a city the size of Cardiff (population: 315,000) with the usual mixture of upper class villas, poor districts of tightly packed houses and industrial estates. In order to root out one percent of the population, the remaining ninety nine percent was put to *some* inconvenience; not fully appreciated in the West, save by the Jewish survivors of Warsaw. Like the Jews, they were advised to leave the city carrying their personal belongings. Those that remained: the very poor, the sick and weak, those who feared for their property or the diminishing number of freedom fighters were now trapped in a situation similar to the rabbits in the corn field.

The assault began in late October 2004, with aerial bombardment and shell fire from large field guns. In order to demonstrate political unity, a small contingent of badly armed new National Iraqi soldiers was brought in to fight. The Americans also requested a reserve battalion of 650 British troops to move into an area south of Baghdad previously occupied by US troops. This would free more US troops to successfully carry out their mission in Fallujah.

On the 18 Oct 2004, the Liberal Democrat MP, Jenny Tonge asked in Parliament, "If we refuse the American request, what penalties are we likely to incur?" Mr Hoon, the Secretary of Defence replied, "There will be no penalty but we will have failed in our duty as an ally.... Were we to refuse the request it would go to the heart of our relationship not only with the US, but with other members of the alliance."[2] The Secretary of State for Defence, who is a barrister as well as an MP, had in this statement confirmed the legal position that allies in war are in partnership. If war crimes are committed, the war crimes of one partner are the war crimes of the other partners. Consequently, US violations become the joint- responsibility of UK nationals, "not withstanding that such violations may have been committed by US forces."[3]

As a result, 650 British Black Watch soldiers were brought in to protect the rear at Camp Dogwood south west of Baghdad. Photographs of this contingent were blatantly used by the CNN television network as propaganda in a ratio of about 4:1 of photographs shown, even though they were outnumbered 23:1 by the 15,000 US soldiers involved. The Black Watch, with the distinctive red flash in their berets provided a tremendous morale boost to the Bush Administration in the run-up to the elections, even though their only contribution was to capture ten men in a small village a few miles from Camp Dogwood, after losing five soldiers.

On 14 November, the main American assault began encircling the city in four pincer movements. Television views of the city showed it rapidly being reduced to burnt out buildings and piles of rubble. Contrary to the laws of war, the water supply was turned off for all the inhabitants. Contrary to the rules of war, the main hospital was attacked; a medical clinic was destroyed killing 20 doctors; medical staff were killed by sniper fire; ambulances were targeted; Red Crescent ambulances were turned away; and Red Crescents activities were threatened by Allawi if they were to criticise the situation.

Food aid was not permitted to enter the city. Children were allowed to die without any medical assistance. Contrary to the laws of war, no quarter was given: Residents who surrendered with white flags or sheets were shot; freedom fighters were killed even though they were wounded and had given up fighting; others were killed in their sleep. Contrary to the laws of war, residents who tried to flee the city by swimming the river were strafed with machinegun fire and shot by US snipers. After three weeks of intense fighting using IDF methods, the city was totally occupied. Industrial estates and housing reduced to rubble. Anything that moved was shot at. In December American tanks were still patrolling the ruins. Refugees were not allowed to return to the city before 24 December and then they had to go through five checkpoints and have their finger prints taken, along with DNA samples and retinal scans. Each citizen was issued with a badge with their address on it, to be worn at all times. Major Francis Piccoli, of 1st Marine Expeditionary force said "Some may see this as a *Big Brother is watching over you* experiment. But in reality, it's a simple security measure to keep the insurgents from coming back."[4]

An officer of the Black Watch returning from Camp Dogwood said "The whole deployment was, of course, politicised from the beginning. Some soldiers criticised Tony Blair by name. There was the feeling that we were being used, and that made it difficult to focus initially on our mission… Was it worth it? Of course we have all got our private thoughts about this war. There was a lot of unease about being identified too much with the Americans and Fallujah… you have to hope at the end that we did some good. Only time will tell."[5] Very little in the way of guns, rockets and ammunition belonging to the rebels was actually found. Many of the rebels had departed, prior to the assault, to fight in Baghdad and elsewhere. They were crushed, but not yet defeated. In the last week of November, the Australian Ambassador was prevented from leaving Baghdad airport for the centre of the city because the freedom fighters were militarily astride the highway.

For the handover of one man a city of a quarter of a million has been destroyed. This will be recorded in history as a war crime comparable to the sacking of Acre by the First Crusade, the destruction of Jerusalem by Titus, Pinochet's coup and other assaults by military might. And the United Kingdom was party to it. Apart from individual acts of brutality, it is not the foot soldiers that should be called to account for the war crimes committed, but (as directed by the Charter of the Nuremberg Tribunal in 1945) the leaders and the field commanders accepting their orders. To place a nineteen-year-old soldier in a burnt out mosque, in the middle of a city ricocheting with bullets, and expect him to differentiate whether a person in a white robe lying on the ground is a freedom fighter or an Iraqi civilian, is expecting a great deal too much. The soldier should not have been there in the first place. In addition, soldiers had been trained by their officers to regard the Iraqi as "the enemy in league with Satan," as we discuss in Chapter 7g: *A Crusade: Religious Persecution*, even though one of the ostensible reason for going to war was to *bring freedom to the Iraqi people.*

The following is a diary of events reflecting what different people had to say about the second siege of Fallujah, as depicted in the newspapers. These quotes illustrate the attitudes of the besiegers and the besieged.

In September 2004 a senior US commander told the *New York Times*, "We need to make a decision on when the cancer of Fallujah is going to be cut out. We would like to end December at local control across the country."[6]

At the end of October 2004, American military officials claimed that there were up to 5,000 Islamic militants, Saddam loyalists and criminals barricaded in the town. Brigadier General Dennis Hejlik, deputy commander of the 1st Marine Expeditionary Force, at a camp near Fallujah said: "We're gearing up to do an operation and when we are told to go, we'll go. When we do go, we'll whack them." [7]

On the night of 14 October US forces launched a major offensive on Fallujah, where the militant leader [Abu Musab al-Zarqawi] is believed to be based. The town was pounded from the air by warplanes and helicopter gunships and heavy artillery and tanks on the ground. Two US Marine battalions began to advance into the town from the north and east...

The Iraqi interim government threatened to declare war on Fallujah. The national Security Adviser, Qassem Dawoud, said: "This cowardly act will not go unpunished. We shall strike them... we shall smash them."[8]

US forces yesterday, 17 October, continued their ferocious assault on Fallujah in a military offensive apparently designed to bring the city back under the control of Iraq's pro-US government. Fierce clashes broke out between US troops and insurgents on a highway east of Fallujah and in the southern part of the city. The road to Baghdad had been blocked. Iyad Allawi, Iraq's pro-US interim prime minister demanded that residents in Fallujah hand over the Jordanian terrorist Abu Musab al-Zarqawi. Yesterday Fallujah clerics said they were willing to negotiate, but this was impossible while US planes were pulverising the city. "We are still ready to go back to the talks and open new channels of dialogue," the negotiator Abdul Hamid Jadou said.

On Saturday hospital officials said that US artillery shells hit a house in Halabsa village, 10 miles south-west of Fallujah, killing a three-year-old girl and injuring four family members, three of them children. In a separate development, Zarqawi's group said in an internet statement that it would take orders from Osama bin Laden and al-Qa'ida from now on.[9]

There have been American bomb attacks on Fallujah on an almost daily basis. Yesterday, the chief negotiator for the city was freed on the orders of Iyad Allawi, Iraq's interim Prime Minister, after his arrest by the Americans on Friday. Mr Allawi had said that he hoped peace talks could restart. But one of the first statements by Sheikh Khaled al-Jumelli after being released was to say that talks with Iraq's interim government will not be resumed as a protest at his detention. He added that three other men arrested with him, said to be the police chief of Fallujah and two of his senior officers, have not been released.

Sheikh Jumelli said: "The fact is that I'm negotiating on behalf of Fallujah people – civilians, children, women – who have no power apart from being represented by somebody. Since the situation has got to this, each side can go wherever they want and we don't want to talk about negotiations."

The interim government's National Security Adviser, Kassim Daoud, insisted yesterday that Fallujah will be attacked unless its people hand over the Jordanian militant leader Abu Musab al-

Zarqawi. Asked when the offensive will begin, he responded: "We have a plan and we will stick to it."[10]

"Our patience is running thin," Mr Allawi said. If no deal was reached, he added: "I have no choice but to secure a military solution. I do so with a heavy heart, for even with the most careful plan there will be some loss of innocent lives. But I owe it to the people of Iraq to defend them from the violence and the terrorists and the insurgents."

One condition demanded by the interim government in talks with a delegation from Fallujah is that they hand over Zarqawi, a demand the city leaders say is impossible to meet. US military commanders say privately that the militant leader may have left Fallujah

In Fallujah, US warplanes and helicopter gunships continued air strikes and ground forces exchanged fire with resistance fighters. Lt-Col Willy Buhl, of the US army, said: "We'll do that when Prime Minister Allawi and President Bush tell us it is time to go."[11]

The Marines will be going in very heavy, with M1 A1 Abrams tanks, tracked armoured personnel carriers equipped with cannons and heavy machine guns, mortars, high-power sniper rifles and a variant of the US Army's Stryker vehicle, which deflects rocket-propelled grenades with metal lattice-work on its outer skin.

"The competence and compassion of my marines will mitigate any civilian casualties," said Lieutenant-Colonel Gareth Brandl when asked how he could control where all this firepower would be directed in the narrow streets and alleys of Fallujah.

Colonel Brandl said he would be quite happy if his marines could just walk into Fallujah, but they were ready for a fight.

The threats include roadside bombs, suicide bombers, booby traps, bombs thrown from roof-tops, mosques used as sniper positions, and a small group of Islamist fighters who believe they are about to seek martyrdom in a holy war.

"The marines that I have had wounded over the past five months have been attacked by a faceless enemy," said Colonel Brandl. "But the enemy has got a face. He's called Satan. He lives in Fallujah. And we're going to destroy him." [12]

"We'll unleash the dogs of hell, we'll unleash them... They don't even know what's coming - hell is coming. If there are civilians in there, they're in the wrong place at the wrong time." Sergeant Sam Mortimer, US marines.[13]

"This is America's fight. What we've added to it is our Iraqi partners. They want to go in and liberate Fallujah. They feel this town's being held hostage by mugs, thugs, murderers and terrorists." Lt-Gen John F Sattler, 1st Marine Expeditionary Force commanding officer.[14]

"You're all in the process of making history. This is another Hue city in the making. I have no doubt, if we do get the word, that each and every one of you is going to ... kick some butt." Sgt Major Carlton W Kent, senior enlisted marine in Iraq.[15]

"Make no mistake about it, we'll hand this city back to the Iraqi people." Lt-Col Mike Ramos, US Marines battalion commander.[16]

"I believe that in Britain we allowed our judgement of the direct consequences of inaction to override our judgement of the even more dire consequences of departing from the rule of law." Sir Stephen Wall, former senior diplomatic adviser on Europe, Speaking at Chatham House, 8 November 2004.

"The American troops' attempt to take over the hospital was not right because they thought that they would halt medical assistance to the resistance. But they did not realise that the hospital does not belong to anybody, especially the resistance." Dr Salih al-Issawi, director of Fallujah Hospital.[17]

"My son got shrapnel in his stomach when our house was hit at dawn, but we couldn't take him for treatment. We buried him in the garden because it was too dangerous to go out. We did not know how long the fighting would last." Mohammed Abboud, a teacher, referring to his nine-year-old son, Ghaith.[18]

"There is not a single surgeon in Fallujah. We had one ambulance hit by US fire and a doctor wounded. There are scores of injured civilians in their homes whom we can't move. A 13-year-old child just died in my hands." Sami al-Jumaili, a doctor at Fallujah Hospital.[19]

"My kids are hysterical with fear. They are traumatised by the sound but there is nowhere to take them." Adil Sabah, trader.[20]

"Every minute, hundreds of bombs and shells are exploding. The north of the city is in flames. Fallujah has become like hell." Fadri al-Badrani.[21]

"The American attack on our people in Fallujah has led and will lead to more killings and genocide without mercy from the Americans" Mohsen Abdel Hamid, leader of the Iraqi Islamic Party.[22]

"My concern now is only one – not to allow any enemy to escape. As we tighten the noose around him, he will move to escape to fight another day. I do not want these guys to get out of here. I want them killed or captured as they flee." Colonel Michael Formica, 1st Cavalry Brigade commander.[23]

Twenty Iraqi doctors and dozens of civilians were killed in a US air strike that hit a clinic in Fallujah, according to an Iraqi doctor who said he survived the strike. "In the early morning the US attacked the clinic, a place that we were using for treating the injured people in the city, "Dr Sami al-Jumaili said, describing the air strike. "I really don't know if they want to tackle the insurgents or the innocent civilians from the city."[24]

"If anybody thinks Fallujah is going to be the end of the insurgency in Iraq, that was never the objective, never our intention, and even never our hope." General Richard Myers, head of the US Joint Chiefs of Staff.[25]

"Anyone who gets injured is likely to die because there's no medicine and they can't get to doctors. There are snipers everywhere. Go outside and you're going to get shot." Abdul-Hameed Salim, volunteer with the Iraqi Red Crescent in Fallujah.[26]

"There's no water. People are drinking dirty water. Children are dying. People are eating flour because there's no food." Rasoul Ibrahim, father of three who fled Fallujah with his family.[27]

"There have been a lot of innocent people killed. The Americans say they are aiming their tanks and aircraft at the Mujahedin, but I know of at least eight other people who have died besides my brother." Suleiman Ali Hassan, whose brother was killed in Fallujah.[28]

It is hard to remember, in the midst of all the brutal, fierce imagery of war and destruction in Fallujah, that the real contest in Iraq is about offering its people peace and dignity. The footage from the American side has been as unrelenting as a macho Hollywood war movie... The onslaught on Fallujah was called "Phantom Fury", which, like the original attack on Baghdad, "Shock and Awe", was designed to instil fear and terror. There were still more pictures of the humiliation of the enemy – with more images of prisoners tied up and blindfolded on the ground.[29]

Our situation is very hard. We don't have food or water. My seven children all have severe diarrhoea. One of my sons was wounded by shrapnel last night and he's bleeding, but I can't do anything to help him." Abu Mustafa, (contacted by telephone in Fallujah by Reuters).[30]

"The Americans have been firing at buildings if they see even small movements. They are also destroying cars, because they think every car has a bomb in it. People have moved from the edges of the city into the centre, and they are staying on the ground floors of buildings. There will be nothing left of Fallujah by the time they finish. They have already destroyed so many homes with their bombings from the air; and now we are having this from tanks and big guns." Aamir Haidar Yusouf, trader.[31]

"The Americans and [Iyad] Allawi have been saying that Fallujah is full of foreign fighters. That is not true; they left a long time ago. You will find them in other places, in Baghdad. We have been saying to Allawi and the Americans that they are not here, but they do not believe us." Mohammed Younis, former policeman.[32]

The US Defence secretary Donald Rumsfeld claimed last week that Iraqi civilians had been warned how to avoid injury. "Innocent civilians in that city have all the guidance they need as to how they can avoid getting into trouble. There aren't going to be large numbers of civilians killed and certainly not by US forces," he said.[33]

The troops can be seen entering the mosque where some injured insurgents had been left following a firefight with a different group of marines the previous day. Rather than being transported away for treatment, the fighters had been left in the mosque, which the second group of marines had erroneously been told had been reoccupied. The video shows one of the marines notices that one of the Iraqis is breathing.

"He's fucking faking he's dead," he says. A second replies: "Yeah, he's breathing." The first marine repeats: "He's faking he's fucking dead." At this point the footage shows the marine point his automatic rifle at the wounded man... The sound of a gunshot can be heard, followed by a voice saying: "He's dead now."

In a report that accompanied the footage, Kevin Sites, a freelance journalist on assignment with NBC, said a total of five injured insurgents were in the mosque, three of whom were severely injured and one who was dead. He said: "The prisoner did not appear to be armed or threatening in any way."

"We follow the law of armed conflict and hold ourselves to a high standard of accountability. The facts of this case will be thoroughly pursued to make an informed decision and to protect the rights of all persons involved." Lt-Gen John Sattler, 1st Marine Expeditionary Force commanding officer.[34]

"The policy of the rules of engagement authorise the marines to use force when presented with a hostile act or hostile intent. So they would have to be using force in self-defence, yes. Any wounded who don't pose a threat would not be considered hostile." Lt-Col Bob Miller, judge-advocate general who is heading the investigation.[35]

"There have been a number of reports during the confrontation alleging violations of the rules of war designed to protect civilians and combatants. Those responsible for breaches – including deliberate targeting of civilians, indiscriminate and disproportionate attacks, the killing of injured persons and the use of human shields – must be brought to justice. I am particularly worried over poor access by civilians still in the city to the delivery of humanitarian aid and about the lack of information regarding the number of civilian casualties." Louise Arbour, the UN high commissioner for human rights.[36]

"Several Red Cross workers have returned from Fallujah as the Americans won't let them into the city. They said the people they are tending to in the refugee camps outside the city are telling horrible stories of suffering and death inside Fallujah." Unnamed official with the Red Cross.[37]

This is a strange time in Fallujah. They say the war is over, but there is no peace. Every day there is shooting, and there are still killings going on. There is very little left of the town now, everywhere there are buildings which have been destroyed...
The Americans say they are just finishing off the insurgents, but then they have been saying that for a few days now, so people here ask: "Who have they got left to finish off?"
I am not staying in Fallujah out of choice. But I am afraid to try to leave. I am 36 years old. The American troops have been arresting any males between the ages of 14 and 45 who have attempted to leave. They say civilians were told to get out of Fallujah, so any man who stayed behind must be in the mujahideen...
The reason I stayed behind is the same as many of the other remaining men here, to protect my house. My wife and parents begged me to go with them when I sent them away to Amiriyah, but I

would not listen. I now realise what a mistake that was. I am staying with relations, and my house has probably been destroyed. The Americans were shooting everywhere, from the air and the ground, when they came into the town... But there is also a lot of damage being caused when they carry out searches of houses...

There is no power or water, and very little food left, and there is simply no medicine left. People I know are very ill, mainly from bad water, but they are not getting treatment. We were told that the Red Crescent and other aid organizations wanted to send food and medicine into the town, but it was stopped on the orders of [Iyad] Allawi...

The Americans say that they have set up centres for distributing food and medicine. They also say that Fallujah hospital has now been open again for more than a week.

This is true in both cases. But the problem is that getting to them is very risky. You can get arrested by the Americans or you might get killed. Two women were shot trying to get food for their families. Abbas Ahmed Ibrahim, Iraqi journalist.[38]

The attack on Yusufiyah began at just after eight in the morning. Round after round of rockets, then mortar shells and machine-gun fire racked the US Marines' base, in an intense and unrelenting barrage.

A relief patrol ran into a well-prepared ambush. Artillery and air strikes had to be called in, but even after that the battle went on for four more hours. The assault was part of a hidden, and largely unreported, war of attrition taking place in the most dangerous part of Iraq. With Fallujah now, in effect, in American hands, the fighting has moved on to north Babil and the so-called Triangle of Death...

Lieutenant Colonel Mark Smith, the commander of the 2nd Battalion based at Mahmudiyah, said: "We have insurgents returning home from Fallujah and finding us on the way. With Fallujah over, the action has moved here. This is now the most dangerous place in Iraq. Increasingly, we are coming up against Zarqawi's people; they are better armed and better trained."

Lt-Col Smith had just returned from an all-night operation, and still had camouflage paint on his face. The raid, on a farm, followed information that Zarqawi was hiding there. They did not find him, but Lt-Col Smith said, they caught two senior militant leaders. "We have had lots of engagements and we have killed a lot. We keep on getting reports that Zarqawi is in this area. If he is we shall find him and we shall capture or kill him."[39]

Colonel Ron Johnson, commander of the 24th MEU said: "This is the heart of the insurgency. If we can stop them here, it'll have a huge effect throughout the rest of Iraq. These are high stakes. If, after Fallujah, the insurgents can hold on to this area, they can rebuild, that is why they are fighting so desperately, and that is why we must destroy them."

A source with links to the insurgents said in Baghdad: "The Americans tried to control that area once before and failed. Why do they think they will succeed this time?

"The people are against them. They are afraid of Abu Musab [Zarqawi], but he is just one man; in the resistance there are many, and they are prepared to fight and die until the invaders are expelled."[40]

"We had five people under treatment and they were killed. We do not know why the clinic was hit. Our colleagues from the Fallujah General Hospital, which was further out in the city, had talked to the Americans and had told us that they would avoid attacking us. "Afterwards, myself and other members of staff went from house to house when we could to help people who had been hurt. Many of them died in front of us because we did not have the medicine or the facilities to carry out operations.

"We contacted the doctors at the Fallujah hospital and said how bad the situation was. We wanted them to evacuate the more badly injured and send drugs and more doctors. They tried to do that, but they said the Americans stopped them.

"One of the things we noticed the most were the numbers of people killed by American snipers. They were not just men but women and some children as well. The youngest one I saw was a four-year-old boy. Almost all these people had been shot in the head, chest or neck." Dr Ali Abbas, 28, from Fallujah, talking in Baghdad.[41]

At the beginning of January 2005, a few of the 250,000 residents of Fallujah started returning wondering what was left of their homes. Still no electricity, running water, or proper sanitation. Shops and schools all closed. The industrial area demolished. Still some sporadic fighting in the city between Americans and freedom fighters.

Some found their houses completely demolished, and their workshops gone. Others found their houses still standing but with added holes blasted in the walls, and their furnishings wrecked. But this they feel is better than living in the tent cities outside the walls.

US handout positions, surrounded by razor wire, distribute food, water, toys and bedding. Lt Colonel Patrick Malay, said, "This is how I like it, just like Disneyland. Orderly lines of people leave with a smile on their face."

One Iraqi found his home was still standing, but was horrified to find his wife's underwear scattered all over the place, and his furnishings smashed. He said sixty per cent of the homes in his area were destroyed or burnt.[42]

Faced with a potential massive increase in the number of insurgents, the Pentagon and CIA are considering using the *Salvador option* in Iraq, that is, clandestine death squads to break the insurgency, even penetrating Syria. The Allawi Interim Government says, "The Sunni population is paying no price for the support it is giving to the terrorists. From their point of view it is cost free. We have to change that equation."[43]

Once the battle is over the press reports dried up. This was partly due to censorship, as coalition leaders do not want the public to know what has really happened in Fallujah, and partly due to the fact that the freedom fighters have unwisely targeted journalists and even held some hostage. However scant, the latest information received continues to be polarised:

This shattered city overrun by U.S. troops to root out terrorists is coming back to life and American officers brag it's now the safest place in Iraq.[44]

IT was the smell that first hit me, a smell that is difficult to describe, and one that will never leave me. It was the smell of death. Hundreds of corpses were decomposing in the houses, gardens and streets of Fallujah. Bodies were rotting where they had fallen – bodies of men, women and children, many half-eaten by wild dogs...[45]

US Lt General James Mattis describing his experience fighting in Iraq as commander of the 1st Marine division that attacked Fallujah: "Actually, it's quite a lot of fun to fight: you know, it's a hell of a hoot. I like brawling: its fun to shoot some people." He has been counselled by Marine Corps, General Mike Hagee and described as a brave and brilliant military leader. There will be no disciplinary charge.[46]

CLAIM: That members of the UK Government and Military, by supporting logistically, militarily, and politically the US assault on the city of Fallujah in November 2004, are in grave breaches of the Rome Statute of the International Criminal Court Article 8: War crimes (2)(a); Protocol I Additional to the Geneva Conventions and relating to the Protection of Victims of International Armed Conflicts, 1977, Article 12; Article 21; Article 51 (1), (2) and (4); and Article 57 (1); and the Charter of the Nuremberg Tribunal 1945.

---

[1] Rory McCarthy, *Guardian*, 14 October 2004.
[2] Hansard, 18 October 2004.
[3] Peacerights, *Report of the Inquiry into the alleged commission of War crimes by Coalition Forces in the Iraq War during 2003*, London, 8-9 November 2003.
[4] Patrick Cockburn and Ken Sengupta, *Independent*, 11 Dec 2004.
[5] Ibid.
[6] Patrick Cockburn & Andrew Buncombe, *Independent*, 20 September 2004.
[7] Hala Jaber, *Sunday Times*, 31 October 2004.
[8] Kim Sengupta, *Independent*, 15 October 2004.
[9] Luke Harding, *Guardian*, 18 October 2004.
[10] Kim Sengupta, *Independent*, 19 October 2004.
[11] Kim Sengupta, *Independent*, 1 November 2004.
[12] Paul Wood, *BBC News*, 7 November 2004.
[13] Channel 4 News, 8 November 2004.

[14] Kim Sengupta, *Independent*, 8 November 2004.
[15] Ibid.
[16] Ibid.
[17] Kim Sengupta & Justin Huggler, *Independent*, 9 November 2004.
[18] Fadel al-Badrani, *Guardian*, 10 November 2004.
[19] 'The day the Americans came to town', *Independent*, 10 November 2004.
[20] Ibid.
[21] Ibid.
[22] Kim Sengupta, *Independent*, 10 November 2004.
[23] Ibid.
[24] Kim Sengupta, *Independent*, 11 November 2004.
[25] Kim Sengupta & Charles Glass, *Independent*, 12 November 2004.
[26] Gethin Chamberlain, *Scotsman*, 13 November 2004.
[27] Ibid.
[28] 'Black Watch in running battles with militants' *Independent*, 13 November 2004.
[29] Anthony Sampson, *Independent*, 13 November 2004.
[30] Michael Georgy & Kim Sengupta, *Independent*, 15 November 2004.
[31] Ibid
[32] Ibid.
[33] Harvey McGavin, *Independent*, 15 November 2004.
[34] Andrew Buncombe, 'Marines will investigate claims of war crimes', *Independent*, 16 November 2004.
[35] Ibid.
[36] Andrew Buncombe, *Independent*, 17 November 2004.
[37] Ibid.
[38] Abbas Ahmed Ibrahim, *Independent*, 20 November 2004.
[39] Kim Sengupta, *Independent*, 22 November 2004.
[40] Ibid.
[41] Kim Sengupta, *Independent*, 24 November 2004.
[42] *New York Times*, 6 January 2005.
[43] Michael Hirsh and John Barry, *Newsweek*, 8 January 2005.
[44] Mark Mooney, *New York Daily News*, 21 February 2005.
[45] Dr Salam Ismael, posted 17 February 2005 http://207.44.245.159/article8093.htm
[46] BBC News, 3 February 2005.

7w. NOT COUNTING THE DEAD. THE STENCH OF DEATH.

"We don't do body counts." General Tommy Franks, US Central Command.

While part of the justification for war put forward by Mr Blair was that Saddam was prepared to kill his own people (referring to the 1983 Hilabja massacre of 5,000 Kurds), the US and UK governments have steadfastly refused to count total Iraqi civilian deaths. This makes it difficult to assess proportionality in war. *Iraqi Body Count*, an independent organisation, assessed deaths by October 2004 to be in the order of 10,000 to 13,000 deaths. When in November 2004 the *Lancet* said that the figure was more likely to be 100,000, the Government said it relied more on the *Iraq Body Count* figure; to which it seems appropriate to use the words of Mandy Rice Davies during the Profumo affair: "They would, wouldn't they?" American soldiers have even prevented journalists from entering hospitals to make body counts of civilians. Both the US and the UK army have been keen to count the casualties victim of firefights, to prove the worth of their efforts to suppress so called *terrorists, insurgents, Islamic militias, Saddam supporters, enemies of democracy* and other riff raff. No total tallies of these deaths have ever been made, even though in humanistic terms the deaths of these men cause great heartache to their families.

French rebels during the Nazi occupation of France were called *The Resistance* and issued with medals. Interesting to notice how language has become distorted to suit.

RELEVANT LAWS AND CONVENTIONS.

1. RELEVANT TO PROPORTIONALITY OF ATTACK:
The Rome Statute of the International Criminal Court, Article 7: *Crimes against humanity;* Article 8: (2) *For the purposes of this*

Statute, "war crimes" means: (a) *Grave breaches of the Geneva Convention of 12 August 1949;* (b) *Other serious violations of the laws and customs applicable in international armed conflict, within the established framework of international law, namely, any of the following acts:* (iv) *Intentionally launching an attack in the knowledge that such an attack will cause incidental loss of life or injury to civilians... which would be clearly excessive in relation to the concrete and direct overall military advantage anticipated.*
Protocol I Additional to the Geneva Conventions, 1977, Article 51: *Protection of the civilian population*; Article 52: *General protection of civilian objects*; and Article 53: *Protection of cultural objects and of places of worship.*

2. RELEVANT TO RESPONSIBILITY OF LEADERS:
Charter of the Nuremberg Tribunal 1945: *Crimes against humanity.*

3. RELEVANT TO INFORMATION ABOUT PoW DEATHS:
Geneva Convention III relative to the Treatment of Prisoners of War, 1949, Article 122: *Upon the outbreak of a conflict and in all cases of occupation, each of the Parties to the conflict shall institute an official Information Bureau for prisoners of war who are in its power... The Power concerned shall ensure that the Prisoners of War Information Bureau is provided with the necessary accommodation, equipment and staff to ensure its efficient working... The Information Bureau shall also be responsible for replying to all enquiries sent to it concerning prisoners of war, including those who have died* in captivity.

4. RELEVANT TO INFORMATION REGARDING CIVILIAN AND BATTLE CASUALTIES:
Protocol I Additional to the Geneva Conventions, 1977, Section III *Missing and Dead Persons,* Article 32: *General principle. In the implementation of this Section... shall be prompted mainly by the right of families to know the fate of their relatives;* and Article 33: *Missing persons.* (1) *As soon as circumstances permit... each Party to the conflict shall search for the persons who have been reported missing by an adverse Party. Such adverse Party shall transmit all relevant information concerning such persons in order to facilitate such searches.*

5. RELEVANT TO RESPECT FOR THE DEAD: Protocol I Additional to to the Geneva Conventions, 1977, Article 34: (1) *The remains of persons who have died for reasons related to occupation or in detention resulting from occupation or hostilities... shall be respected*; Article 61: (1)(a) (m) *emergency disposal of the dead*; and Article 81: *Activities of the Red Cross and other humanitarian organizations.*

Geneva Convention I relative to the Wounded and Sick, 1949, Article 15: *At all times, and particularly after an engagement, Parties to the conflict shall, without delay, take all possible measures to search for and collect the wounded and sick, to protect them against pillage and ill-treatment, to ensure their adequate care, and to search for the dead and prevent their being despoiled;*

Article 16: *Parties to the conflict shall record as soon as possible, in respect of each wounded, sick or dead person of the adverse Party falling into their hands, any particulars which may assist in his identification. These records should if possible include: (a) designation of the Power on which he depends; (b) army, regimental, personal or serial number; (c) surname; (d) first name or names; (e) date of birth; (f) any other particulars shown on his identity card or disc; (g) date and place of capture or death; (h) particulars concerning wounds or illness, or cause of death.*

As soon as possible the above mentioned information shall be forwarded to the Information Bureau described in Article 122 of the Geneva Convention relative to the Treatment of Prisoners of War of 12 August 1949, which shall transmit this information to the Power on which these persons depend through the intermediary of the Protecting Power and of the Central Prisoners of War Agency.

Parties to the conflict shall prepare and forward to each other through the same bureau, certificates of death or duly authenticated lists of the dead. They shall likewise collect and forward through the same bureau one half of a double identity disc, last wills or other documents of importance to the next of kin, money and in general all articles of an intrinsic or sentimental value, which are found on the dead. These articles, together with unidentified articles, shall be sent in sealed packets, accompanied by statements giving all particulars necessary for the identification of the deceased owners, as well as by a complete list of the contents of the parcel;

Article 17: Parties to the conflict shall ensure that burial or cremation of the dead, carried out individually as far as circumstances permit, is preceded by a careful examination, if possible by a medical examination, of the bodies, with a view to confirming death, establishing identity and enabling a report to be made. One half of the double identity disc, or the identity disc itself if it is a single disc, should remain on the body.

Bodies shall not be cremated except for imperative reasons of hygiene or for motives based on the religion of the deceased. In case of cremation, the circumstances and reasons for cremation shall be stated in detail in the death certificate or on the authenticated list of the dead.

They shall further ensure that the dead are honourably interred, if possible according to the rites of the religion to which they belonged, that their graves are respected, grouped if possible according to the nationality of the deceased, properly maintained and marked so that they may always be found. For this purpose, they shall organize at the commencement of hostilities an Official Graves Registration Service, to allow subsequent exhumations and to ensure the identification of bodies, whatever the site of the graves, and the possible transportation to the home country. These provisions shall likewise apply to the ashes, which shall be kept by the Graves Registration Service until proper disposal thereof in accordance with the wishes of the home country.

As soon as circumstances permit, and at latest at the end of hostilities, these Services shall exchange, through the Information Bureau mentioned in the second paragraph of Article 16, lists showing the exact location and markings of the graves, together with particulars of the dead interred therein.

EVIDENCE OF VIOLATIONS: At the end of April 2004, 52 retired diplomats wrote an open letter to the Prime Minister. "We the undersigned, former British ambassadors, high commissioners, governors and senior international officials, including some who have had long experience in the Middle East... have watched with deepening concern the policies which you have followed... The Iraqis

238

killed by the coalition forces probably total between ten and fifteen thousand (it is a disgrace that the coalition forces themselves appear to have no estimate), and the numbers killed last month in Fallujah alone is apparently several hundred, including many civilian men, women and children. Phrases such as "We mourn the loss of life, we salute them and their families for their bravery and their sacrifice," apparently referring only to those who have died on the coalition side, are not well judged to moderate the passions these killings arouse..."[1]

In September 2003, in a letter to a newspaper referring to a published article, Llew Smith, Labour MP for Blaenau Gwent, commented that it highlighted "the indifference of the US occupying forces to Iraqi civilians they are killing. Sadly, Britain has adopted a similar policy towards Iraqi deaths. In a written parliamentary reply to me, published on 8 September, the Defence Minister Adam Ingram said: 'Whilst the Ministry of Defence has accurate data relating to the number of UK service personnel that have been killed or injured during Operation Telic, we have no way of establishing with any certainty the number of Iraqi casualties.'

"In a further question, I asked the Defence Secretary if he would examine reports of Iraqi deaths from eyewitness correspondents embedded with the military in the invasion of Iraq; request the Coalition Provisional Authority to make a survey of deaths reported in hospitals in Iraq from 19 March to 1st May, arising from military conflict; and make the estimating of Iraqi military deaths part of the aim of interrogation of Iraqi military commanders in custody. Mr Ingram's reply stated, 'Any loss of life, particularly civilian, is deeply regrettable, but in a military operation the size of Operation Telic it is also unavoidable. Through very strict rules of engagement and the use of precision munitions, the coalition did everything possible to avoid unnecessary causalities. We do not, therefore, propose to undertake a formal review of Iraqi casualties from 19 March to 1st May.' Surely this is both an inhumane and unacceptable position. As at least part of our aid to post-war Iraq must be targeted at assistance to families left without breadwinners, who have been killed or seriously injured by the invasion, then our planners are going to have to calculate the numbers of families left destitute by their loss." [2]

One of the reasons for justifying the war was that Saddam Hussein had gassed his own citizens, killing 5,000 Kurds at Halabja. As soon as George W Bush declared the end of the war, mass graves were exposed to illustrate Saddam's ruthlessness in repressing Shia and Kurdish uprisings a decade earlier. Body counts were made of the skeletons, revealing the extent of his wickedness. What was not mentioned in respect of this terrible evidence was that in 1992 John Major's government encouraged the Kurds in the north and the Shia in the south to revolt against Saddam's regime –which they did. What these people were not to know was that they would be abandoned by the British and left to die in vast numbers, slaughtered by superior forces and cunning. The southern marshes were drained, leaving the marsh Arabs literally high and dry. If ever there was a moment to justify British military intervention against genocide, this was it. However, the last thing the West actually wanted was a division of Iraq with a powerful fundamentalist Shia Islamic state in the south. All that the British were prepared to do was fly fast jets over Iraqi air space, leaving Saddam's forces on the ground to do whatever they wanted. Cynical realpolitik delayed military intervention for 12 years.

In May 2003, Ann Clwyd, UK Special Humanitarian Envoy, was duly dispatched on a tour of the mass graves and declared that it was a just war, on account of these countless killings. In her travels she also discovered some unpalatable facts such as an Iraqi woman in her seventies who was put in a harness and made to walk on all fours and ridden like a donkey by American troops.[3]

It becomes rather difficult to justify a just war, when your side refuses to count the deaths caused by your own forces. If your declared aim is to prevent a tyrant killing his own people, at what point in this mathematical equation does a just war become an unjust war? Or are you trying to hide something? The Coalition refuses to count bodies except of their own soldiers. American soldiers have even prevented journalists from entering hospitals to record deaths. It has been left to private institutions to assess their numbers. *Iraq Body Count* has collated information from hospitals and mortuaries and other sources and has arrived at a figure of 16,000 Iraqi civilian deaths since the start of hostilities, of which a large proportion are children. This figure is continuously updated.[4]

However not everyone agrees with this assessment. In October 2004 *The Lancet*, a very reputable journal of the British medical establishment, came up with very different figures.[5] By careful extrapolation of a small area of Iraq, they assessed that 100,000 Iraqis had died violent deaths since the commencement of hostilities. This calculation was immediately discredited by the UK Government, and their spokesman said that they found the Iraq Body Count figures of 10,000 to 13,000 more reliable.   Nor is there an assessment of the number of injured adults and children. How many have had their limbs blown off, or been blinded, or psychologically traumatised by seeing their relatives killed by high-tech weapons and other horrors of war that President Chirac of France said should be avoided at all costs? In rough statistical terms, it can be estimated that the number of physical injuries is four times higher than deaths. Thus if *The Lancet* figures are correct, the number of Iraqi wounded is in the order of 400,000, making the total number of deaths and injured approaching half a million, without counting psychologically damaged people. Saddam's killing of his own people has now been assisted by the UK and USA in no small measure.

Geoff Hoon, the Secretary of State for Defence, justifies the various weapon systems on the grounds of military expediency. The same justification is implicit in the Prime Minister's statements about "blood sacrifice" and the inevitable casualties of war "and collateral damage." In other words, the proportional effect of an attack.

This question of proportionality is discussed at great length in the Peaceright Report of the Inquiry into the alleged Commission of War Crimes by Coalition Forces in the Iraq war during 2003. The argument hinges on Articles 52 and 53 of the 1977 Protocol I Additional to the Geneva Conventions and the idea that to justify an attack there must be some relationship between the military advantage gained and the estimated civilian casualties. This idea of proportionality is also implicit in the Rome Statute of the ICC International Criminal Court, Article 7, Crimes against humanity.

If, for instance, someone knocked out a machine gun post killing four soldiers, but at the same time killed 1,000 children in the school playground in which the block house was situated; the military objective would not have justified the action taken and would therefore have been considered a war crime. Consequently, if no assessment was ever made of the numbers of children killed in an attack on a residential district of Baghdad; neither Mr Hoon, Mr Blair, Mr Ingram nor Ms Clwyd can contend that the proportion of civilian casualties justifies the military attack in that area. If "as a matter of principle" they never make assessments of Iraqi deaths in any of their actions, how can they justify any of those actions?

The truth is they haven't a clue, don't want to have a clue, don't want the public to have a clue, and are only panicked when a journal with a high reputation like *The Lancet* makes public an estimation which is unfavourable to them. If there are no measurements of "collateral damage" caused by depleted uranium cluster bombs, cluster shells or *Storm Shadow* robotic rockets, I am perfectly justified in saying that Messrs Blair, Hoon, Ingram and Clwyd are acting contrary to the Geneva Conventions, because the military they direct are in no position to judge whether the ordnance used complies with their terms. Nor is the British public able to judge whether Ms Clwyd's "just war" is actually just, or is just a bloodbath. Meanwhile the Arabic public have made their assessment of the situation. Their assessment is that the West treats them as a different species.

In the matter of keeping an Information Bureau as required by the Geneva Conventions, the slap dash and *ad hoc* adherence to this was recorded in a television documentary aired in October 2003. It shows that there is a chronic failure to keep proper records of the location of PoWs and civilian prisoners in 17 US-run Iraq jails. Iraqis are seen trying to locate imprisoned relatives at an enquiry office in Baghdad opened several months after their capture. There is a very long queue of anxious Iraqis outside the office. A single young American soldier is seen attempting to locate the prisoners from a list in a small laptop computer. He is accompanied by an Arabic interpreter. All the names on the computer have been transcribed into American script. (It is notoriously difficult to make accurate transcriptions from Arabic. For instance, Hammoudi is also spelt Hamoodi). The American soldier is having extreme difficulty in locating the Iraqi names. He is unable to find the place of detention. The family members are given a small scrap of paper. The Iraqis leave not knowing where in Iraq their relative is held. Is he in a British camp in the south… or a US camp in the north? Or is he dead? Or indeed is the name on the scrap of paper they are handed the correct one? They are told to go to the police to locate the prisoner. The police are unable, or unwilling to do so. They say, "Come back tomorrow". They may be the very Ba¹athist police who abducted or killed the prisoner in the first place.[6]

Asked about the number of Iraqi dead, Lt Col Ellen Krenke, Pentagon spokesperson said. "It is something that is not done. We just never have. We keep a count of our own, but not the enemy." This slip of the tongue shows that the Iraqi people, who were to be *liberated*, have become "the enemy."[7]

CLAIM: That by not counting the Iraqi dead, or respecting the dead, or not being able to assess proportionality, members of the UK government and military are in breach of the following laws and customs of war:

The Rome Statute of the International Criminal Court, Article 7 and Article 8, (2)(a) and (2)(b);

Protocol I Additional to the Geneva Conventions, 1977, Article 32; Article 33; Article 34 (1) Article 51; Article 52; Article 53; Article 61 (1)(a)(m); and Article 81;

Charter of the Nuremberg Tribunal 1945;

Geneva Convention I relative to the Wounded and Sick, 1949, Article 15; Article 16; and Article 17; and

Geneva Convention III relative to the Treatment of Prisoners of War, 1949, Article 122.

---

[1] Letter to Blair: Your Middle East policy is doomed, say diplomats, *Independent*, 27 April 2004.

[2] Letter to *Independent*, signed by Llew Smith MP, 18 September 2003.

[3] Andrew Gilligan, *Evening Standard*, 5 May 2004

[4] http://www.iraqbodycount.net

[5] *Lancet*, October 2004.

[6] Channel 4 documentary, *Iraq: Journey into Madness*, 19 October 2003.

[7] Andrew Buncombe, Severin Carrell, Raymond Whitaker, *Independent*, 12 December 2004.

WAR CRIMES OR JUST WAR?

CONCLUSION.
JUST ONE MORE TIME

"One may smile, and smile, and be a villain." **Hamlet**

One of my most vivid childhood memories is looking out of my bedroom window and clearly seeing the faces of the two pilots and navigators of two Heinkels flying just fifty feet from the ground. After that I would spend my days pretending to be a British soldier, complete with tin helmet, wooden gun, and an army of miniature jeeps and field guns. I never imagined I would one day feel I was on the wrong side of a war.

The preceding case studies of the Iraq war clearly illustrate that something has gone terribly wrong. Many in the Middle East share the perspective that this war is a great crime, a humiliation of Arabs and Islam, and a wreckage of civilization's history. The war also has proved how easy it is to continue enjoying a pleasant existence while foul deeds are being committed in your name; and how easy it is not to protest. To protest against the established authorities requires a considerable effort, a leap into unchartered territory, away from the false security offered by silence. Outspoken dissent can have unexpected consequences. In the case of George Galloway, it cost him the membership of the party he loved. In the case of Dr. Kelly, it led to his death.

The fact that the RAF has been bombing Iraq off and on since 1920 belies the notion that all British actions in Iraq are always altruistic. That Iraq is sitting on the second largest reserve of oil in the world (estimated at 115 billion barrels), undoubtedly must be a factor in the equation. Of course the crimes of Saddam, especially the draining of the marshes, required retribution. But as Chirac wisely said, "war must be the last resort".

Nor is war detached from expediency. In Northern Ireland, Gerry Adams, of Sinn Fein, was, for a period of years, not allowed to be

245

heard on the BBC. His voice was dubbed by an actor. Now he has a seat in Parliament.

Colonel Gaddafi's tent was bombed by US aircraft flying from the UK. His daughter was killed. Now he is feted for UK arms and engineering contracts worth millions. No one could have imagined the bloodless implosion of communist Russia in 1961.

Nor can we exclude – in the equation of a just war to "liberate the Iraqi people" – America's history. Especially the period which involved the destruction of the Red Indians, and America's fostering of a rebellion in Tripoli as far back as 1801. The early twentieth century presidents propounded a vision of global world capitalism supported by God, American flags and troops.

Nor can we ignore that some of the most ruthless dictatorships in the world were and are supported, even appointed, by America. When the Americans arrive, they bring with them a large bundle of historical baggage.

It would appear that when engaging in this *War on Terror*, America and Britain have chosen the wrong target. Instead of addressing the root causes of al-Qa'ida, they have chosen to bomb and occupy a country militarily weak but extremely important economically. In so doing, they have entered a political hornets' nest, which may prove very difficult to escape. There are those who believe that this is primarily a war to demonstrate America's might to its own people, and at the same time it serves as an exploitive war.

Until America's grotesque greed (25% of the world's resources) is restrained; until Britain stops manufacturing and selling arms (its most important industry), and acting as a perfidious fig leaf; until the West stops regarding an endless supply of cheap oil as its God-given right, until the Palestinians are granted a viable and safe state; and until there is genuine respect for foreign cultures, forms of government and religions, envy and malevolence will flourish.

Although the International Criminal Court has begun formally to investigate claims about the Iraq war, it is very unlikely that members of the UK government and military will have to account for themselves at the ICC. The Statutes were written by people who never envisaged themselves as the defendants. Many of its articles are in fact weaker than the more specific Hague Conventions and Nuremberg Charter. Cynically we could argue that that the ICC was set up to further the interests of the West by controlling the excesses of African, Latin American and other rogue governments around the world.

Similarly, the fact that the *High Contracting Parties* to the Geneva Conventions have to initiate proceedings themselves when the Conventions have been breached, make it unlikely that anything worse is going to happen than a request for US and UK ambassadors to visit the offices of the Red Cross at Geneva. Nevertheless, the Geneva Conventions remain a yardstick for reasonable behaviour in the uncivilised action of war.

Until the Iraq war, it was generally agreed combatants were not to shoot up ambulances or hospitals. Soldiers, we would have hoped, would afford PoWs humane treatment expecting a certain reciprocity if they were taken prisoner. Before Fallujah, we would have hoped that *proportionality* would come into play and that countless civilian homes would not be destroyed in order to eradicate 3,000 freedom fighters from a population of 250,000.

The Hague Conventions of 1907 served a similar purpose of restraint, even though they were followed seven years later by the *Great War*, one of the most catastrophic wars in history. During the Second World War Montgomery, who was a stickler for the Hague Conventions, set the high moral tone. This meant that Tunisia did not descend into violence after it was captured by British forces – as Iraq has now done under joint US and UK occupation.

The 1945 Charter of the Nuremberg Tribunal was written with great optimism. By defining 'aggression' as a *crime against peace* it hoped to prevent aggressive war. It also established the principle of the culpability of leadership. It established that the seizure of a state's assets was a war crime, and that genocide and slavery should not go unpunished. Unfortunately, the Blue Books, its twenty volumes of protocols, gathered dust with the advent of the Cold War. Hopefully, it is the Nuremberg Protocols, but not its punishments that may be due for a dusting off. Since General Pinochet's arrest in London in 1998, its pages may be turned with renewed interest. It is my hope that Pinochet's arrest may prove very significant. If, twenty years after committing a monstrous crime, someone can visit a *friendly* country for whatever reasons and suddenly be arrested for extradition to a *not-so-friendly* country, there is hope that leaders might be more cautious about committing acts of torture, or taking a country to war, and more circumspect in war's conduct.

HYPOTHETICAL SCENARIO: A group of farmers in the Hilla region (whose farm houses have been trashed by cluster bombs and aggressive patrols and whose children have been maimed or killed during a war that has been declared illegal by the Secretary General of the United Nations), determine that the compensation offered by the British Government (£500-£800 per family) is inadequate to cover their loss and decide to sue Mr Blair personally. Mr Blair, meanwhile, has retired and lives in a townhouse valued at £3.6 million in Connaught Square. In 2014, Mr Blair takes his family on holiday to Petra. In the intervening time the Hashemite Kingdom of Jordan has signed an extradition treaty with a legitimate sovereign state called Iraq with a sympathetic Shia government. The principles of extradition have in the meantime been extended to include not only torture but also grave breaches of the Geneva and Hague Conventions. While viewing the beauties of Petra, Mr Blair is surprised to see a detachment of Jordan police approaching him on camels...

I hope that the case studies, of what appear to be examples of war crimes, crimes against peace, and crimes against humanity, stimulate debate.

Do we really want a world in which hooding and the use of plastic cable ties is considered standard practice for detention..? Do we want armed mercenaries or private armies to protect private companies and be no longer beholden to the laws of the sovereign state in which they operate..? Do we want torture and the use of dogs to be standard practice..? Are cluster bombs and depleted uranium missiles acceptable weapons..? Do we want the rights granted in the Magna Carta..? Do we want Christianity to be used as a weapon against Islam..?

These are all issues that involve our democratic choice at the moment. Before long we will have no choice. I for one do not want my grandchildren to live in a culture which is represented by US army specialist Charles Graner, who said of his work in Abu Ghraib: "The Christian in me says it's wrong, but the corrections officer in me says I love to make a grown man piss himself." Nor do I want a prime minister who says that Guantanamo Bay is "providing useful information". Even less a prime minister who deceives a nation into going to war.

Perhaps it is best that this book ends with a recent e-mail sent by an Iraqi doctor, Dr Salam Ismael, after he returned to Fallujah at the beginning of the year, following the American siege in November 2004. In his own words:

> "The First step I put inside Falluja .. I smell the death and what a smell? It was offal .. I saw the bodies .. woman, men and children .. torn bodies ..eaten by dogs .. every where in the streets, in the gardens inside the houses .. only two pictures I want to copy it to u .. I wish that u can see it by my eyes and close ur eye to imagine ..
>
> "A child blown her head by a bullet lie down over the chest of her father which torn by many many bullets, the 2 bodies on the side of the road as they were running away ..
>
> "Another picture of a young girl tell me her story while the tears covering her eye and the atrocity fending her voice … atrocity of a child saw the American soldiers killing her mother and her elderly father on the front gate of the house while he is trying to explain to them that there were no body in the house only women … and she saw how the American soldiers entered the house and killed her 2 elder sisters and her 13 year old brother .. and she was hiding behind the refrigerator … she stayed with the bodies for three days in the same room …, with no food with no water .. then the red crescent found her …"

But on 23 February 2005, the newspaper lies on the doormat as yet unread. What stories does it contain..? Condoleezza Rice flitting the globe, like one of the Eumenides in a puppet play, issuing dire warnings to Syria and Iran..? Or of US secret negotiations with the Sunnis, "For God's sake we don't want a government of Shia clerics running Iraq"..? Or of US tanks and artillery surrounding Ramadi to deliver yet another decisive blow against the *Axis of Evil*..? Or of our Prime Minister, surrounded by a circus of flying pigs and Shylocks, asking us with a shy smile (rehearsed..?) to move on, and believe in his beliefs just one more time..?

STOP PRESS.

19 JANUARY 2005. On 15 May last year, Major Dan Taylor ordered soldiers to round up detained looters and "work them hard" in operation Ali Baba. These were looters to the Army's humanitarian food warehouses half a mile west of Basra. About 9 NCOs rough treated the captured Iraqis. One Iraqi was hoisted while tied to a fork lift truck. Two were made to strip and perform sexual acts in front of a camera. Another was put in a net and trampled on. The NCOs went to Court martial for acts contrary to section 66 and 69 of the Army Act 1955 on 28 January 2005 in Germany. Major Dan Taylor did not face charges.

19 JANUARY 2005. John Simpson reported in a *BBC TV* news broadcast that Baghdad now only had four hours of electricity a day.

21 JANUARY 2005. The *Washington Post* says that, according to the 119- page CIA NIC (National Intelligence Council) report, Iraq had provided terrorists with a training ground, a recruiting ground, and the opportunity for enhancing technical skills "At the moment Iraq is a magnet for the international terrorist activity" There they have found tons of unprotected weapons caches, now used against American troops. By 2020, Al-Qa'ida "will be superseded" by these new groups.

26 JANUARY 2005. The *Independent* formally asked to see, under the Freedom of Information Act, the full text of the Attorney General's memo authorising the war with Iraq, and was refused. Clare Short asked "Who is the Attorney General's client? Who is the Attorney General accountable to? It should be to the country, not ministers. It wasn't even shared with the full Cabinet."

9 FEBRUARY 2005. According to the *Independent*, the Shia, United Iraqi Alliance party, which obtained the largest vote in the 30

January 2005 election, is likely to follow Ayatollah Ali-al-Sistani's views and adopt Islamic law. Such things as playing chess, or music for pleasure, and alcohol will be banned, together with restrictions on women's rights and compulsory wearing of veils. This will be a major set back for Sunni professional women.

16 FEBRUARY 2005. The *Independent* reported that six bodies were being exhumed by the UK Army Prosecuting Authority in connection with investigation of deaths of Iraqis by UK soldiers. Compensation received by the families of those killed ranged from £550 to £825. [It seems Whitehall still thinks in terms of fobbing the *natives* off with strings of beads, and cannot see that such sums are a grotesque insult.]

15 FEBRUARY 2005. Blair's speech to the Labour Party Conference outlining his desire for a third term at the coming general election. "I understand why some people feel angry, not just over Iraq but many of the difficult decisions we have made. And as ever, a lot is about me," said Blair. "I am still the same person. Older, a little wiser, I hope. But still with the same commitment and belief." [Depressingly, it seems the general public is going to swallow this leftover charm, all wedding-party-humour and hypnotic stuff, and vote for him again. The country will have to endure a liar for a prime minister for a further five years.]

TIMELINE OF THE IRAQ WAR 2003 - 2005

17 MARCH 2003. Final ultimatum by US President Bush for Saddam to leave Iraq within 48 hours or face consequences.

18 MARCH 2003. Twenty groups of US and UK special forces infiltrate into Iraq before battle commences, some dealing with missile sites directed against Israel; others contacting Kurdish fighters in the Kurdish region; others to stop oil wells being fired.

20 MARCH 2003: Stealth bombers drop one-ton bombs on Saddam Hussein hideout. Land assault begins from Kuwait. British tornadoes and American planes take out radar installations within Iraq. *Shock and Awe* begins on Baghdad with cruise missiles and precision bombs fired from UK and US warships and planes. Umm Qasr attacked by US and UK marines.

22 MARCH 2003: UK forces reach outskirts of Basra. US thrust towards Baghdad. Nasiriyah and Najaf skirted by US forces. Local Iraqis do not rise up against Saddam as had been expected, but Saddam fedayeen harry supply lines. Long supply line takes 48 hours from Kuwait to US advance forces.

25 MARCH 2003: Sandstorms stop coalition operations for two days.

26 MARCH 2003: Kurdish peshmerga paramilitaries are assisted by US paratroops.

28 MARCH 2003: US reaches Karbala and Al Kut. UK forces begin to penetrate Basra. Missile strikes Baghdad market killing many civilians

1 APRIL 2003: Najaf taken by US forces. Saddam's Iraqi Republican Guard forces flee northwards and disperse.

2 APRIL 2003 : Hilla reached by US soldiers. Cluster bomb attacks on villages near Hilla. Kurdish and US forces reach Mosul and Kirkuk.

4 APRIL 2003: US troops reach Baghdad Saddam International Airport.

8 APRIL 2003: British take Basra. US tanks enter centre Baghdad. Looting begins. Records disappear when ministries are ransacked.

14 APRIL 2003: Major military operations end when Tikrit is taken.

21 APRIL 2003: General Jay Garner appointed head of Office of Reconstruction and Humanitarian Assistance (ORHA) in Green Zone of Baghdad.

1ST MAY 2003: Bush arrives on USS Abraham Lincoln aircraft carrier (as co-pilot of Navy S-3B Viking jet) and declares that "Major combat operations in Iraq have ended."

6 MAY 2003: Paul Bremer takes over from Jay Garner as head of renamed Coalition Provisional Authority (CPA).

20 DECEMBER 2003: Saddam Hussein captured in farm underground hideout near Tikrit.

28 MARCH 2004: Muqtada al-Sadr's Al-Hawza newspaper shut down by US occupation authorities followed by widespread revolt by Muqtada's Shia supporters.

APRIL 2004: US combat Muqtada al Sadr's Shia militias in Karbala, Sadr City, Najaf and Nasiriyah. Truce finally brokered between chief Shia cleric Grand Ayatollah Ali al-Sistani and US. First major US attack on Fallujah. Increase in guerrilla war (largely Sunni) against US.

MAY 2004: Abu Ghraib prison atrocities revealed.

28 JUNE 2004: Ilyad Allawi appointed interim PM, supported by 1,300-strong US diplomatic mission headed by John Negroponte (former US Ambassador to Honduras during civil war)

NOVEMBER 2004: Second major assault on Fallujah. 250,000 refugees evacuate city.

DECEMBER 2004: British Embassy declares Baghdad Airport road unsafe to travel.

30 JANUARY 2005: Elections for National Assembly: Sistani Shias take 48% of vote; Kurdish Alliance 26%; Ilyad Allawi's party 13.8%. Sunnis abstain. UK Hercules transport plane crashes – possibly shot down – north of Baghdad killing ten UK troops. Total US death toll reaches 1,400 with 10,000 seriously wounded. UK death toll reaches 86. Iraqi deaths: unknown.

INDEX